The Study of Language in England,
1780 - 1860

Là où les passions humaines intervien-
nent, le champ de l'imprévu est immense.

The Truth is, he who shall duly consider these Matters, will find that there
is a certain *Bewitchery*, or Fascination
in Words, which makes them operate
with a Force beyond what we can naturally give an account of.

Saasnart vi opdage Grændsen for vor
Kundskab, gruble vi uden Ro paa
Midler til at udvide den; vi søge lige
begjerlig at kige tilbage i det forsvundne
og frem i det tilkommende.

Ce qu'il y a de consolant, c'est qu'on
arrive nécessairement quelque part.

THE STUDY OF LANGUAGE
IN ENGLAND, 1780-1860

BY HANS AARSLEFF

GREENWOOD PRESS, PUBLISHERS
WESTPORT, CONNECTICUT

Library of Congress Cataloging in Publication Data

Aarsleff, Hans.
    The study of language in England, 1780-1860.

    Reprint of the ed. published by Princeton University
Press, Princeton, N.J.
    Includes bibliographical references and index.
    1. Linguistic research--Great Britain--History.
2. Languages--Philosophy--History. I. Title.
[P81.G7A62 1978]   401   78-13573
ISBN 0-313-21046-2

Reprinted with the permission of Princeton University
Press

Reprinted in 1979 by Greenwood Press, Inc.
51 Riverside Avenue, Westport, CT 06880

Printed in the United States of America

10 9 8 7 6 5 4 3 2 1

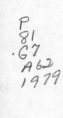

Preface

THE present work had its origin in an examination, begun some ten years ago, of the background and history of the Early English Text Society. It soon became evident, however, that our accounts of the history of philology and the study of language did not offer an adequate foundation for such a task. In spite of their great virtues, the detailed nineteenth-century histories reveal the limitations that generally characterize early historiography, and they are, in any event, almost wholly concerned with Continental scholarship. Later, especially in this country, the general tendency of linguistics became pugnaciously anti-historical, treating all previous work as the product of a dark age and worthy only of contempt. Under these circumstances, I chose to deal with the study of language in England from Horne Tooke to the period when the final plans for the *Oxford English Dictionary* were prepared. I hope that my work makes a small contribution to the history of ideas in a field which has so far received little attention.

An earlier and substantially different version was submitted as a doctoral dissertation at the University of Minnesota. Among other differences, it examined the rationalist and empirical, Cartesian and Lockian traditions in greater detail, a subject which I hope to treat in the future in a study of the relations between language and natural philosophy in the seventeenth century.

I wish to thank my friend and former colleague, Professor John W. Clark of the University of Minnesota. As my advisor, he was always ready with help, advice, and encouragement, yet allowed me to work in my own way, a true service for which I will always be grateful. At Princeton, I have been especially thankful for the interest and encouragement of Professor C. C. Gillispie. I also owe a great debt of gratitude to the late Professor Paul Diderichsen of the University of Copenhagen, who was greatly

v

interested in my work and gave willingly of his time, both in correspondence and in discussion. His monograph on Rasmus Rask and the grammatical tradition is fundamental to any understanding of the history of language study, whether construed in the narrower philological sense or seen in the larger context of intellectual history. I am also grateful to many friends in Princeton for their willingness to listen and endure with patience. Finally, for aid in the concluding stages, my thanks go to Eve Hanle of the Princeton University Press.

I am indebted to the Annan Fund and the Research Fund of Princeton University for financial support at various stages.

Princeton   Hans Aarsleff
October 1966

Contents

The Study of Language in England,
1780 - 1860

Introduction

It happens on occasion that history produces curious and disturbing coincidences which rightly considered cast doubt on our previous assumptions. Confined within the limits of our own interests and controlled by the outlook of our age, we tend to remember the forward-looking events but forget or suppress those that were too contemporary to enjoy success. Positive achievements, as we call them, give us a sense of comfort mixed with pride, which only in our better moments may give way to admiration. The rest, if we remember them at all, make us impatient and annoyed, and we flatter ourselves that we have overcome their errors and limitations. In thought and learning, in the history of science, ideas and scholarship, nothing succeeds like success. But the fabric of history is rarely so simple. Error may be as influential as truth. It is only in retrospect that the difference stands out clearly. We see the line of truth as a record of progress, but forget that the record of progress is not the same as history. To the historical understanding, the pseudo-science of an age may be as important as its science. It is here that coincidences may alert us to problems we have smoothed over or forgotten. To the study of language in England, 1786 is a crucial year. In that year Horne Tooke brought out the first volume of his *Diversions of Purley* in London, and in February, Sir William Jones delivered his famous discourse "On the Hindus" to the Asiatic Society of Calcutta. Both had a profound influence on the course of language study—Tooke's work in England and Jones's chiefly on the Continent, where it gave the impulse to the development of the new historical and comparative study which a generation later was imported into England in opposition to the influence of Tooke. It is easy to decide who was right and who was wrong, to judge between success and failure; but history is not so simple that 1786 was the end of one tradition and the beginning of another. It was a beginning for both, and in England the battle lasted for two generations. In 1860, the Philological Society of London committed itself to the final plan for the dictionary which is now known as the *Oxford English Dictionary*. It is unquestionably one of the chief philological monuments of the century. The plan for the dictionary depended upon the methods and results of the new philology, but behind it lay the desire to oppose and overcome the Tooke tradition and the popularity it had gained in the materialist philosophy of the Utilitarians. We may think of the study of language as an activity that has few practical and intellectual consequences outside its own domain, whose territory may of course shift, expand, and contract from one period to another. But during the years under consideration, language study—even when called philology —was not merely a matter of knowing the forms, syntax, phonology, historical relationships, and other aspects of particular languages. It involved questions of wider significance. What, for instance, was the origin of thought? Did the mind have a material basis? Did mankind have a single origin? Was the first language given by revelation or had man invented it in the process of time? Could etymology be made instructive without lending support to skepticism? It is possible to separate philology as a scholarly discipline, characterized by certain methods and subject matter, from these questions. But it is not possible to deal with its history without including them, provided that the aim is not merely to record but also to seek to understand and explain the connections between events. It is the aim of the present work to give an historical account of the intellectual development that links the philosophically oriented preoccupations of the 1780's with the philological concerns of the 1850's.

This attempt has not previously been made, and its success depends on the thesis that is central to my plan. Before the middle of the nineteenth century, language study was a mixture of philosophy and philology, and its history must be written in those terms. It is characteristic that Dr. Johnson, Sir William Jones, Friedrich Schlegel, Jacob Grimm, and N. F. S. Grundtvig all considered language study a means to an end rather than the end itself, though they differed somewhat in their conception of that end. Nineteenth-century philology has its historical origin in the seventeenth century, both in the study of the early vernacular and in the philosophical exploration of the nature and function of language and words. Francis Junius' edition of Caedmon, William Somner's Anglo-Saxon dictionary, and George Hickes' grammar were still indispensable to Rask, Bopp, and Grimm, who found no recent work that answered their needs so well as these old volumes. The eighteenth century did not continue the study of Old English in that tradition. On the contrary, this early philology fell into abeyance and had virtually ceased to exist by the middle of the century, not to be revived until the 1830's with frequent reminders that England to its shame had neglected and forgotten its philological inheritance. During the eighteenth century, the study of language became centered on the twin problems of universal grammar and the origin of language, the former being the legacy of Cartesianism and the latter of Locke's philosophy as extended by Condillac. In our terms both were philosophical rather than philological problems. When these two approaches, one quasi-comparative and the other etymological, were joined by renewed interest in national origins and the study of old texts and distant languages, the result was the beginning of what in English is generally called philology, or, for a while at least, the "new philology"—to distinguish it from classical philology which had its own tradition and did not mix with the new. Comparative and historical philology did not, as we have often been told, spring ready-made from the brain of Friedrich Schlegel; and the history we seek will gain neither continuity nor coherence if we in advance decide to limit it to such work as may deserve the name of philology in the narrower sense, a decision that has by and large been left to German scholars.

These considerations will already have suggested why I use the term "study of language" rather than "philology." By study of language I refer not only to philology in the conventional sense but to any reasonably coherent and clearly formulated discussion that is specifically directed toward problems that arise in relation to language. Here belong, for instance, certain passages in Bacon, some aspects of the program and much important work of the early Royal Society, the Port-Royal Grammar and Logic, the Third Book and some other parts of Locke's *Essay*, and works by du Marsais, Condillac, Turgot, Monboddo, Bentham, James Mill, and several of the Scottish philosophers—to mention only a few. None of these can be properly understood if they, or parts of them, are assumed to be philological; and yet, the history of philology itself cannot be understood apart from them. In its early formative stages, philology proper was nourished and guided by expectations that it might yield answers to questions that had arisen in other contexts. In this respect, the situation of philology and its history is not unique. Even natural science did not have its origin in unalloyed, disinterested, nearly angelic objectivity about the phenomena of nature, though it is still widely believed, indeed often dogmatically asserted against the testimony of the evidence, that the early Royal Society had only the purest of scientific motives, almost as if it were founded by Newton—or rather by the later image of

Newton. The error has the same origin in both cases, that of confounding the formal criteria of a discipline in its maturity—or at least its present state—with the motives and influences that brought it into being, allowing no concern to operate in the latter that is not admitted in the former, combined perhaps with a rather narrow and anything but disinterested fear that any foreign ingredient in the early makings corrupts even the present constitution. Professor Kristeller has observed that "the historian of science will do well to recognize that the positive scientific discoveries of the past were never unrelated to the theoretical and philosophical assumptions of the investigating scientist, whether they were true or false from our point of view, whether consciously expressed or tacitly accepted by him." Kepler's contributions to astronomy and mathematics, for instance, can be assessed in the context of those disciplines, but their history, even in the narrower sense, remains incomplete without an understanding of his mystical motives and his great admiration for Proclus. If we restrict our view to what we now call scientific, "the history of science becomes nothing but a catalogue of disconnected facts, and a modern version of hagiography."[1]

In recent years the best history of science has abandoned hagiography, though hagiography will always be popular. The history of the study of language is not so fortunate. The misconceptions have their origin in two quarters. One derives from the more traditional accounts of the development of philology I have referred to above, based on too narrow a conception of the material that is relevant. This view has been codified in the well-known and still useful works of Theodor Benfey and Rudolf von Raumer, who both also show a heavy bias toward the

[1] Paul Oskar Kristeller, *Renaissance Thought: The Classic, Scholastic, and Humanist Strains* (New York: Harper Torchbooks, 1961), p. 67.

belief that all good work and advances in philology have been the product of German ingenuity. This attitude, though without the German bias, was clearly stated by Vilhelm Thomsen in 1902. Referring to Herder's prize-essay and Tooke's *Diversions* as characteristic examples of the eighteenth-century mode, he granted that they might have some relevance in the history of ideas, but he also believed that they had little to do with philology (*sprogvidenskaben*) and that they had not, either directly or indirectly, brought it one inch forward. Being subjective speculations, they were bound to miscarry for lack of any concept of philological empiricism, of the principles of the history of language, and of the life of language in general. One may of course decide that Herder and Tooke have nothing to do with philology, and in that case it becomes irrelevant whether they have moved it one or many inches or feet forward or backward. But the implication that philology would have become what it is without them is either so hypothetical as to be useless, or else must, more reasonably, be decided by looking at the facts of history. If we choose the latter, they cannot be denied their importance. It is, of course, no concern of history whether the movement at any given stage has been forward or backward as we see it; all that matters is what it was. Part of the problem here seems to be that Vilhelm Thomsen shows traces of a positivist conception of the forward march of history, of progress, a conception that will invariably give less than the history that is my concern. With this sort of outlook, no history of learning or scholarship can ever achieve more than a deceptive coherence.

The other misconception is of more recent date. It has found expression in the opinion that Monboddo and Horne Tooke, if they had applied what little scientific method they possessed and had paid some attention to the documents available, might have saved eighteenth-

century and later grammarians from many foolish statements. Here it is not the forward march that misleads but
rather the conviction that the top has been reached. The
chief prop of this historically inadmissible assumption is
fondness for the prestigious appellations of "science" and
"scientific," almost as if the thing becomes so by the mere
use of those terms and becomes more so in proportion to
the frequency of their use. In this view all earlier study of
language is seen as a rather malicious conspiracy against
the future and the present enlightenment, and history
gains attention only as a sort of inverted self-flattery. It
has become fashionable to pick forerunners, though it is
rarely clear whether the runners were engaged in the same
race or even that they were running toward the same goal.
But Koyré's remark about the history of philosophy also
holds for philology: "La manie de la recherche des
'précurseurs' a bien souvent irrémédiablement faussé
l'histoire de la philosophie." Not only does the forerunner
approach fail to produce history—though that it does
seems to be the assumption. But failing to be history, it
also carries no guarantee that the foremost runner has
been correctly identified. With his famous name and frequent concern with easily recognizable philological matters, Leibniz has been a favorite. But it is rarely asked
what his influence was and precisely when and where it
made itself felt. The answers to these questions would
make it evident that his influence did not equal Locke's,
who was also beyond a doubt more firmly versed in a
variety of languages. Nor is the question asked that is of
direct relevance to the forerunner approach—whether
Leibniz was in fact on all counts as original as is generally
assumed. If it was, it would be seen that much that is being credited to him derives from seventeenth-century
scholars, a fact that might have the effect of cooling the
current interest in him as a precursor. Quite apart from
not producing history, the misconception I have de-

scribed here is harmful because it tends to discourage that sympathetic study of past work which may often yield fruitful results. During the last two or three decades, it has, for instance, been fashionable to ridicule eighteenth-century grammar. It was not realized that this grammar, with its foundation in *grammaire générale et raisonnée*, had a very respectable intellectual ancestry, though even hasty reflection might have tended to suggest that Descartes, Pascal, and Arnauld could have something interesting to say on language, even without being "scientific linguists." Recently a reassessment has occurred, but not from the same quarter that formerly ridiculed the eighteenth century. It is a common observation that brilliant—or perhaps merely well-articulated and systematically pursued—errors are often much more suggestive than the common, unquestioned truths of workaday scholarship.

The history of the study of language is still largely unexplored, and it ought not to go wrong at the outset. The task of gaining the proper depth of historical perspective within a given period can only be satisfied by seeking to recapture all relevant contemporary knowledge without reference to or misguidance by the later accumulation of scholarly opinion and assignment of influences, which are far too often and too easily accorded the status of unquestioned doctrine. My work is an essay in the application of that method. Readers will therefore look in vain for specific treatments of past opinion and work on such topics as morphology, phonology, semantics, dialectology, and the like. They were studied, but both their nature and their relevance were determined by their place in the context of historical development I have attempted to describe. Any effort to study them apart from that context will give less than a full understanding and most likely so much less that it will amount to misunderstanding. In the interest of history, I have deliberately avoided any attempt to force the subject matter into the molds of current doctrine and terminology. Similarly, the history of Paracelsism cannot be written in current medical terminology, and the history of medieval mechanics would be of little use if written according to the canons of quantum mechanics.

I wish to emphasize the limited purpose of Chapter One. Its aim is to provide the background that is necessary to an understanding of the context in which Horne Tooke and his contemporaries found themselves. It is not the aim of that chapter to provide a full account of the philosophy of language in the mid-eighteenth century. A full account would need to pay much more attention to Locke and the career of universal grammar, with emphasis on the early work of du Marsais, whose importance still remains largely unexplored, though a heavy and quite useful monograph has been devoted to him. Condillac is far and away the most important figure, even in the history of Lockianism in general, and I have therefore chosen to deal with his work in some detail. He also seems to have received less attention than he demands. Among the Englishmen whom Horne Tooke singled out for special dislike were James Harris and Lord Monboddo; I have chosen to deal with Monboddo because I find him both more interesting and more representative than Harris. Harris' *Hermes* belongs in the tradition of universal grammar, but with very significant differences which make it a poor representative of its kind. On this subject, readers will find an excellent exposition and analysis in Otto Funke's *Studien zur Geschichte der Sprachphilosophie* from 1927. Seven years later, Otto Funke published another monograph which also deserves more attention than it has received: *Englische Sprachphilosophie im späteren 18. Jahrhundert.* This work does include de Brosses and Monboddo, but Condillac has no place in Funke's scheme. The latter half is devoted to "Horne Tooke als Sprachphilosoph."

CHAPTER I

Eighteenth-Century Doctrines
Concerning Language and Mind

The chief business of Tooke's *Diversions of Purley* was
not philology but philosophy. It was his ambition to demonstrate the dependence of thought on language and to
create a "system of Language" which when applied to
"all the different systems of Metaphysical (i.e. verbal)
Imposture"[1] would entirely do away with metaphysics,
which in his view included "all general reasoning, all
Politics, Law, Morality and Divinity."[2] Rejecting Locke's
concern about the imperfections of language, he believed
that "the perfections of Language, not properly understood, have been one of the chief causes of the imperfections of our philosophy."[3] His system was raised on the
basic doctrine that "the business of the mind, as far as it
concerns Language, appears to me to be very simple. It
extends no farther than to receive Impressions, that is, to
have Sensations or Feelings. What are called its operations, are merely the operations of Language."[4] Thus the
mind is passive, a mere recording instrument and store-
house; its active powers reside in language alone. To
achieve this materialist reduction, Tooke presented two
separate lines of argument. Etymology was the tool that
gave the proof and produced the "discovery" which so
greatly astonished his contemporaries. But he also insisted that the truth of his doctrine did not depend on that
method of proof, which was merely a way of arguing because he knew "that the generality of minds receive conviction more easily from a number of particular in-

[1] *Diversions of Purley*, II, 51b. Cited hereafter as *DP*. For the
text of the *Diversions*, see Ch. 2, n. 1.
[2] *DP*, II, 121.   [3] *DP*, I, 37.   [4] *DP*, I, 51.

stances, than from the sure but more abstracted arguments of general proof." As for himself, he asserted that he was ignorant of etymology when he first formed his theory of language and that "it was general reasoning *à priori*, that led me to the particular instances; not particular instances to the general reasoning."[5] With his theory and his demonstration, Tooke was trying to play a Newton to language and mind, but neither the attempt nor the set of doctrines that sustained it was his own invention. Both were borrowed from earlier eighteenth-century efforts to explain the mind and the understanding in a manner that joined the philosophical legacies of Descartes and Locke on the one hand and the current interpretation of scientific achievement, especially Newton's, on the other. The aim was the natural history of understanding, of thought, of mind. To explain why and how the study of language came to play a crucial role in these efforts is the design of the present chapter, but only insofar as this background is a prerequisite to the right understanding of Tooke's work. A full historical account of the tradition would need to include a great deal more. The main figure is Condillac, who based his explanation of the operations of mind and the origins of human knowledge on a new and original doctrine of signs, which in turn rested on two foundations: the rational principles of universal grammar and the Lockian doctrine of the origin of ideas in sensation.

Universal grammar was the first of the two to postulate a connection between language and thought. It was based on the simple consideration that if discourse is the image of thought and if thought is subject to the laws of reason, then discourse itself must reveal and illustrate the laws of reason. This view was summed up in the popular and suggestive metaphor which said that language or speech is a painting or a copy of the mind—"la parole est une

[5] *DP*, I, 130-133.

peinture de l'esprit." The original being the same to all people regardless of the language they speak, it follows that their individual copies must of necessity reproduce the same form or structure of this original, though the colors, the actual words and expressions, may differ. Thus this kind of grammar is universal; it comprises all the general principles which no particular grammar can fail to illustrate.[6] These principles were set forth in Claude Lancelot's and Antoine Arnauld's *Grammaire générale et raisonnée*, known also as *L'art de parler* or the Port-Royal Grammar, which soon after its appearance in 1660 gained an authority which through numerous reissues lasted for more than a hundred years, aided by the even greater fame of its companion piece *La logique, ou l'art de penser*, which first appeared in 1662.

The *Grammaire générale et raisonnée* does not, as we might perhaps have expected, pay much attention to syntax; its main concern is to give a rational explanation of the parts of speech and of the grammatical categories such as case, gender, tense, mood, and number. For all of these must conform to the laws of the mind, to reason, since language is the "invention"—or perhaps better the creature—of the mind. That Latin and French are practically the only languages that figure in the analysis is no obstacle, since the initial postulate gives sufficient warrant that one language will do as well as another. Each part of speech must serve the particular purpose for which it was invented, and it is the nature of this purpose that must be explained in rational terms—and none fail to

---

[6] The metaphor occurs frequently in Beauzée's articles in the *Encyclopédie*; see, e.g. *Encyclopédie méthodique: Grammaire et littérature*, II (Paris & Liège, 1784), 411b (s.v. "langue") and p. 361b (s.v. "Inversion"). The metaphor is first fully developed in [Bernard Lamy], *De l'art de parler* (Paris, 1675) in Ch. 2 "La parole est un tableau de nos pensées." Cf. Pascal, *Pensées*, ed. Brunschvicg, No. 26: "L'eloquence est une peinture de la pensée."

gain their explanation. Pronouns, for instance, were invented because it was found inconvenient to repeat the same noun when it occurred several times in the same context. This analysis, however, treats only their distribution in a complete scheme of person, case, gender, and number, without any suggestion that the pronouns could be dispensed with by repeating the noun and thus might be considered later and secondary creations. It is in this sense that "invention" has a special meaning, totally devoid of any concept of creating step by step as the need arose. Rational analysis explains "les diverses formes de la signification des mots," reason accounts for grammar, but it is never suggested that the irregularities, the omissions, or redundancies of language may have a bearing on the subsumed conception of "invention."[7] Thus the *Grammaire générale et raisonnée* includes no concept of development. It seeks no reduction to basic elements, to the original parts out of which all the rest might perhaps, by conjecture, be seen to have evolved. It presents only a rational view, which precisely because it is rational is assumed to make things easier and rules not so hard to grasp and remember. Universal grammar was not a mere intellectual exercise, but also sought immediate, practical ends. It was on these grounds that Destutt de Tracy, in spite of his high admiration for the Port-Royal Grammar, regretted that its authors had not paid sufficient attention to the formation of ideas.[8] Destutt de Tracy spoke long after Locke and Condillac, whose philosophical disciple he was. The solution to this problem was offered by Condillac, who made Locke's *Essay* his point of departure. To the static view of universal grammar, he added the di-

---

[7] On the meaning of "invention," see Guy Harnois' cogent remarks in *Les théories du langage en France de 1660 à 1821* (Paris [1928]), pp. 24-25.

[8] Sainte-Beuve, *Port-Royal*, ed. Maxime Le Roy (Paris: Pléiade, 1954), II, 477.

mension of time, which in turn brought etymology into the picture.[9]

It is a curious fact that Condillac, who himself never devoted as much as a short chapter to etymology, should all the same be responsible for the persistent concern with etymology and the origin of language which is one of the most characteristic features of philosophical activity in the latter half of the eighteenth century. Still, without Condillac, it is impossible to understand that de Brosses had in mind when he said that "l'art étymologique est un excellent instrument pour disséquer les opérations de l'esprit, & en découvrir la contexture."[10] The work that

[9] The principles of universal grammar are at least as old as the High Middle Ages, but Cartesianism had given them new life. On the rare occasions when the *Grammaire générale* takes an historical view of language, it does so with reference to usage but not with reference to etymology and the original constituents of language. A remarkable example occurs in Part II, Chapter 10, which presents a brilliant critique of Vaugelas' rule "qu'on ne doit pas mettre le relatif après un nom sans article," which is revised to read: "Dans l'usage présent de notre langue, on de doit point mettre de *qui* après un nom commun, s'il n'est déterminé par un article, ou par quelque autre chose qui ne le détermine pas moins que feroit un article." After further discussion and citation of examples in support of the revised rule, the chapter concludes: "S'il y a d'autres façons de parler, qui y semblent contraires, & dont on ne puisse pas rendre raison, par toutes ces observations, ce ne pourront être, comme je le crois, que des restes du vieux style, où on omettoit presque toujours les articles. Or c'est une maxime, que ceux qui travaillent sur une langue vivante, doivent toujours avoir devant les yeux, que les façons de parler qui sont autorisées par un usage général & non contesté, doivent passer pour bonnes, encore qu'elles soient contraires aux regles & à l'analogie de la langue; mais qu'on ne doit pas les alléguer pour faire douter des regles & troubler l'analogie, ni pour autoriser par conséquence, d'autres façons de parler, que l'usage n'auroit pas autorisées. Autrement, qui ne s'arrêtera qu'aux bizarreries de l'usage, sans observer cette maxime, fera qu'une langue demeurera toujours incertaine, & que n'ayant aucuns principes, elle ne pourra jamais se fixer." Arnauld, *Oeuvres*, XLI (Paris, 1780), 42-45.

[10] *Traité de la formation méchanique des langues, et des principes physiques de l'étymologie*, 2 vols. (Paris, 1765), II, 124 (par. 181).

17

introduced this novel and astoundingly productive doctrine was Condillac's *Essai sur l'origine des connoissances humaines*, which in the first edition of 1746 bore the subtitle: "Ouvrage où l'on réduit à un seul principe tout ce qui concerne l'entendement." Condillac admired Locke as the greatest of all metaphysicians, in fact as the only metaphysician whose philosophy made any sense, but he also felt that Locke had not gone far enough. True, Locke had sought the origin of all our knowledge in experience alone, even of "those sublime Thoughts, which towre above the Clouds, and reach as high as Heaven it self,"[11] but he had reduced ideas not to a single origin in sensation, but to a dual origin in sensation and reflection. Unhappy about the active but unexplained operations of the latter, Condillac wished to demonstrate that reflection could be derived from sensation. To achieve this reduction, Condillac invented a new principle which made it possible to explain all ratiocination and thinking as the ultimate product of sensation and of man's instinctive reaction to the needs of the circumstances in which he found himself, to the promptings of nature. This new principle, the single principle that accounted for all the operations of the understanding, was the connection of ideas, "la liaison des idées," which in turn—in all but its most primitive form—depended on the use of signs. The unique advantage of this explanation, he said, was its demonstration that "le bon sens, l'esprit, la raison et leurs contraires naissent également d'un même principe, qui est la liaison des idées les unes avec les autres; que, remontant encore plus haut, on voit que cette liaison est produite par l'usage des signes; et que, par conséquent, les progrès de l'esprit humain dépendent entièrement de l'adresse avec laquelle nous nous servons du langage. Ce principe est simple, et

---

[11] *Essay*, II, i, 24. Throughout I refer to the 5th edition of 1706, the last to receive Locke's own revisions.

répand un grand jour sur cette matière: personne, que je sache, ne l'a connu avant moi."[12] Thus the progress of mind and knowledge goes hand in hand with the progress of language. Language is not merely, as Locke had been content to maintain, the necessary means of communication and an aid to memory. It is more than that, for thinking could neither begin nor continue without it. The crucial problem in Condillac's account of the understanding is therefore the origin of language.

Now, since the invention and use of signs are only within the capability of the more advanced operations of mind, Condillac must first show how these can be brought into being by a gradual rise from sensation to reflection. The first of these operations is perception, which is the *impression* produced on the mind by the agency of sense. It is a simple fact of experience that the mind cannot help always having a certain number of perceptions, and they may further be accompanied by a certain awareness that the mind has such perceptions. At this stage the mind has arrived at *conscience*, which in turn may rise to *attention* if certain perceptions are singled out for particularly lively awareness of their impression on the mind. This capacity for attention predisposes the mind to take note of changes in its perceptions, so that the mind will become aware both of their disappearance and of their recurrence. In the latter case the result is *réminiscence*, which is the very beginning of experience, for without it, every moment would appear to be the first in our existence. It cannot be explained, but has its foun-

[12] *Essai* in Georges Le Roy (ed.), *Oeuvres philosophiques de Condillac* (Paris, 1947), I, 36b. To facilitate cross reference to other editions, I shall also give the part, section, chapter, and—where applicable—the paragraph numbers, in this case I, ii, xi, par. 107. The latter half of this passage—after "l'usage des signes"—is only in the first edition, but not in the *Oeuvres* of 1798. Condillac's "liaison des idées" is, of course, not the same as Locke's association of ideas.

dation in the unique nature of the union of the body and the soul. Attention has the further effect of linking certain perceptions together in such a manner that they become inseparable; this is the first beginning of the *liaison* which is the foundation both of *imagination* and *mémoire*. The former occurs when one of the perceptions connected with an object is enough to reproduce the entire object as if it were present; here the imagination for a moment takes entire possession of the mind. Memory occurs when the reproduction is less complete, making present to the mind not all the connected perceptions but only some of them, such as the name or the circumstances in which the object was first perceived. The mind may, for instance, recall the name of a flower or the place where it was seen but fail to recall its odor. Both imagination and memory depend entirely on the "liaison des idées" which is the product of attention, whose selection is completely governed by the needs and passions that arise in particular situations. As yet, however, both are beyond the active control of the mind, for neither will occur except by the chance encounter of a perception that will elicit a particular imagination or memory; but insofar as this occurs, that perception acts as a sign that sets the rest of the operation in motion. It is this circumstance that raises the possibility of an active and deliberate use of signs; if the mind could somehow have a sufficient stock of signs at its disposal, it would also be able to control its imagination and memory and thus become its own master. And as soon as that occurs, reflection is born from memory and imagination. But only one kind of sign will serve this function, namely those arbitrary signs which the mind itself has made for that purpose. Here, it would seem, is a deadlock, for, as Condillac says: "Il semble qu'on ne sauroit se servir des signes d'institution, si l'on n'étoit pas déjà capable d'assez de réflexion pour les choisir et pour y attacher des idées: comment donc, m'objectera-t-on peut-être, l'exercice de la réflexion ne s'acquerroit-il que par l'usage des signes?" But the answer is clear: "Je réponds que je satisferai à cette difficulté lorsque je donnerai l'histoire du langage."[18] If Condillac can show the natural means by which the origin and progress of language puts arbitrary signs within the reach of the mind, he has solved his problem. His single principle will then successfully have explained how reflection and all discursive thought derive from perception and have their origin in sense alone.

Condillac now again returns to first origins, though not of course to Adam and Eve, for they were—"par un secours extraordinaire"—at once capable of reflection and communication. A philosopher, however, cannot have recourse to extraordinary means; he must explain how things may have come about by natural means. He imagines instead that two infant children of either sex are placed alone in a desert some time after the Flood. How will they arrive at the first signs of language, granted that living together they will try to make themselves understood to each other? At this point Condillac introduces a new concept—though it has a familiar and ancient ancestry—which he borrowed from William Warburton: the language of action which is altogether involuntary, the product of instinct alone and thus part of the nature which man shares with the animals. In a passage in the *Divine Legation of Moses*, which Condillac cites at length, Warburton had observed that there is a "way of expressing the thoughts by action," and that "in the first ages of the world, mutual converse was upheld by a mixed discourse of words and actions . . . ; and use and custom, as in most other affairs of life, improving what had arisen out of necessity, into ornament, this practice subsisted long after the necessity was over; especially amongst the eastern people, whose natural temperament

[18] *Essai* in *Oeuvres*, I, 22b (I, ii, v, par. 49).

inclined them to a mode of conversation, which so well exercised their vivacity, by motion."[14] This language of action consisted of all manner of bodily gestures—with the head, hands, arms, eyes, and every other part of the body—as a particular need arose for one of the two children to call the other's attention to something. But most important of all were the gestures they produced with their voice, the "cris naturels"—or interjections—which gave expression to some inward passion—desire, want, hunger, fear. Now the first beginning was made, for in their limited world they would often come upon the same situation and produce the same involuntary responses, including the articulated sounds. By this occasion for frequent repetition of the same vocal gesture, the two children—or now perhaps grown-ups—would in time gain power to recall it at will and thus also to reproduce it as a sign for each other's information, a procedure that was in fact tantamount to using the original, involuntary natural sign with the same function as an arbitrary sign. They would gradually come to do by reflection what they had previously done by instinct alone: the machinery of the mind would have made the first significant motion, sufficient to start all the rest. The deliberate use of a few simple vocal signs would extend the operations of the mind, which in turn would improve the signs, increase their number, and make them more firmly familiar. The mind and the use of signs would interact to the mutual advantage of both.

At this point the mind was prepared to make the most decisive of all its forward steps. Condillac imagines that the two isolated beings would by now quite accidentally,

[14] *Works* (London, 1788), II, 405-408 (in Book IV, Section iv). Part I of the *Divine Legation* was published in 1737, Part II in 1741. In 1744 Book Four, except for the first section, was published in Paris in two volumes as *Essai sur les hieroglyphes des Egyptiens*. Condillac's citation occurs in *Oeuvres*, I, 62a-b (*Essai*, II, i, i, par. 6).

as their needs demanded, have acquired the habit of connecting a few of their ideas to nonvocal, arbitrary signs. This lesson taught the next step: "Les cris naturels leur servirent de modèle pour se faire un nouveau langage. Ils articulerènt de nouveaux sons, et en les répétant plusieurs fois, et les accompagnant de quelque geste qui indiquoit les objets qu'ils vouloient faire remarquer, ils s'accoutumèrent à donner des noms aux choses."[15] The process would be very long and slow, extending through many generations—not least because the vocal apparatus would also need time to develop; but the crucial beginning had been made. Having left two beings alone to face nature, Condillac had shown that they could develop the rudiments of discursive thought from the simple beginnings of perception and instinct, their own basic nature interacting with Nature. For a long time, speech would be accompanied by the signs of the language of action, but the latter would in time be found less serviceable than the former. "The dominion of Speech," as Horne Tooke said, "is erected upon the downfall of Interjections."[16] The language of arbitrary signs, of words, had opened the way to the highest operations of the mind.

From his demonstration of the dependence of thought on language, Condillac derived several important consequences. First of all, language remains the medium of thought. Initially, language was made possible by a certain decomposition of the connected perceptions that sense presented to the mind, a decomposition which at this stage was the product of attention alone. But with the use of artificial signs, language puts thought in control of itself. A thought is instantaneous, it has no succession in time. Succession is found only in discourse, which decomposes the thought into the ideas it contains. Now the mind will not merely have a thought, but also know

[15] *Oeuvres*, I, 61b (*Essai*, II, i, i, par. 6).
[16] *DP*, I, 62.

what it is doing—"nous pouvons nous en rendre compte; nous pouvons par conséquent, apprendre à conduire notre réflexion. Penser devient donc un art, et cet art est l'art de parler."[17] In this fashion the words of language perform the same function as the signs of mathematics. The concept of the number one thousand, for instance, is retained only by the sign or word which distinguishes that particular collection of units, and it is consequently impossible to calculate without the use of signs. If so, Condillac argues, "les mots ne doivent-ils pas être aux idées de toutes les sciences ce que sont les chiffres aux idées de l'arithmétique?"[18] Like arithmetic, speech is "une méthode analytique," and we must follow the same procedure to gain the right use of its words. The concept of one thousand is the product of the steady addition of the original number one; the meaning of words is not so easy to fix, but the same principle holds that we must go back to their origin—"*principe* est synonyme de *commencement*, et c'est dans cette signification qu'on l'a d'abord employé."[19] This search for origins was the "point de vue plus lumineux qu'on n'a encore fait"—a perspective more useful than all the rules of the logicians and their formulation of principles and definitions, which were usually mere plays on words not properly understood, leading more often to obscurity than to clarity. The philosophers had in fact done great harm to language by ruining the natural perfection of the first languages. No one then asked whether the word "substance" could mean other than "*ce qui est dessous*," or whether "*pensée* signifie autre chose que *peser, balancer, comparer*. En un mot, on n'imaginoit pas de faire les questions que font

[17] *Oeuvres*, I, 403b, in "Discours préliminaire" to the *Cours d'études pour l'instruction du Prince de Parme* (Parme, 1775; Paris, 1776). The first part of the *Cours* is the *Grammaire*, to which Horne Tooke refers several times, e.g. *DP*, I, 65 and 309.

[18] *Oeuvres*, I, 42a (*Essai*, I, iv. i, par. 5).

[19] *Oeuvres*, II, 403b (*Logique*, II, vi).

aujourd'hui les métaphysiciens: les langues, qui répondoient d'avance à toutes, ne permettoient pas de les faire, et l'on n'avoit point encore de mauvaise métaphysique."[20] In other words, the right understanding of etymology would recover right thinking and do away with all metaphysics, except the Lockian kind.

Condillac's explanation of the origin of ideas and language had another consequence. Since language had developed slowly from its first simple words, one might ask which sorts of words came first and in what order one could imagine that the rest were added. The grammatical categories, for instance, could not all have arisen at the same time; which parts of speech then were primary? For Condillac naturally attempts to explain them by reference to their origin, following the traditional listing illustrated in the Port-Royal Grammar: nine parts of speech, with separate categories for the article, the interjection, and the adverb, though the last—again according to tradition—is considered unnecessary because *sapienter* can be replaced by *cum sapientia*. He accepts the traditional autonomy of the noun, both substantive and adjective, and of the only true verb, the verb substantive *être* which by its union with adjective ideas creates all other verbs, though in practice he prefers to assign the verbs to their own part of speech; for "d'après l'étymologie, *verbe* est la même chose que *mot* ou *parole*. . . . Il est en effet l'ame du discours."[21] He leaves the interjections in their usual indefinite position, noting merely that grammar has nothing to say about them. He treats the article only in terms of its use in French, except for remarking at the end that it is not absolutely necessary since one cannot imagine that Latin is the poorer for not

[20] *Oeuvres*, II, 400b (*Logique*, II, iv). The same point is made *Oeuvres*, I, 461b (*Grammaire*, II, i).
[21] *Oeuvres*, I, 467b and 445b (*Grammaire*, II, vi and I, viii). So also *Grammaire générale* in Arnauld, *Oeuvres*, XLI (Paris, 1780), 49-50.

having it. But he has more to say about the remaining three: the pronoun, the conjunction, and the preposition. The pronouns receive a very curious explanation with reference both to etymology and to function, but the result is the same. Some are true nouns and some are adjectives which by ellipsis have come to occupy the position of the noun substantive. In Condillac's example, *"voulez-vous me donner cela,"* vous, me, and *cela* designate, respectively, the person speaking, the person spoken to, and that which is requested; properly speaking they are not at all pronouns but nouns which have found their place in discourse in the same fashion as the regular nouns.[22] The same is universally true of the first and second person pronouns, for it would not give the same meaning if the names of the persons speaking and addressed were put in their place.[23] *On* and *l'on* are corruptions of *homme* and *l'homme*—"ce mot est un vrai substantif: il n'est mis à place d'aucun nom: il ne se rapporte même à aucun, et il ne laisse rien à suppléer." But it is very different with the third person pronouns *il, elle, le,* and *la*, which are all derived from Latin *ille* and *illa*, "or en latin, *ille* est proprement un adjectif exprimé ou sousentendu." Thus, if speaking of a peach tree, one says *"il est en fleurs,"* il really stands for "il pêcher," in which case ellipsis has occurred so that *pêcher* must be supplied by subaudition, to use the terminology of Horne Tooke who makes subaudition one of the cornerstones of his language doctrine.[24] Finally, *qui, que, dont, lequel,* and *laquelle*, along with the demonstrative pronouns, are all adjectives, to be explained by ellipsis and subaudition.[25]

The conjunctions receive a somewhat similar treat-

[22] *Oeuvres*, I, 89a (*Essai*, II, i, x, par. 109).
[23] *Oeuvres*, I, 468a (*Grammaire*, II, vii).
[24] *Oeuvres*, I, 468b (*Grammaire*, II, vii).
[25] *Oeuvres*, I, 490b-494a (*Grammaire*, II, xviii-xx).

ment, for one can in all cases imagine their replacement by a fuller—though more cumbersome—sequence of words. They work by ellipsis, are explained by subaudition, and are introduced for the sake of abbreviating the discourse. For example, in the sentence "je vous assure *que* les connoissances sont sur-tout nécessaires aux princes," the conjunction stands for "*cette chose qui est.*" This, of course, does not quite do the trick, so Condillac resorts to a bit of etymological legerdemain by supposing that the more original form was "que est" rather than "qui est," in which case the conjunction *que* has been explained as the result of ellipsis. It is in this fashion that he believes all conjunctions to have arisen.[26]

The preposition is a more interesting case. Owing to the seemingly high order of intellectual sophistication required for its creation, it had often caused difficulty to eighteenth-century grammarians. Condillac, however, has a solution. He imagines that prepositions were originally conceived as the names of gestures which indicated direction. By this simple device he manages to retain it among the four parts of speech that are original and essential: the two sorts of nouns, the verb, and the preposition. Consistent with this explanation, he also maintains that two different prepositions can never be used in the same situations. In the three phrases "être dans le royaume, être en Italie, être à Rome," for instance, each preposition indicates a particular relationship; each has a fixed and unvarying meaning. Prepositions are at first capable of referring only to the relationship of sensible objects, but they may by analogy be transferred also to other relations, for instance from "de la ville à la campagne" to "de la vertu au vice"—with an amusing choice of examples.[27]

[26] *Oeuvres*, I, 459b-460b (*Grammaire*, I, xiv). It is worth noting that he takes refuge in an etymological assumption.
[27] *Oeuvres*, I, 478a-481b (*Grammaire*, II, xiii). For the group-

Condillac's treatment of the parts of speech shows that he was not satisfied with the traditional grouping of the *Grammaire générale*; he reduced adverbs and pronouns to other parts of speech, assumed that articles and conjunctions are useful rather than necessary, and gave a novel explanation of the preposition on the basis of the doctrine of the language of action. But he introduced considerable confusion in the process and did not achieve the ideal of reducing all the parts of speech to a single one. Still, he did make an effort to solve the problem which Locke had raised in his brief chapter "Of Particles,"[28] when he said that these words "are not truly, by themselves, the names of any *Ideas*," a statement which Locke's eighteenth-century readers found equivalent to an admission of inconsistency in his philosophy.

It is, of course, too evident to require demonstration that Condillac's *Essai* cannot be imagined without Locke's *Essay*—in fact, the subtitle of the first English translation in 1756 advertised the *Essai* as being "a supplement to Mr. Locke's Essay on the Human Understanding."[29] Even Condillac's doctrine of signs and lan-

---

ing of the preposition with the two nouns and the verb, see *Oeuvres*, I, 445b (*Grammaire*, I, viii): "On pouvoit . . . après avoir montré deux lieux différens, marquer, par un geste, celui d'où l'on venoit, et par un autre celui où l'on alloit. Voilà donc deux gestes, l'un équivalent à la préposition *de*, et l'autre à la préposition *à*. D'autres gestes pouvoient également être équivalens à *sur*, *sous*, *avant*, *après*, *etc.*; or, dès qu'on a eu démêlé ces rapports, dans la pensée décomposée par le langage d'action, on trouvoit d'autant moins de difficultés à leur donner des noms, qu'on avoit déjà nommé beaucoup d'autres idées. . . . Il ne faut que quatre espèces de mots pour exprimer toutes nos pensées: des substantifs, des adjectifs, des prépositions, et un seul verbe, tel que le verbe *être*."

28 *Essay*, III, vii.

29 Thomas Nugent (tr.), *An Essay on the Origin of Human Knowledge*; the translation is dedicated to William Warburton with flattering mention of Condillac's use of his *Divine Legation*. The author's name does not occur on the title page since the *Essai*

guage, which most sharply sets him apart from Locke, has close affinities with Locke's suggestion that some words play an active role in thought. Our ideas of mixed modes, for instance, exist only by virtue of the word which, like a knot, ties together a bundle of voluntarily joined ideas. Locke, however, was more concerned about the harmful effects of words: "That which has most contributed to hinder the due *tracing* of our *Ideas*, and finding out their Relations, and Agreements or Disagreements one with another has been, I suppose, the ill use of *Words*."[30] Condillac drew the converse inference that the right use of words promotes the tracing of our ideas, a reasonable inference for him since by right use he would understand an awareness of their origins, of their generation at a time when language was more suited to philosophical thinking than it now is. It was in this fashion that men might gain a clearer understanding of their signs and become like the mathematicians whose use of clear signs Locke so often referred to as a model. Locke and Condillac were both, and for similar reasons, suspicious of principles and definitions. The distance between Locke and Condillac is not so great as it may appear, even though one was chiefly concerned with the "imperfections" of language and words, the other with their "perfections." The underlying conception is the same, though only the second alternative could produce Condillac's theory of the dependence of all discursive thought on the use of language.

Condillac's analysis of the origin of language and words had one more consequence which was especially important since it had been anticipated by Locke. In the *Essay*, Locke had occasionally suggested that a consid-

---

did not appear under Condillac's name until the edition of the *Oeuvres* in 1769, though its authorship was widely known many years earlier.

[30] *Essay*, IV, iii, 30.

eration of words might give information about man's need for particular concepts, about their origin, and about the progress of the mind. In the chapter "Of Other Relations" in Book Two, he had remarked that we have words for the family relationships among men such as *father, son, brother,* and *cousin-german,* but we have no corresponding terms for the same relationships in animals because we do not have the same occasion to use them. He then continued: "This, by the Way, may give us some Light into the different State and Growth of Languages; which being suited only to the Convenience of Communication, are proportioned to the Notions Men have, and the Commerce of Thoughts familiar amongst them."[31] This suggests that a study of words may provide information about the people who speak them and about their society, its needs and concerns. In another place he had argued that men are more likely to admit infinite duration than infinite expansion, an argument he supported by references to analogy and etymology: "If the Names of things may at all direct our Thoughts towards the Originals of Mens *Ideas,* (as I am apt to think they may very much,) one may have occasion to think by the Name *Duration,* that the Continuation of Existence, with a kind of Resistance to any destructive Force, and the Continuation of Solidity, (which is apt to be confounded with, and if we will look into the minute anatomical parts of Matter, is little different from Hardness,) were thought to have some Analogy, and gave occasion to Words, so near of kin as *Durare* and *Durum esse.*"[32] The same sort of observation may give information about another matter which lies at the center of Condillac's entire argument. Locke derived all experience from sensation and reflection, but he had admitted that reflection comes on the scene after sensation, for "the first Years are usually

[31] II, xxviii, 2.
[32] II, xv, 4.

employ'd and diverted in looking abroad." The mind cannot begin to reflect until it has stored up a sufficient number of ideas of sensation to have something to reflect on.[33] But although reflection is chronologically secondary, Locke does not draw the conclusion that the capacity for reflection is reducible to the effects of sensation. This, however, was precisely the point at which Locke, according to Condillac, had failed to go far enough. On that question, the *Essay* contained a passage which superbly fitted Condillac's doctrine of the primacy of sensation and the historical dependence of thought on language. After Condillac, this passage became the unquestioned rationale for all etymological searching for the history of thought. It is so fundamental that it must be quoted at length. In the first chapter of Book Three, Locke had said:

> It may also lead us a little towards the Original of all our Notions and Knowledge, if we remark, how great a Dependance our *Words* have on common sensible *Ideas*; and how those, which are made use of to stand for Actions and Notions quite removed from sense, *have their rise from thence, and from obvious sensible* Ideas *are transferred to more abstruse Significations,* and made to stand for *Ideas* that come not under the cognizance of our Senses; v.g. to *Imagine, Apprehend, Comprehend, Adhere, Conceive, Instill, Disgust, Disturbance, Tranquillity,* &c. are all Words taken from the Operations of sensible Things, and applied to certain Modes of Thinking. *Spirit*, in its primary Signification, is Breath; *Angel*, a Messenger.

In the last two illustrations, Leibniz foresaw a tendency toward impiety, soon to find expression in later materialist interpretations, although of course neither Locke nor Condillac had any intention of transgressing the bounds of

[33] II, i, 8, 20, 24.

orthodoxy when they assumed that man in his present state is banished to a world of sense. Locke continued:

And I doubt not, but if we could trace them to their Sources, we should find, in all Languages, the Names, which stand for Things that fall not under our Senses, to have had their first rise from sensible *Ideas*. By which we may give some kind of guess, what kind of Notions they were, and whence derived, which filled their Minds, who were the first Beginners of Languages; and how Nature, even in the naming of Things, unawares suggested to Men the Originals and Principles of all their Knowledge: whilst, to give Names, that might make known to others any Operations they felt in themselves, or any other *Ideas*, that came not under their Senses, they were fain to borrow Words from ordinary known *Ideas* of Sensation, by that means to make others the more easily to conceive those Operations they experimented in themselves, which made no outward sensible Appearances; and then when they had got known and agreed Names, to signify those internal Operations of their own Minds, they were sufficiently furnished to make known by Words, all their other *Ideas*; since they could consist of nothing, but either of outward sensible Perceptions, or of the inward Operations of their Minds about them.[34]

Quoting and borrowing from this passage, Condillac came to this conclusion: "On voit évidemment comment tous ces noms ont été figurés dans leur origine."[35] Touching all aspects of Condillac's account of the origins of

[34] The observations and illustrations in the first part of this passage were not original with Locke. For this and Locke's treatment of words in general, see "Leibniz on Locke on Language" in the *American Philosophical Quarterly*, I (1964), 165-188.
[35] *Oeuvres*, I, 87b (*Essai*, II, i, x, par. 103).

human knowledge, Locke's tentative but suggestive illustration had an effect that could only have been equaled by the revered philosopher's return from the dead to proclaim the truth of the as yet anonymous *Essai*. The individual's introspection into the operations of his own mind and its growth could now, so it seemed, be replaced by the philosopher's study of the origin and progress of language, of etymology, both in regard to words and grammar. The principle was neatly expressed in Turgot's summary phrase: "Les langues sont la mesure des idées des hommes."[36] The long paragraph in the first chapter of Book Three of the *Essay* made it possible to attribute the great discovery to Locke himself. The impact on Condillac's contemporaries was almost immediate.

The first printed work that fully stated the philosophical significance of the study of language was Turgot's article on "Étymologie," which appeared in the *Encyclopédie* in 1756. People might object, Turgot said, that introspection would suffice to convince us of the sensible origins of spiritual ideas. True, "mais cette verité n'est-elle pas mise, en quelque sorte, sous les yeux d'une manière bien plus frappante, et n'acquiert-elle pas toute l'évidence d'un point de fait, par l'étymologie si connue des mots *spiritus, animus . . . pensée, délibération, intelligence*, etc.?" Turgot was convinced that this was a better and surer approach to the problem.

> Je crois qu'il est très désirable qu'on s'en occupe un peu d'après ce point de vue. En effet, l'esprit humain, en se repliant ainsi sur lui-même pour étudier sa marche, ne peut-il pas retrouver, dans les tours

[36] "Tableau philosophique des progrès successifs de l'esprit humain. Discours prononcé en latin dans les écoles de Sorbonne . . . le 11 decembre 1750," in *Oeuvres*, ed. G. Schelle (Paris, 1913), I, 223.

singuliers que les premiers hommes ont imaginés pour expliquer des idées nouvelles en parlant des objets connus, bien des analogies très fines et très justes entre plusieurs idées, des rapports de toute espèce que la nécessité toujours ingénieuse avait saisis, et que la paresse avait depuis oubliés? N'y peut-il pas voir souvent la gradation qu'on a suivie dans le passage d'une idée à une autre et dans l'intervention de quelques arts et, par là, cette étude ne devient-elle pas une branche intéressante de la métaphysique expérimentale?[37]

The same justification of etymology and its importance was developed at greater length in Charles de Brosses' *Traité de la formation méchanique des langues et des principes physiques de l'étymologie,* which soon became the chief text on etymological study.[38] In fact, de Brosses not only quoted Locke's passage in full but was so carried away by enthusiasm that he changed the cautious opening words into a categorical assertion—" 'Rien ne peut, dit le célebre Locke, nous approcher mieux de l'origine de toutes nos notions & connoissances . . . .' "[39] The unique importance of the *Traité,* however, was not its advocacy of the Locke-Condillac doctrine which was by now familiar enough. It lay, rather, in the practical demonstration that the doctrine worked. De Brosses tried to show that words might take their origin not only in interjections, but also in such "necessary words" as *papa* and *mama* which all children would automatically produce, in words associated with the particular organs of

[37] *Oeuvres,* I, 506. A few lines later in the same paragraph and context, Locke and Condillac are credited with these views.

[38] 2 vols. (Paris, 1765). French contemporaries remarked that demand had greatly increased its price before the reissue in 1801. A German translation appeared at Leipzig in 1777 as *Über Sprache und Schrift,* tr. Michael Hissman.

[39] *Traité,* II, 93 (par. 171). Coste's French version has nothing of the sort, but is a correct rendering of the original.

the mouth—such as *gorge, langue, dent, bouche*—in "les mots qui peignent par onomatopée," and in the invariable symbolic "meanings" of particular sound combinations such as *st-* for something firm and steadfast and *fl-* for something flowing or liquid.[40] These observations are, of course, much older than de Brosses, but he was the first to put them all together in this context. He further gave a wealth of examples in favor of the doctrine and paid close attention to the *cognatio literarum*—or phonological correspondence of sounds—which governed regular procedures in etymology.[41]

With the aid of this doctrine, de Brosses managed to produce a number of startling etymologies, for instance the derivation of *ratio* from *res*, for, as he said, "on ne pouvoit meiux peindre la force de cette opération de l'entendement qu'en y appliquant le mot *res*, pour faire entendre que la *raison* c'étoit la *chose* même toute réelle & toute vraie."[42] Philosophically, this sort of etymology tended toward materialism and skepticism, but there are no grounds at all for believing that either Condillac or de Brosses had any such aim in mind. Their aim was set entirely on giving a natural explanation of the origins of language and the operations of the mind. Horne Tooke, however, was certainly interested in the materialism and in showing that the nature of truth was not fixed but relative, as dependent on the observer as left and

[40] I, 222-269 (pars. 69-80).

[41] The procedures were none too certain but widely accepted at the time, on the authority of the influential "Prolegomena" to Johann Georg Wachter's *Glossarium Germanicum* (Leipzig, 1737), which remained a standard reference into the second decade of the nineteenth century. In *Traité*, II, 158-159 (par. 190), de Brosses gave this summary: "En étymologie dans la comparaison des mots, il ne faut avoir aucun égard aux voyelles, & n'en avoir aux consonnes qu'autant qu'elles seroient de différens organes." He believed that languages were distinguished by their consonants, but dialects only by the vowels.

[42] *Traité*, II, 254 (par. 212).

right. And whether materialist or not, Condillac and de Brosses could not escape the imputation that they had greatly reduced the range of activity that was necessary for the mind to achieve all its operations. If reflection was an operation that only language could set in motion and if, as Condillac said, "les langues sont l'ouvrage de la nature,"[43] then the mind was very passive indeed; and that was precisely the view of the skepticism which Locke's philosophy had produced in England. It was therefore quite reasonable that one line of attack might wish to show that language involved much more than nature, need, and instinct could produce, that its creation presupposed nonnatural, spiritual, active faculties, which could not be explained but only assumed to be inherent in the mind. This was the argument pursued by James Harris and Lord Monboddo, whom Horne Tooke considered the most typical representatives of the philosophy he wished to destroy with his etymological proof that the operations of the mind are merely the operations of language.[44]

The title of Monboddo's great work was an announcement that he intended to make language the pivotal issue

[43] *Oeuvres*, I, 432b (*Grammaire*, I, ii).

[44] Charles de Brosses exercised a greater influence than the date of the *Traité* appears to indicate. The *Traité* was largely based—though to what extent is not known—on two memoirs which he read to the *Academie des Inscriptions et Belles-Lettres* in Paris in June 1751. Originally intended for inclusion in the *Encyclopédie*, they passed into the hands of Diderot, who later lent them to Turgot after the latter had agreed to do the article on etymology. Turgot gives evidence of having borrowed from de Brosses, but would not necessarily have the Locke-Condillac doctrine from him. The influence of the two memoirs also spread through other articles, as acknowledged, for instance, in Nicolas Beauzée's article "Interjection." Articles in the *Encyclopédie* that appeared from 1765 onward frequently quoted the *Traité* at great length, e.g. the article "Onomatopée." See Th. Foisset, *Le Président de Brosses* (Paris, 1842), pp. 547-552 and 579, as well as de Brosses' "Discours préliminaire" to the *Traité* and Turgot's own acknowledgment at the end of "Étymologie."

in his argument against the prevailing tendencies of the philosophy of his time: *Of the Origin and Progress of Language.*[45] But Monboddo's critique embraces much more than language, which is only the example that illustrates his contention that man's attainments are more artificial and less natural than had been claimed. What right, for instance, did the natural school have to assume that it was man's basic nature to be rational? None at all, says Monboddo, for this is precisely the question at issue. He therefore begins with a distinction between natural man, who is the work of God, and man as "the work of man," a "creature of art," which is the state in which we now observe him. The natural history of man has two aspects, the material or physiological, which has already been carefully studied, and "the natural state of his better part, the mind," which has been neglected.[46] Hence the unique importance of the study of the origin of language "as it is by language that we trace, with the

[45] 6 vols. (Edinburgh, 1773-1792). Only Volumes I and III were reprinted, in 1774 and 1776; I am using the 2nd edition of Volume I, which is the only one that concerns us here. Monboddo stated in the "Preface," pp. ix-x, that his knowledge of the contents of Condillac's *Essai sur l'origine* derived not from the work itself, but from the excerpts he had read in a review of Thomas Nugent's English translation in the *Critical Review*, II, (1756), 193-218, where one may assume he also found the title he used, the review correctly giving the subject of the *Essai*'s II, i, as "origin and progress of language" (p. 202). Monboddo further wrote that he gathered that he and Condillac were in basic agreement; but he still believed that Condillac's work did not make his own superfluous, "as his [Condillac's] book is chiefly upon the operations of the mind, so that a small part of it only is employed upon language, I do not think it could have been of great use to me. The subject, therefore, may still be considered as new." Monboddo is of course mistaken, for Condillac's II, i, "De l'origine et des progrès du langage," is the title of a third of his work, but there would have been no way of knowing this from the review, which also failed to show why Condillac and Monboddo would not agree, in spite of many obvious similarities.
[46] I, iii (Preface).

37

greatest certainty, the progress of the human mind."[47] He defines language as *"the expression of the conceptions of the mind by articulate sounds,"* thus altogether ruling out the language of action, gestures, facial grimaces, and "signs, such as our dumb persons use,"[48] all of which can at best be called language in a metaphorical sense—little did Monboddo know how much he disagreed with Condillac. Empirical evidence shows that man alone—or rather *homo sapiens*—has achieved language, the defining characteristic of his humanity. First of all, even conceptions of the mind are so hard to come by that the simplest sensations need the active interpretation of the mind before they can become ideas—even the sight of a horse will, without "a *discursus mentis,* and a conclusion of reason, as I call it,"[49] remain a mere picture in the bottom of the eye. Here the mind must already exercise its first active faculty which, though it may be acquired by habit, must proceed from a much higher original. Abstraction makes no sense without the Platonic doctrine of ideas. But granted that this difficulty has been overcome, language is still very hard to attain. Evidence again shows that meaningful articulation is so demanding that man alone has it. It is not natural, for "not only solitary savages, but a whole nation, if I may call them so,

---

[47] I, 154. At this point Monboddo refers to the famous passage in Locke's *Essay* on the etymology of words that apply to modes of thinking. Cf. I, 214-215: "I said, in the beginning of the work, that it was an inquiry that would lead me back to the very origin of the human race; and it has so happened. For I could not give the philosophical account I proposed, of the origin of language, without inquiring into the origin of ideas." And further I, 574: "It appears, that, from the study of language, if it be properly conducted, the history of the human mind is best learned, especially in the first steps of its progress, of which it is impossible there can be any other record than what is preserved in language." It is worth noting that Monboddo does not attribute skepticism to Locke himself, but only to the misunderstandings of his followers.
[48] I, 5-6.   [49] I, 37.

have been found without the use of speech." At this point enters the celebrated orang-outang. "This is the case of the Orang Outangs. . . . They are exactly of the human form; walking erect, not upon all-four, like the savages that have been found in Europe; they use sticks for weapons; they live in society; they make huts of branches of trees, and they carry off negroe girls, of whom they make slaves."[50] The inclusion of the orang-outang in the species man was a brilliant stroke; certain learned people had assumed that they were monkeys "not men, because they did not speak, proceeding upon the vulgar error, that language is natural to man; and that therefore whatever animal does not speak, is not a man."[51] Clearly, they did not lack certain basic arts if they could build huts nor did they lack some understanding. Monboddo had seen a stuffed one in Paris in the king's cabinet of natural curiosities. "He had exactly the shape and features of a man . . . lived several years at Versailles . . . died by drinking spirits . . . had as much of the understanding of a man as could be expected from his education, and performed many little offices to the lady with whom he lived; but never learned to speak." Monboddo had also heard of another who "belonged to a French gentleman in India, who used to go to market for him, but was likewise mute."[52] And to guard against the objection that the apes lacked speech for physiological reasons, we are told that this specimen "had the organs of pronunciation as perfect as we have."[53] With its social state, the orang-

[50] I, 187-188. Monboddo notes that he has his information from Buffon.

[51] I, 257. [52] I, 189.

[53] This was, of course, a delicate point in the argument. In 1779 the *Philosophical Transactions of the Royal Society*, LXIX, 139-159, carried an article by the famous Dutch anatomist Peter Camper under the title "Account of the Organs of Speech of the Orang Outang," complete with illustrations and proof of "the true organical reason . . . the absolute impossibility there is for the Orang and other monkies to speak." It is hard not to believe

outang solved another crucial problem. Rousseau had criticized Condillac for surreptitiously avoiding the question whether language or society came first by placing the boy and the girl alone in the desert, for the family itself, Rousseau objected, involved social structure; Rousseau, therefore, did not see how the problem could be solved.[54]

After these long preliminaries, Monboddo is ready to give an account of the origin of language, which must be a highly artificial product. *Homo sapiens* first began to articulate in imitation of the natural cries of animals, just as he also, by his unique capacity for imitation, learned the art of weaving from the spider.[55] From this beginning, language would grow by slow degrees, "words still multiplying, till at last the language became too cumbersome for use; and then art was obliged to interpose, and form a language according to rule and method."[56] Thus at this stage, Monboddo's account of the origin of language is very similar to Condillac's, but with the enormous difference that Monboddo's man had already at this point, and without language, developed far beyond the moment when, according to Condillac, language was beginning to give man the first glimmerings of reflection. Monboddo had not brought man into company with the orang-outang in order to debase him; on the contrary, even at this seemingly close range, there is a vast distance between natural and artificial man; and the difference is entirely a product of those active powers and energies for whose development the speaking man alone had re-

---

that this communication was designed to nullify Monboddo's argument. De Brosses was disturbed by the same problem; in his notes for additions to the *Traité* was found a query why the orang-outang does not speak if it has the same speech organs as man; he answers: "Sans doute que les différences échappent à l'art de l'anatomiste." Foisset, *op.cit.*, p. 451.

[54] Monboddo, I, 215ff. and Rousseau, *Oeuvres complètes*, I (Paris: Hachette, 1905), 96 (*Discours sur l'origine de l'inégalite*).
[55] I, 489ff.　[56] I, 481-482.

ceived the disposition.[57] And that was what Monboddo wanted to show.

Samuel Johnson was afraid that "Monboddo does not know he is talking nonsense," and called his examination of the primitive state of man "all conjecture upon a thing useless, even were it known to be true." His estimate misses the wide implications and the philosophical sophistication of Monboddo's argument, but it is probably a typical expression of contemporary opinion, which paid much attention to the orang-outang but little to the argument in which it appeared. By contrast, James Beattie's *Essay on the Nature and Immutability of Truth* ran through eight editions between 1770 and 1800 and saw as many again during the next twenty-five years. As early as 1773, it brought its author a pension of two hundred pounds from the king, who admitted that he never "stole a book but one, and that was yours."[58] Beattie expressed similar philosophical views in his "Theory of Language," which held that language was given by inspiration, an opinion also accepted in Hugh Blair's phenomenally successful *Lectures on Rhetoric*. This work could boast ten editions in England between 1783 and 1806, not to mention the American reissues and one French (1797), one Italian (1801), and one Spanish (1816) version.

Monboddo's reputation fared much better in Germany. Herder suggested that his work be translated, and in 1784-1785 appeared, at Riga, *Des Lord Monboddos Werk von dem Ursprunge und Fortgange der Sprache*, which was a somewhat abbreviated version of the first

[57] Actually Condillac's view is very similar to Monboddo's, but not having Monboddo's grounds for being on guard against skepticism, he left it a rarely stated assumption. In the *Traité des animaux*, however, he said: "Il n'est pas étonnant que l'homme, qui est aussi supérieur par l'organisation que par la nature de l'esprit qui l'anime, ait seul le don de la parole" (*Oeuvres*, I, 361b).

[58] *DNB*, s.v. "James Beattie."

three volumes. Herder himself wrote the Preface, in which he pointed out that the work had had a poor reception in England because the metaphysicians scorned the attack on Locke, the men of science the critique of Newton (in *Antient Metaphysic*), and the reviewers the contempt for modern literature. But Herder believed that the book would have success in Germany where such objections could not prevail. Monboddo had nothing to fear from German philosophers for the significant reason that "Locke geht uns nicht weiter an, als sofern er der Wahrheit diente, und wir sind lange schon durch Leibnitz gewöhnt, auch schwache Seiten seiner Philosophie zu finden"—a statement that goes far to explain the difference between English and German thought, not least in regard to the history and the concerns of language study in Germany. With the great authority of his own prize-essay on the origin of language, Herder gave the highest possible praise in these words: "Vorzüglich, dünkt mich, ist unserm Verfasser der Hauptzweck seines Werks, die Untersuchung vom Ursprung und den Fortschritten der Sprache gelungen; so dass ich ihm hierinn, da ich ziemlich alles gelesen, was über diesen Gegenstand geschrieben ist, und selbst darüber beschrieben habe, willig die Palme reiche."[59] The works of Monboddo and Harris, whose *Hermes* had also been translated into German, would at last make possible a "Philosophie des menschlichen Verstandes" when the small deficiencies of the present work had been removed "durch weitere Untersuchungen in unserm Sprachgelehrten philosophischen Vaterlande"—another prophetic phrase.

Horne Tooke would not have accepted Herder's estimate, and here lies the reason why the study of language in England and Germany came to be pursued along widely diverging lines during the next generation, in spite

[59] B. Suphan (ed.), *Herders Sämmtliche Werke* (Berlin, 1877-1913), XV, 179-183.

of the profound influence which Lowth, Harris, Monboddo, and several others exercised in Germany. But Horne Tooke did agree with Monboddo's succinct statement of the doctrine that the study of language was the best aid to the study of the human mind: "It appears, that, from the study of language, if it be properly conducted, the history of the human mind is best to be learned, especially in the first steps of its progress, of which it is impossible there can be any other record than what is preserved in language."[60] As to the hopeful outcome of that study, however, he would have agreed with Turgot that the study of language was the best remedy against innate ideas and the innumerable imaginery beings that were the result of giving reality to the abstractions of the mind, against virtualities, formalities, entities, quiddities, etc. "Rien, je parle d'après Locke," said Turgot, "n'est plus propre à en détromper, qu'un examen suivi de la manière dont les hommes sont parvenus à donner des noms à ces sortes d'idées abstraites ou spirituelles, et même à se donner de nouvelles idées par le moyen de ces mots."[61] This was the path Horne Tooke set out to pursue.

[60] I, 574.

[61] G. Schelle (ed.), *Oeuvres*, I, 505 ("Étymologie"). The original text of the *Encyclopédie*, VI (1756), 108, has "par le moyen de ces noms." Here as elsewhere, Schelle's text differs in detail from the text printed in the *Encyclopédie*.

CHAPTER II

The Diversions of Purley

Horne Tooke's ΕΠΕΑ ΠΤΕΡΟΕΝΤΑ, *or the Diversions of Purley* took the form of a dialogue with three participants, one of whom was the author. In the first volume the other two were William Tooke, who owned the country estate near Croydon where the "diversions" occurred and whose name John Horne respectfully adopted in 1783; and the author's good friend from the Cambridge days, now master of Jesus College, Richard Beadon. In the second volume his place was taken by another good friend, Sir Francis Burdett, and William Tooke was no longer present—or said nothing. But all three say only just enough to feed the right questions to the author whose answers are so long, and so full of examples, etymologies, and footnotes, that the illusion of dialogue is soon lost during the reading of the work, which exceeds one thousand pages. The first volume, which incorporated *A Letter to Mr. Dunning* of 1778, appeared in 1786 and was reissued in 1798, while the second volume was published in 1805. A third volume was to have contained the completion of the system, but it never appeared. We are told that the manuscript was nearly finished when, during his last illness shortly before his death in 1812, Horne Tooke threw it on the fire together with his large correspondence. Horne Tooke's philosophical and philological reputation rests entirely on these two volumes, which also earned him between four and five thousand pounds.[1]

[1] I am using the standard edition—hereafter abbreviated *DP*—which consists of the 1st edition of Volume II (1805) and the 2nd edition of Volume I (1798), which includes the *Letter to Mr. Dunning* in Chapters vi, vii, and viii, "except some small

The *Diversions* open in the middle of a debate which has led Horne Tooke to maintain, against the opinion of William Tooke, "that all sorts of wisdom and useful knowledge may be obtained by a plain man of sense without what is commonly called Learning," a familiar eighteenth-century motif which we have already encountered in Condillac. William Tooke now tries to put his friend to the test by asking him whether this would also hold for grammar. Beadon suggests that the matter does not appear very difficult to him, for English grammar can be easily learned from the "excellent Introductions of Doctor Lowth: or from the *first* (as well as the *best*) English grammar, given by Ben Jonson"; and if one should wish to go farther, from James Harris's *Hermes*. But William Tooke and the author do not agree with Beadon, for the former has asked "after the causes and reasons of Grammar," a subject which the author finds difficult but also "absolutely necessary in the search after philosophical truth," acknowledging "philosophical Grammar . . . to be a most necessary step towards wisdom and true knowledge." Truth, he believes, "has been improperly imagined at the bottom of a well: it lies much nearer to the surface; though buried indeed at present under mountains of learned rubbish." He differs from all those who have gone before him and proposes to offer an altogether new theory. The stage is set.[2]

Horne Tooke first explains how traditional grammar

---

alterations and additions" according to Horne Tooke's own statement (*DP*, I, 74); he also says here that his interest in language goes back some thirty years. The *Letter* is separately reprinted in the Appendix to Richard Taylor's edition of *DP* (London, 1829, 1840, 1857, and 1860). Another edition was published in Philadelphia in 1806-1807. For biographical information and further references, readers are referred to Leslie Stephen's article in *DNB* and to Minnie Clare Yarborough's *John Horne Tooke* (New York, 1926).

[2] *DP*, I, 1-15 (Introduction).

has gone astray, ending in utter confusion. Words being the signs of things, grammar rightly began by admitting only as many parts of speech as there were sorts of things; but at best, this division only led to four parts: noun, verb, conjunction, and article. Finding it impossible to fit all words into these four groups, the grammarians reversed the process and instead postulated as many differences of things as of signs. Having been "misled . . . by the useful contrivances of language, they supposed many imaginary differences of things: and thus added greatly to the number of parts of speech, and in consequence to the errors of philosophy."[3] Matters did not improve when grammarians, substituting ideas for things, referred the parts of speech to the operations of the mind. Now, as soon as they ran into difficulty, they solved the problem by supposing additional operations of the mind to the further detriment of philosophy. The result was "dispute, diversity, and darkness." This is the problem that was suggested by the Port-Royal Grammar and for which Condillac had attempted to offer at least a partial solution. Horne Tooke is now ready to present the explanation which will overcome the confusion.

From Locke he borrowed two time-honored axioms about the nature of language: its first aim is to communicate our thoughts, its second to do so quickly or "with dispatch," in order to make the speed of discourse more nearly approach the speed of thought. Investing this doctrine with a new meaning, Horne Tooke makes abbreviation the cornerstone of his theory of language. In all languages, the words can be divided in two groups: those that are immediately the signs of things or ideas and those that "are merely *abbreviations* employed for dispatch, and are the signs of other words."[4] These are the "artificial wings of Mercury . . . and do not, like those of other

[3] *DP*, I, 22. [4] *DP*, I, 27.

winged deities, make a part of his body." To study language, we must "loose the strings from his feet, and take off his cap"—as illustrated in the frontispiece to the first volume. The first group, containing all the words necessary to communication, comprises only two parts of speech, the noun and the verb. The nouns are easily accounted for; they are the signs of the impressions that sensation makes on the mind, the names of ideas. But Horne Tooke also allows the verb in this group on the grounds that it "must be accounted for from the necessary use of it in communication."[5] All other words are abbreviations of words in the first group. "General reasoning *à priori*" had brought him to this conclusion. The etymological proof was secondary and did not occur to him until many years later, "and it occurred to me suddenly, in this manner;—'If my reasoning concerning these conjunctions is well founded, there must then be in the original language from which the English (and so of all other languages) is derived, literally *such* and *such* words bearing precisely *such* and *such* significations.' "[6] By this means Horne Tooke achieved the reduction which others had sought but failed to find. He had produced a theory of language which agreed entirely, so it seemed, with the more radical eighteenth-century interpretations of Locke's doctrine of the origin of ideas in sense. He could confidently claim that "the business of the mind, as far as it concerns Language . . . extends no farther than to receive Impressions, that is, to have Sensations or Feelings."[7] The verb, of course, was worrisome. Early in the first volume he promised to deal with it as one of the parts of speech necessary to communication, but he was diverted—or avoided it—before he came to it. The question was not raised again until the very end of the *Diversions*, when Sir Francis Burdett bluntly

[5] *DP*, I, 51.   [6] *DP*, I, 131-132.   [7] *DP*, I, 51.

asked: "What is the *Verb*? What is that peculiar differ-
ential circumstance which, added to the definition of a
Noun, constitutes the *Verb*?" But time was running out.
"We will leave off here for the present," said Horne
Tooke. "It is true that my evening is now fully come, and
the night fast approaching; yet, if we shall have a toler-
ably lengthened twilight, we may still perhaps find time
enough for a farther conversation on this subject." But
this was the manuscript that went up in smoke some
seven years later. Still, abbreviation was the great discovery which to his contemporaries made Horne Tooke
the immortal "philologer," who in the words of Erasmus
Darwin had "unfolded by a single flash of light the whole
theory of language, which has so long lain buried beneath the learned lumber of the schools."[8] Or as he said
poetically with personification in the *Temple of Nature*
(1802) at the end of Canto III, on the "Progress of the
Mind,"

> Last steps Abbreviation, bold and strong,
> And leads the volant trains of words along;
> With sweeth loquacity to *Hermes* springs,
> And decks his forehead and his feet with wings.

To understand the impact of this discovery of the role of
abbreviation in language, we may first take a closer look
at the doctrine and its adaptation in Tooke before turning
to some typical examples from the *Diversions*.

Traditional grammar had often invoked abbreviation
as a sort of force that operated in language, though without explaining what it was, looking only to the effect but
not to the cause. The Port-Royal Grammar, which Horne
Tooke always mentions with respect, had for instance
used it to account for the contraction of phrases into
single words, in this case adverbs: "Le désir que les

[8] *Zoonomia*, I (New York, 1796), 392 (Sect. xxxix, 8); 1st
edn., London, 1794.

hommes ont d'abréger le discours, est ce qui a donné lieu aux adverbes: car la plupart de ces particules ne sont que pour signifier en un seul mot, ce qu'on ne pourroit marquer que par une préposition & un nom: comme *sapienter*, sagement; pour, *cum sapientia*, avec sagesse." The influential French universal grammarian, du Marsais, had emphatically stated that this was a universal principle which operated in all languages because the reason for it was the same in all: "L'empressement que nous avons tous à faire connoître nos pensées dans le discours, a introduit l'usage d'abréger les expressions qui reviennent souvent."[9] Condillac, as we have seen, used the same explanation to account for adverbs and certain conjunctions and pronouns by ellipsis, again in all cases to shorten the discourse for the sake of keeping up with the speed of thought. But in the *Traité de la formation méchanique*, de Brosses had altered the conception somewhat and thus came a good deal closer to Tooke, though, for reasons which will appear later, Tooke did not agree. Referring to prepositions, de Brosses had said: "Elles sont des formules abrégées dont l'usage est le plus frapant & le plus commode dans toutes les langues pour circonstancier les idées: elles sont elles-mêmes racines primitives; mais je n'ai pas trouvé qu'il fut possible d'assigner la cause de leur origine: tellement que j'en crois la formation purement arbitraire." De Brosses further thought that the same was true of all the particles, of articles, pronouns, conjunctions, and all the other little words that are used to "tie the discourse together."[10] Here abbreviation is not used to explain the contraction of a construction, but to describe the nature of the particles,

[9] *Oeuvres* (Paris, 1797), I, 18, in *Exposition d'une méthode raisonnée pour apprendre la langue Latine* (1722).

[10] *Traité*, II, 187-188 (par. 198). This passage is quoted in *DP*, I, 314-315.

though with the ready admission that their origin cannot be explained.

There is, however, another and no less important kind of abbreviation, which the mathematicians and the philosophers often mention. In "De l'esprit géométrique et de l'art de persuader," Pascal discussed the definitions and signs that are used in geometry. "Leur utilité et leur usage," he said, "est d'éclaircir et d'abréger le discours, en exprimant, par le seul nom qu'on impose, ce qui ne pourrait se dire qu'en plusieurs termes."[11] Locke had used the same principle to illustrate how language works by abbreviation—though normally without the speaker's awareness—most evidently in the names of complex ideas of mixed modes and substances. Of the former he said:

> Though these complex *Ideas* be not always copied from Nature, yet they are always suited to the end for which abstract *Ideas* are made: And though they be Combinations made of *Ideas*, that are loose enough, and have as little union in themselves, as several other, to which the Mind never gives a connexion that combines them into one *Idea*; yet they are always made for the convenience of Communication, which is the chief end of Language. The use of Language is, by short Sounds to signify with ease and dispatch general Conceptions.

[11] *Oeuvres complètes* (Paris: Pléiade, 1954), p. 577. For Pascal's contributions to the Port-Royal *Grammaire* and to the *Logique*, see *Oeuvres*, eds. Brunschvicg, Boutroux, & Gazier, IV, 77-78 and IX, 231-239. Cf. Galileo in *Dialogues Concerning Two New Sciences*, trs. Henry Crew and Alfonso de Salvio (Evanston, 1946), p. 28: "Note by the way the nature of mathematical definitions, which consists merely in the imposition of names, or, if you prefer, abbreviations of speech established and introduced in order to avoid the tedious drudgery which you and I now experience simply because we have not agreed to call this surface 'circular band' and that sharp solid portion of the bowl a 'round razor.'"

A few sections later he said: "Though therefore it be the Mind that makes the Collection, 'tis the Name which is, as it were, the Knot, that ties them fast together." It is characteristic that Horne Tooke in his copy of the *Essay* heavily underscored the latter part of both passages and put multiple brackets in the margin.[12] Both passages, along with a number of others in the *Essay*, suggested that language or words may in some fashion perform an active role, a suggestion which agreed with and may have helped fix Tooke's belief that the operations of mind are really operations of language. The philosophical and the grammatical conceptions of abbreviation came together in Tooke's system, thus explaining both the origin and true meaning of the particles, as well as the bases of abstraction in language.

Abbreviation has a threefold application in language: in terms, in sorts of words, and in construction. The best guide to the first is Locke's *Essay*, and "numberless are the authors who have given particular explanations of the *last*." It is, Horne Tooke says, the second that is his province, but only for the present, with reference to conjunctions and prepositions, for it soon becomes apparent that he will also deal with the third application, which works by ellipsis and requires subaudition for its explanation. What does Horne Tooke mean when he says that he considers "the *whole* of Mr. Locke's Essay as a philosophical account of the *first* sort of abbreviations in Language"?[13] Somewhat in the manner of Condillac, he means that the

---

[12] *Essay*, III, v, 7, 10. Tooke's copy was the 15th edition (London, 1760), now in the British Museum. Tooke underlined a similar passage in III, vi, 32 ("Of the Names of Substances"): "But Men, in making their general *Ideas*, seeking more the convenience of Language and quick dispatch, by short and comprehensive signs, than the true and precise Nature of Things. . . ." On abbreviation, see also Hume's *Treatise*, ed. Selby-Bigge, pp. 20-21.

[13] *DP*, I, 30.

so-called composition of ideas is a contrivance of language, a composition in terms, so that it is "as improper to speak of a *complex idea*, as it would be to call a constellation a complex star." Only terms are general and abstract; ideas never are.[14] Locke had proposed to deal with the "force and manner of Signification" of words, but had in fact—even in Book Three—never gone beyond their force, except in the brief chapter "Of Particles." "The force of a word," Tooke says, "depends upon the number of Ideas of which that word is a sign," which makes it the same as the first sort of abbreviation, "which is by far the most important to knowledge, and which he [Locke] supposed to belong to Ideas."[15] In this sense, the force of words is the same as abstraction.

Locke, however, had rightly divided all words into two categories, names of ideas and particles, which corresponded to Tooke's two categories of words that are necessary for communication and words that are necessary only for "quickness and dispatch." Thus the chapter "Of Particles" in Book Three "should have contained an account of every thing but *Nouns*"—a contention which again suggests that the verb is an awkward intruder in Tooke's system. But could language really get along with nouns—and perhaps verbs—alone? Tooke thought so and was naturally forced into that position if he wished to remain consistent in his opinion that the mind had no other business than to have sensations. It would be difficult and cumbersome, but it could be done. And it was precisely to meet this difficulty that words had taken

[14] *DP*, I, 37. He found the example in the *Essay*, II, xxiv, 3. In the analytical table of contents to Book II, he put "none" opposite the headings of Chapters xii, xxiii, xxiv, xxix, xxx, xxxi, xxxii. To the marginal summaries of II, xxiv, 2 and 3, he wrote "no," and to the phrase "that it be considered as one Representation, or Picture, though made up of never so many Particulars," in II, xxiv, 1, he remarked "one word, that is all."

[15] *DP*, I, 40-43. Locke's phrase is in III, ix, 21.

wings, in the abbreviation both of terms and of the manner of signification, the latter of which, we now see, refers
not only to abbreviation in sorts of words but also in construction. This conception had gained acceptance as a
seemingly natural consequence of Condillac's account of
the origins of knowledge, though he had failed to achieve
a convincing reduction of the parts of speech. But de
Brosses had suggested that a man who lived alone and
had no need to communicate would also have no need for
the particles. He could formulate "sa phrase mentale"
from "les seuls termes principaux" alone, which were, so
to speak, sufficient to create "la peinture de l'esprit."[16]
Tooke can therefore confidently agree that what Locke
had called "the composition, abstraction, complexity,
generalization, relation, &c. of Ideas, does indeed merely
concern *Language*."[17] And he can triumphantly assert
that "perhaps it was for mankind a lucky mistake (for it
was a mistake) which Mr. Locke made when he called
his book, An Essay on Human *Understanding*. For some
part of the inestimable benefit of that book has, merely
on account of its title, reached to many thousands more
than, I fear, it would have done, had he called it (what
it is merely) A *Grammatical* Essay, or a Treatise on
Words, or on *Language*."[18] In the light of Condillac's
doctrine of the fundamental dependence of thought on
the use of signs and language, that statement is not so
absurd as it may appear at first. But Tooke differs from
Condillac in doing away with even that dependence; all
the operations of thought reside in language alone. He
does not need the doctrine that language makes thought
possible, for language is thought. It is enough for him to
stand by Locke's doctrine that the purpose of language
is communication—even memory he does not need to
consider, for that also is contained in words and language.

[16] *Traité*, II, 188.   [17] *DP*, I, 39.   [18] *DP*, I, 31.

It would be easy to maintain that Horne Tooke's philosophy does not ultimately make sense, but there can be no doubt that it is radical—even though it contains the germs of a very romantic and nearly mystical notion of language, germs that were quite as numerous and potent in Condillac. If thought resides in language, then one may also think that language has a soul and a genius. "Tout confirme donc," Condillac had said, "que chaque langue exprime le caractère du peuple qui la parle."[19]

Horne Tooke is now ready to go to work on the sort of abbreviations that have their cause in the need for dispatch, all of which he intends to refer to the two primary parts of speech, the noun and the verb. His best tool is etymology which, he says in a revealing metaphor, "like a microscope . . . is sometimes useful to discover the minuter parts of language which would otherwise escape our sight."[20] But he begins with the word that had been the occasion for the *Letter to Mr. Dunning*, the word *that*, which provides him with the opportunity to assert against Harris and other grammarians that the same word never fluctuates among different parts of speech. Harris, for instance, had maintained that *that* was sometimes an article, and at other times a pronoun or a conjunction. This Tooke cannot admit, for the consequence would also be different meanings, which of course goes against the basic doctrine. The error lay in not properly considering the construction so as to reveal that the manner of signification remains the same. *That* is an article and never a conjunction, as may be seen by "resolving" the sentence "I wish you to believe that I would not wilfully hurt a fly" into "I would not wilfully hurt a fly; I wish you to believe *that* (assertion)." Another illustration is the famous example from the trial for sedition: "She knowing *that* Crooke had been indicted for forgery, did so and so,"

[19] *Oeuvres*, I, 98b (*Essai*, II, i, xv, par. 143).
[20] *DP*, I, 531-532.

54

is resolved into "Crooke had been indicted for forgery; she, knowing *that* (fact), did so and so."[21] Since this account will be found to hold for all languages, it follows that the explanation is correct and not merely based on an adventitious occurrence in the English language, though the resolution will not always be as easy as with *that*. In such cases, etymology may be required to show the connection that has been lost, for the particles are especially prone to change on the principle that "Abbreviation and Corruption are always busiest with the words which are most frequently in use. Letters, like soldiers, being very apt to desert and drop off in a long march, and especially if their passage happens to lie near the confines of an enemy's country."[22] If Tooke here seems to be taking a light view of etymological procedures in our sense, it must be remembered that his contemporaries had none better to offer, a very important fact since the etymological proof of the a priori doctrine would not have succeeded if it had been attempted a hundred years later. Tooke was using all the etymological dictionaries of his day, though he did not feel bound to follow them if they did not suit his doctrine. He can now begin the detailed consideration of a large number of prepositions and conjunctions, having been urged by his interlocutor Beadon to do so for the sake of complete conviction and proof.

The method is best illustrated by the citation of a few typical examples. With a little speculation and quickness of his own, the reader can easily construct others that will come out nearly as well as Horne Tooke's. Harris had given *from* several different meanings, and Dr. Johnson had distributed it into no less than twenty separate cate-

[21] *DP*, I, 86-87.

[22] *DP*, I, 94. The first sentence of this quotation is in italics. I have simplified Tooke's—or the printer's—extravagant use of italics and of small and large capital letters. It occurs chiefly in the citation of examples.

gories, such as privation, transmission, abstraction, distance, and so forth. But Tooke explains that "*from* means merely *beginning*, and nothing else. It is simply the Anglo-Saxon and Gothic noun *Frum: Beginning, Origin, Source, fountain, author*." Thus the phrases "figs came from Turkey," "lamp falls from ceiling," and "lamp hangs from ceiling," do not, as Harris had said, illustrate uses of *from* that give it the varying meanings of detached relation of body, motion, and quiescence. To show that *from* retains the same meaning of *beginning*, the phrases need merely be resolved in the following manner: "figs came—beginning Turkey," "lamp falls—beginning ceiling," and "lamp hangs—beginning ceiling." And these again can be further resolved into the simpler formulae "Turkey the place of beginning to come," "ceiling the place of beginning to fall," and "ceiling the place of beginning to hang." Similarly "From morn till night th' eternal Larum rang," is resolved "the Larum rang beginning morning"; for the meaning of *from* retains the same basic meaning whether in relation to place or time. A footnote calls attention to the great utility of this sort of explanation, for "if the meaning of this word *from,* and of its correspondent prepositions in other languages, had been clearly understood; the Greek and Latin Churches would never have differed concerning the *Eternal Procession* of the Holy Ghost *from* the Father, or *from* the Father and the Son. . . . If they had been determined to separate, they would at least have chosen some safer cause of schism." The conclusion is that this preposition "continues to retain invariably one and the same single meaning," in spite of all the separate denotations—"which, I believe, are above seventy"—given in Johnson's *Dictionary*.[23] In other cases, prepositions are reduced directly to the names of real objects, as for instance the English *through* which "is no other than the

[23] *DP*, I, 341-347.

Gothic substantive *dauro*, or the Teutonic substantive *thuruh*: and like them means *door, gate, passage*." This explanation is further illustrated with English, Anglo-Saxon, Dutch, German, and other Germanic forms.[24] Other words such as *before, behind, below, beside, besides* are "merely the imperative *be*, compounded with the nouns *fore, hind, low, side*, which remaining still in constant and common use in the language; as—the *fore part*, the *hind part*, a *low place*, the *side*,—require no explanation."[25]

Where a noun reduction is not available, the imperative is used instead. Skinner had explained *unless* as "oneless," but Tooke derives it from the imperative of the Anglo-Saxon verb *onlesan*, with a *ðe* either expressed or understood: *onles ðe* is simply "dismiss that."[26] Similarly *still* is from Anglo-Saxon *stellan*: to put; *yet* from *getan*: to get; *but* with short *u* from *botan*: to boot; with long *u* from *beon-utan*: to be without; and *since* is the participle of *see* with *ðe* added, meaning "seeing that." Other words are so transparent in their formation and construction that they require no explanation at all, for example, *notwithstanding, albeit, save that, saving that,* and *except that*. The preposition *with* is a more interesting and complicated example. He chooses the phrases "a house *with* a party-wall" and "a house *without* a roof." The meaning of *with* in the former is explained as the imperative of a verb for *join*, the only difference between the two being "that the other parts of the verb *wiðan, to join* . . . have ceased to be employed in the language," though still retained in the substantives *with* or *withe, withers*, and *wither-band*. This reduction, however, will not do for the second phrase, which requires *with* to be derived from the Anglo-Saxon verb *wyrðan, to be*, a derivation which is supported by the observation

[24] *DP*, I, 334-338.   [25] *DP*, I, 405.   [26] *DP*, I, 171.

that *by* and *with* are often synonymous, "for *by* is the imperative of *beon, to be.*" The resolution of the two original phrases can now be achieved: "A house *join* a party-wall" and "a house *be-out* a roof."[27] But what then is the explanation of *out*? Indeed, this question later occurs to Beadon, who asks Tooke how he would account for *in, out, on, off,* and *at.* He gets no answer, however, for the remarkable thing happens that Tooke for once shows a little humility, admitting that he has neither the knowledge nor the skill to explain them, though he is nearly convinced by his own conjecture that *in* derives from a word meaning "interior pars corporis" and *out* from one that meant "skin."[28]

The etymological derivation of prepositions and conjunctions has demonstrated, Tooke hopes, that "instead of *invention*, the *classes* of them spring from *corruption*," which disproves Monboddo's contention that "every kind of *relation* is a *pure idea of intellect*, which *never can be apprehended by sense.*" His doctrine of language being false, it follows that his metaphysic is nonsense.[29] Tooke has also justified his statement, that "wherever the evident meaning and origin of fhe Particles of any language can be found, *there* is the certain source of the whole,"[30] against Locke's belief that the particles "are not truly, by themselves, the names of any *Ideas.*" His proof could not, however, be established without a method of derivation which to us appears very arbitrary because he allowed meaning to be his only guide; but this procedure was normal in the eighteenth century and had the authority of de Brosses, who had

----

[27] *DP*, I, 320-323.

[28] *DP*, I, 456-457. He justifies his position by quoting de Brosses: "La preuve connue d'un grand nombre de mots . . . doit établir un précepte général sur les autres mots de même espece, à l'origine desquels on ne peut plus remonter." *Traité*, II, 270-271 (par. 215).

[29] *DP*, I, 397-399.   [30] *DP*, I, 147.

made it the first rule of etymology that "la langue étymologique parle à l'esprit plutôt qu'aux yeux ou qu'aux oreilles," which again was the inescapable consequence of universal grammar and its basic assumption that language is studied by reference to mind.[31] Initially, universal grammar had made little or no use of etymology, but Condillac's interpretation of Locke had, as it were, added the dimension of time for the sake of reducing the parts of speech to those that could be referred to names of impressions. De Brosses himself had made a suggestive beginning by deriving the French *chez* from the Italian *casa* "in the house," a derivation Tooke cites in favor of his account of *through*; but not believing that all particles could be similarly explained, de Brosses had come to the conclusion that their formation was "purement arbitraire," an opinion which it is now evident that Tooke could not share, though here again he was not entirely original. In his *Histoire naturelle de la parole*; *ou Grammaire universelle et comparative*, Court de Gébelin had reasoned that if modern prepositions such as *nonobstant, malgré, attendu, pendant,* and *durant* had evident significations, we could believe no less about the older ones which did not appear so easy to explain, for the ancients could not have failed to find suitable words "dans la Nature." "Nous pouvons donc être assurés que toute Préposition s'est formée d'un mot connu, dont elle a eu toute l'énergie; & que c'est en vertu de cette analogie qu'elle est devenue propre à être le signe d'un raport entre deux objets." In Tooke's manner, he gave examples

[31] *Traité*, II, 422 (par. 257). So also Turgot in "Étymologie": "Le sens est le premier guide qui se présente: la connoissance détaillée de la chose exprimée par le mot, et de ses circonstances principales, peut ouvrir des vues. Par exemple, si c'est un lieu, sa situation sur une montagne ou dans une vallée; si c'est une rivière, sa rapidité, sa profondeur; si c'est un instrument, son usage ou sa forme" (*Oeuvres*, ed. G. Schelle, I, 484). The choice of these examples may have been influenced by Leibniz.

to prove his assertion, showing for instance that *sur* came from Latin *super*, which again derived from a Greek *hup-er,* whose root meant "elevation" and in turn explained English *up* "qui signifie *en haut,* d'où *up-land,* pays élevé, pays de montagnes." Like Tooke, Court de Gébelin came to the conclusion that all prepositions, adverbs, and conjunctions derive from nouns and that they all have a fixed meaning, though he was neither as doctrinaire nor as consistent and explicit as Tooke.[32] Against Beadon's charge of "etymological legerdemain," Tooke had shown that there was no "capricious irregularity in any part of language";[33] this also meant that inflectional endings "were not originally the effect of premeditated and deliberate *art,* but separate words by length of time corrupted and coalescing with the words of which they are now considered as the *Terminations.*"[34]

The first volume of the *Diversions* had only dealt briefly with abstraction. It was the same as abbreviation in terms, the subject to which Locke's *Essay* was the best guide. In that connection, Tooke had also explained that from the "necessity of *General Terms,* follows immediately the necessity of the *Article*: whose business it is to reduce their generality, and upon occasion to enable us to employ *general* terms for *Particulars.*"[35] Thus, being necessary for the communication of thought, the article occupied an anomalous position in the system and could not be put in the same class as the particles. But by the

[32] *Monde primitif,* II (Paris, 1784), 304-305 and 323. Tooke cites Court de Gébelin twice, in *DP,* I, 279 and 305, in the first case to reject Monboddo's opinion that verbs are the parent words in all languages, in the second for authority that prepositions have a proper meaning of their own. Court de Gébelin's work is an attempt to carry out the program laid down by de Brosses. An earlier version of the *Histoire naturelle* had appeared in 1772 and 1776, which seems to have been the one Tooke used.

[33] *DP,* I, 502.

[34] *DP,* I, 352.

[35] *DP,* I, 69.

time the second volume was ready in 1805, Horne Tooke
had found a solution to this dilemma: "*The* (our *Article*,
as it is called) is the Imperative of the verb *ðean*: which
may very well supply the place of the correspondent
Anglo-Saxon article *se* which is the Imperative of *seon,*
videre: for it answers the same purpose in discourse to
say—*see* man, or, *take* man." He found an equally convenient etymological solution to *that* which in the first
volume he had declined to explain. It means "*taken,*
assumed, being merely the past participle of the Anglo-
Saxon verb *ðean* . . . to *the,* to *get,* to *take,* to *assume*."[36]
But most of the second volume is devoted to what Tooke
rather inappropriately calls "abstraction," a term which
covers every sort of noun for which he can find an explanation, but especially metaphysical terms such as
heaven, accident, luck, destiny, fate, truth, right, and
wrong. He says at the end that he hopes he has said
enough "to discard that imagined *operation of the mind,*
which has been termed *Abstraction*: and to prove, that
what we call by that name, is merely one of the contrivances of language, for the purpose of more speedy
communication."[37]

[36] *DP*, II, 59-60.

[37] *DP*, II, 396. In the *Table Talk*, Coleridge has said: "All
that is worth anything (and that is but little) in the Diversions
of Purley is contained in a short pamphlet-letter which he addressed to Mr. Dunning." This statement is misleading; the *Letter*
to Mr. Dunning had said nothing about abstraction, which most
clearly brings out the philosophical implications of Tooke's theory
of language. He also said: "All that is true in Horne Tooke's
book is taken from Lennep, who gave it for so much as it was
worth, and never pretended to make a system of it" (*Table Talk*,
4th edn. [London, 1851], pp. 65-66 [May 7, 1830]). This also
is hardly correct. The main statement of Lennep's doctrine was
contained in his posthumous *Etymologicum linguae Graecae*,
published in two volumes by Ev. Scheid in 1790. Tooke may have
been influenced by an earlier member of the Dutch etymological
"Schola Hemsterhusiana," Albert Schultens, but the differences
are too many to involve simple influence. The point had been
raised in an early critique of the 1st ed. of the *Diversions*, I, Cas-

The opening chapter presents some of his best known and most typical etymologies. "*Right* is no other than *rect-um* (*regitum*), the past participle of the Latin verb *regere*. Whence in Italian you have *ritto*; and from *dirigere, diritto, dritto*; whence the French have their antient *droict*, and their modern *droit*. The Italian *dritto* and the French *droit* being no other than the past participle of *direct-um*."[38] Similarly, *just* is the past participle of the Latin *jubere*, with the consequence that "when a man demands his *right*, he asks only that which it is *ordered* he shall have"; this is illustrated with a number of examples such as "a *right* conduct is, that which is *ordered*," and "a *right* line is, that which is *ordered* or *directed*—(not a random extension, but) the shortest between two points."[39] "A thing may be at the same time both *right* and *wrong*, as well as *right* and *left*. It may be *commanded* to be done, and *commanded* not to be done. The *law, laeʒ, laʒ*, i.e. that which is *laid down*, may be different by different authorities."[40]

Tooke's interlocutor, Sir Francis Burdett who has now taken Beadon's place, finds these examples very interesting, but wonders whether the same sort of explanation will also account for "*abstract ideas*, whose existence you deny." Tooke thinks so, and now begins a very long list of examples which are all designed to illustrate the principle that these terms "are generally (I say *generally*) Participles or Adjectives used without any Substantive to which they can be joined; and are therefore, in *construction*, considered as Substantives. An *act*—(aliquid)

---

sander's [John Bruckner] *Criticisms on the Diversions of Purley* (London, 1790). Tooke discusses this matter *DP*, I, 240-246. On Tooke's derivation of the particles, James Bonar wrote in his article on "Language" in the *Edinburgh Encyclopedia* that Tooke was "not the first who struck into that path, similar views having previously been entertained, though probably unknown to him, by the Dutch etymologists Schultens, Hemsterhuis, and Lennep."
[38] *DP*, II, 7.   [39] *DP*, II, 8-9.   [40] *DP*, II, 13-14.

act-um. A *fact*—(aliquid) *fact*-um. *Incense*—(aliquid) *incens*-um," and so forth.[41] *Heaven*, for instance, is "some place, any place *heav*-en or *heav*-ed," *leaven* is from the French *lever* "to raise, i.e. that by which the dough is raised."[42] *Truth* and *true* are both referred to the verb *to trow*, meaning "to consider, to think, to believe firmly, to be thoroughly persuaded of." Horne Tooke can, in line with his philosophy, confidently assert that "there is therefore no such thing as eternal, immutable everlasting *truth*. . . . Two persons may contradict each other, and yet both speak *truth*: for the *truth* of one person may be opposite to the *truth* of another." The Latin *verus* receives a corresponding explanation: "*Res*, a thing, gives us *reor*, i.e. I am *thing-ed*: *ve-reor*, I am strongly *thinged*; for *ve* in Latin composition means *valde*, i.e. *valide*. And *verus*, i.e. strongly impressed upon the mind, is the contracted participle of *vereor*." To Burdett's objection that *reor*, though a deponent verb, means "I think," Tooke answers that deponent verbs exist only for the convenience of translation; one would not call *think* a deponent verb, and "yet it is as much a deponent as *reor*. Remember, where we now say, *I think*, the antient expression was—*me thinketh*, i.e. *me thingeth*, *it thingeth me*."[43] It is an understatement to say that these explanations are fantastic, but they are part and parcel of Tooke's system and no more fantastic than the doctrine and the method that produced them. He was convinced that "these words, these Participles and Adjectives, not understood as such, have caused a metaphysical jargon and a false morality, which can only be dissipated by etymology."[44] His etymological derivations from *bar* is perhaps the most fantastic of all: "A *bar* in all its uses, is a *defence*: that by which any thing is fortified, strengthened, or defended. A *barn* (*bar-en, bar'n*) is a

[41] *DP*, II, 17.   [42] *DP*, II, 71.   [43] *DP*, II, 402-406.
[44] *DP*, II, 18.

63

covered inclosure, in which the grain &c. is protected or defended from the weather, from depredations &c. A *baron* is an armed, defenceful, or powerful man. A *barge* is a strong boat. A *bargain* is a confirmed, strengthened agreement. . . . A *bark* is a stout vessel. The *bark* of a tree is its defence: that by which the tree is defended from the weather &c. . . . The *bark* of a dog is that by which we are defended by that animal."[45] In the midst of these etymologies, it is comforting to be told that "there is nothing strictly arbitrary in language."

All these etymological explanations rest on the assumption that a word which originally followed the participle or the adjective has since disappeared and must now be understood or supplied to complete the construction before the right etymology will emerge. In the second volume Tooke called this principle "subaudition" and equated it with abstraction, thereby again referring an imagined operation of the mind to the operation of language. Subaudition was not a new concept; it had long been used in traditional grammar to make elliptical and irregular phrases that were sanctioned by usage conform to the same pattern as supposedly normal constructions, thereby reestablishing the missing analogy and the regularity which universal grammar always looked for. In the first volume, Beadon had already noted that Tooke reconciled the uses of *that* both as an article and a pronoun "by a *subauditur* or an abbreviation in Construction."[46] In other words, subaudition is a principle which accounts for abbreviation in construction, the third sort of abbreviation originally listed by Tooke. It had been used by Condillac, de Brosses, and Court de Gébelin. The Port-Royal Grammar had observed that the names for various professions such as *roi, philosophe, peintre, soldat,* must originally have preceded the word for man,

[45] *DP*, II, 182-183.
[46] *DP*, I, 84.

which being the same and obvious in all cases could be dropped without harm, "parce qu'on l'y peut sous-entendre sans aucune confusion, le rapport ne s'en pouvant faire à aucun autre. Et par-là ces mots ont eu, dans l'usage, ce qui est particulier aux substantifs, qui est, de subsister seuls dans le discours."[47] Du Marsais was especially fond of this principle, which he justified by referring to such authorities as J. C. Scaliger, Sanctius, and Vossius. In a passage which occurred in a work that was in Tooke's library, he called it the basic principle of all syntax, the Ariadne thread that guided us through the labyrinth of transpositions and ellipses: "On doit toujours rapprocher les mots de leurs corrélatifs, et exprimer ceux qui sont sous-entendus, lorsque l'on veut pénétrer le sens de l'auteur qui, dans le temps même qu'il ne l'énonce qu'en peut de mots, parle toujours conformément à l'analogie de sa langue, et imite les façons de parler où tous les mots sont exprimés."[48] Thus, like abbreviation subaudition was an old grammatical concept which Tooke assigned a new and much expanded role in order to achieve his reduction of all thought to the operations of language.

Tooke was aware that his subaudition had put a very heavy burden on adjectives and participles, so heavy indeed that it might endanger his fundamental principle that all words could ultimately be reduced to nouns— and perhaps verbs. He therefore devoted the last hundred pages of the second volume to those two classes. Being true abbreviations, adjectives are not, he argues, necessary to language—another philosophical triumph which does away with "qualities, accidents, substances, sub-

[47] Arnauld, *Oeuvres*, XLI, 19.
[48] *Oeuvres*, III, 400, in "Fragment sur les causes de la parole," which was included in his *Logique et principes de grammaire* (Paris, 1769); it is listed in the sale catalogue of Tooke's library, now in the British Museum.

strata, essence, the adjunct natures of things, &c. &c."
He hopes his listener "will perceive in the misapprehen-
sion of this useful and simple contrivance of language,
one of the foundations of those heaps of false philosophy
and obscure (because mistaken) metaphysic, with which
we have been bewildered."[49] In support of his argument,
he can refer first of all to instances of the adjectival use
of the substantive as in gold-ring, brass-tube, and silk-
string as well as to compounds such as sea-weed, ivory-
wand, shell-fish, river-god, weather-board, hail-storm,
laundry-house, and family-quarrel; and also to cases in
which the substantive and adjective are convertible
"without the smallest change of meaning: As we may
say—a perverse nature, or, a natural perversity." Secondly, the characteristic endings, as in *golden* and *silken,*
which had led grammarians to say that the adjective cannot stand by itself, are only a grammatical feature of the
adjective which still remains the name of a thing, for "if
indeed it were true that Adjectives were not the names of
things, there could be no *Attribution* by Adjectives: for
you cannot *attribute Nothing.*"[50] Tooke can finally refer
to a language which altogether manages to do without
adjectives, namely that of the Mohegans, who "have no
Adjectives in all their language. Although it may at first
seem not only singular and curious, but impossible, that
a language should exist without *Adjectives*, yet it is an
indubitable fact."[51] If one language could do without adjectives, none needed them.

The participle caused much more difficulty since it
raised the problem of the verb which Tooke had planned
to solve in the third volume. For the present, however,

[49] *DP*, II, 458-459.
[50] *DP*, II, 442.
[51] *DP*, II, 463. Tooke quoted those words from Jonathan Ed-
wards' "Observations on the Language of the Muhhekaneew
Indians . . . Communicated to the Connecticut Society of Arts
and Sciences" (London, 1788).

he was only prepared to make a very complicated division of the verb adjective, as he called it, into no less than six categories. There are first "the simple verb adjective," which is the same as the present participle; the "past tense adjective," which is the past participle; and the "future tense adjective," as in *venture* and *adventure*. There are in addition three adjective moods: the "potential mood passive" which refers to all adjectives ending in *-able* or *-ible*; the "potential mood active" which is formed with an ending borrowed from the Latin as in *purgative, vomitive,* and *operative,* or from Greek as in *cathartic, emetic,* and *energetic,* an explanation which also serves to reduce some abstract nouns to concrete ones, as for instance *provocative, palliative,* and *motive*; and finally the "official mood passive," which refers to the "manner of using the verb, by which we might couple the notion of duty with it," as in *legend, reverend, dividend,* and *memorandum.*[52] The non-English endings of all but two of these categories are abbreviations which for the sake of convenience were borrowed from Latin and Greek, languages which in this respect are more perfect than English.

But all the ingenuity does not bring us any closer to the reduction of verbs to nouns, except insofar as Tooke treats verbs in much the same manner as nouns. He insists that "every *Verb* has a signification of its own, distinct from *Manner* and *Time,*"[53] a contention that was forced upon him because Harris had said the opposite, maintaining that "the nature of verbs and participles being understood, that of adjectives becomes easy. A verb implies both an attribute, and time, and an assertion. A participle implies only an attribute and time, and an adjective only implies attribute." Tooke reversed the order; he began with adjectives, to which he then reduced the

[52] *DP*, II, 497-503.
[53] *DP*, II, 468.

participles, and denied that the verb implied any assertion. "No single word can. Till one single thing can be
found to be a couple, one single word cannot make an
Ad-sertion or an *Ad-firmation*: for there is *joining* in that
operation; and there can be no junction of one thing." To
the objection that the Latin *ibo* is an assertion, he answers,
"Yes indeed it is, and in three letters. But those three
letters contain three words; two verbs and a pronoun."[54]
In the same manner he says that, just as case, gender, and
number are not parts of the noun, so "*Mood, Tense,
Number, Person* are no parts of the Verb. But these same
circumstances frequently accompanying the Verb, are
then signified by other words expressive of these circumstances: and again, in some languages, these latter words,
by their perpetual recurrence, have coalesced with the
Verb; their separate significance has been lost sight of
(except in their proper application), and these words
have been considered as mere artificial terminations of
the Verb."[55] And at that he left it.

Did Horne Tooke perhaps near the end find himself
in so hopeless a quandary over the ultimate foundation of
his system that he despaired of ever finding the solution?
It is reasonable to assume that in the final, projected
volume of the *Diversions* he would have been forced to
face the problem of the origin of language in order to
decide whether the verb or the noun was the ultimate,
primary part of speech. On that issue he had produced so
much confusion and contradiction that even his greatest
admirers did not agree on any single answer. The
Diversions only once made reference to the beginnings of
language, if not to its origin. This passage explained that
prepositions and conjunctions were the result of corruption rather than invention and that consequently the
savage languages were in the same situation as the so-

54 *DP*, II, 431-432.
55 *DP*, II, 473.

called languages of art, "except that the former are less corrupted: and that savages have not only as *separate and distinct ideas* of those relations as we have but that they have this advantage over us (an advantage in point of intelligibility, though it is a disadvantage in point of brevity) that they also *express* them separately and distinctly"[56]—an opinion which agrees with Condillac's belief in the greater philosophical perfection of the early state of language. If language does not take its origin from invention—a view Tooke was obviously forced to dismiss out of hand—then it must have its origin in nature, most likely in imitation as many of his predecessors had said. But Tooke never makes anything of onomatopoeia, and he had dismissed the interjections as suitable only for the expression of feelings but not of thought. Perhaps the answer is to be found at the very beginning of the *Diversions* where Tooke clearly states that his investigation will not deal with "the organical part of language," for this was a matter his admired de Brosses had made much of in his account of the origin of language. Tooke also appears to take an ambivalent view of the career of language. If the present state of language is the result of corruption, then the beginning must have been perfect; still, he clearly believes that language is now better than it was. His predecessors had held either one or the other of these views, but not both. The use he made of abbreviation, however, makes it possible for him to accept both without contradiction. What has been lost in clarity of expression has been gained in dispatch. The more or less extensive use of abbreviation is a measure of how cultivated a language is; thus Anglo-Saxon must not be derived from the Greek as Junius had done,[57] and Tooke is convinced that the founders of Rome came from the north of Europe because the language proves it.[58] This confusion may be surprising, but it is understandable

[56] *DP*, I, 399.   [57] *DP*, I, 148.   [58] *DP*, II, 140.

and was nearly universal (whether in this form or some other) before Sanskrit with its undisputed high antiquity, so to speak, lined up the old European languages in a new and more fruitful perspective.

It is easy to criticize the *Diversions* in the light of later modes of language study. But even without that unfair advantage, it would seem easy to raise a host of material objections against Tooke's doctrines and his use of etymology "to get rid of the false philosophy . . . concerning language and the human understanding."[59] Still, the virtual absence of any such objections is a fact and at the same time a measure of the undoubted authority which his doctrines, aims, and procedures had already gained within the context of the study of language in the latter part of the eighteenth century. The *Diversions* had spread the light which most students believed that one could reasonably expect language study to cast on the philosophy of mind. A few statements were perhaps too bold, some of the etymologies perhaps mistaken, but the system and the discovery would stand against caviling at a few details. Who could doubt that Horne Tooke was a very learned man? He displayed a seemingly profound knowledge of a wealth of languages—Anglo-Saxon, Middle English, Gothic, Old German, Danish, Swedish, Latin, Greek, occasionally Persian and even more remote languages. And he had revealed a close knowledge of a wide number of works on language, philosophy, and grammar in Latin, Greek, French, Italian, and English, including Quintilian, Vossius, Scaliger, Campanella, Jonson, Wallis, Hickes, Skinner, Lye, Minshew, Junius, Johnson, and Tyrwhitt. His range was truly wide and impressive, and must have helped to make his reputation safe even with men who might for other reasons have felt little inclination to find virtue in his work. Those who had no use for the philosophy still admired the etymol-

[59] *DP*, I, 148.

ogies. Bentham was convinced that Tooke's discovery had at last laid firm foundations for universal grammar and expected great things from its application to the learning of foreign languages, not least for the benefit of missionaries.[60] Hazlitt stated the grounds for the appeal of the *Diversions* to an age impressed by the method of natural science and its recent successes:

> Mr. Tooke . . . treated words as the chemists do substances; he separated those which are compounded from those which are not decompoundable. He did not explain the obscure by the more obscure, but the difficult by the plain, the complex by the simple. This alone is proceeding upon the true principles of science: the rest is pedantry and *petitmaîtreship*. Our philosophical writer distinguished all words into *names of things*, and directions added for joining them together, or originally into *nouns* and *verbs*.[61]

Even the sale of books from his library showed that the world expected great philological and philosophical benefits from Tooke's mind. His copy of Johnson's *Dictionary* "with a great number of MS. notes, alterations and emendations by Mr. Tooke" was sold for the fantastic price of two hundred pounds, accounting for nearly one-sixth of the proceeds of the sale. His copy of Lye's *Dictionarium Saxonicum* (1772) with "MS. notes" went for thirty-four pounds, Locke's *Essay* for thirteen, and the *Works* for eighteen, both with "MS. notes by Mr. Tooke." It would be a good while before anyone would pay attention to the opinion that "with all his swaggering upon the subject, even he was barbarously ignorant of all the Teutonic tongues; and owes what reputation he has en-

[60] *Works*, ed. Bowring, VIII, 185 and 188 in the Appendix to the *Chrestomathia* (1817).
[61] "The Late Mr. Horne Tooke" in the *Spirit of the Age* (1825) in *Complete Works*, eds. P. P. Howe *et al.* (London, 1932), XI, 55-56.

joyed solely to a happy knack of outbullying his opponents upon subjects with which he and they were alike
conversant."[62]

Tooke himself had been convinced "that all future
etymologists, and perhaps some philosophers, will ac-
knowledge their obligation to me."[63] He was almost right,
for the next generation had greater veneration for Horne
Tooke than even he, without hyperbole, could have
imagined.

[62] J. M. Kemble in "Letter to Francisque Michel" in the latter's *Bibliothèque Anglo-Saxonne*, Part II (Paris and London,
1837), pp. 24-25.
[63] *DP*, I, 146.

CHAPTER III

Horne Tooke's Influence and Reputation

The reputation of Tooke's *Diversions* is one of the most remarkable phenomena in the intellectual and scholarly life of England during the first third of the nineteenth century. For thirty years it kept England immune to the new philology until the results and methods finally had to be imported from the Continent in the 1830's, and even then they met strong opposition. Only a variety of factors can explain this state of affairs, but of these the most important by far was Tooke's successful marriage of philology and philosophy. The discovery that all words can be reduced to names of sensation was eagerly accepted by the philosophic radicals, who took the proof to lie in the etymologies which they had neither the desire nor the competence to judge. Erasmus Darwin, Thomas Belsham, James Mill, Bentham, Mackintosh, Brougham, and Hazlitt were all too dazzled by the flash of light to examine its source. Coleridge might wish to stem the tide of materialism, but where was the philologist who had the courage and the knowledge to show that the system was wrong? Besides, Tooke did not pretend that he could explain all words in the language, nor even that some of his etymologies were not subject to question; but enough of them were right to prove his a priori system. It was in the nature of the case that philology could not disprove the system which was accepted by the philosophers, who, paradoxically, believed that philology had already proved its truth. There was, furthermore, the uncomfortable awareness that even the best philology tended to make reductions that were similar to Tooke's, a circumstance that made it possible to believe that Tooke had been a forerunner of the new philology. Had he known its results, he would have been forced to change many—or all —of his etymologies; but the fact would remain that all words were still derived from names of sensation and the discovery would still prove the material bases of mind against idealism, both at home and abroad. Philologists might ignore Tooke's work, but they could not escape being judged—or ridiculed—on its grounds. Only time, accumulated evidence, and the abandonment of the philosophy could decide the outcome, and for long the Tooke tradition remained the stronger, casting its shadow even into the 1850's when the *New English Dictionary* was being planned. The philosophical authority of Tooke made it very hard for the new philology to gain acceptance in England, and when it finally came, it was in some quarters deliberately used as a Germano-Coleridgean challenge to the false prophets of Utilitarian thought. In the meantime, the reviews were ecstatic and the philosophic radicals happy, while the study of language fell to a few inferior minds who posed no threat to Tooke. Only Dugald Stewart raised fundamental objections which prepared for a change of attitude.

From the first notice of the *Letter to Mr. Dunning* in 1778 until 1810, Tooke's work was reviewed, outlined, quoted, and excerpted in fifteen different publications in nearly twenty articles totalling over two hundred pages. A few might question the philosophy, disapprove of the politics, and take issue with this or that etymology, but they were all, with a single exception, unanimous in their opinion of the "unspeakable value of Mr. Tooke's hypothesis," which had demonstrated that words in the art of reasoning were not merely Bacon's *vestigia mentis,* but "the machines used by the mind; and the lever, the wheel, or the screw, are but faint representations of their

74

power and their utility." Plato had composed an elaborate and "most erroneous" dissertation "on that very part of grammar, in which an acuter mind was destined to discover the truth, more than 2,000 years after the *Cratylus*, or Dialogue on Etymology, was published."[1] Others found that the work was "the most valuable contribution to the philosophy of language, which our literature has produced";[2] that "the entire and undisputed merit must for ever remain with its author, of having alone conferred that importance on the science of etymology, from which all future discoveries must derive their value."[3] One reviewer hoped that Horne Tooke's twilight may be long enough to allow completion of the section of the verb to round off the system,[4] while yet another, who saw "some truth, some false philosophy, and something which, to our ears, sounds very like nonsense," still found it "needless to add, that on the subject of *philology* there is no work in the English language, or indeed in any language with which we are acquainted, that stands higher in our estimation."[5] The single exception to this chorus of praise was the *Eclectic Review*. It criticized the a priori method as a source of error in the false selection of proof and too ready assent to what would fit the hypothesis. It concluded that if Tooke had "really aimed at *truth*, it would have compelled him altogether to relinquish his hypothesis," but feared at the same time that "the abuse with which the author overwhelmed most of his grammatical precursors, and the

[1] *Monthly Review*, New Series, XXVII (December, 1798), 423-425.

[2] *Annual Review*, IV (1805), 675-679.

[3] *Monthly Magazine*, XII (September-October, 1801), 112-113, 210-213.

[4] *Monthly Review*, N.S., LI (December, 1806), 387-408.

[5] *British Critic*, XXIV (May-June, 1807), 461-480, 631-650. Quotations from pp. 466, 647.

contempt which he poured even on the objects at which he aimed, were but too likely to be mistaken, by many readers, for proofs of superior knowledge and genius."[6]

The fears were well founded. Tooke did not influence a single etymologist whose work was not so much worse than its model that it failed to gain any stature at all, with the significant exception of Charles Richardson's *New Dictionary of the English Language*, whose importance will be discussed in a later chapter. Even nonsense found its way into print. A case in point is the work of Samuel Henshall, a fellow of Brasenose College, who in 1798 published a short work entitled *The Saxon and English Languages Reciprocally Illustrative of Each Other*. This book was designed to prove that the Latin translation that had commonly accompanied old texts "was insufficient to produce a correct knowledge of the Idioms of the Anglo-saxonic Language, which has little similarity with a Latin Construction."[7] What he meant may be gathered from his handling of these lines from Caedmon's hymn, one of the numerous examples he gave:

> He erest gescop aelda bearnum heofon
> *He erst shaped elder Barns   Heavens*
>
> to rofe halig Scyppend, tha middan
> *to roof holy Shaping;   then middle*
>
> geard mon cynnes weard ece Drihtne
> *earth men's kind world eke Do-right*
>
> aefter teode, firam foldan frea Aelmihtig.
> *after tied,   free folds   from (the) Almighty.*

A note to "world" for "weard" tells the reader that "the omission of a letter here, l, is sometimes not to be much regarded," and "free folds from the Almighty" is glossed "men created free beings." Toward the end, Henshall out-

---

[6] Volume II (April-May, 1806), 245-254, 353-361.
[7] Pages 2-3.

lined his new mode of Anglo-Saxon study with heavy reliance on Tooke, whose *Diversions* contained "much useful information to the Saxon and English student, and supply some excellent elementary Rules"—although Henshall detested Tooke himself as a "self-consequential snarler" and a "venomous viper of democracy." The construction of the verb, for instance, can be understood in this Tookian fashion: "Present singular, I love, or do love, thou love-in-is, or lovenest, by abbreviation lovest, and loves,—he love-do or loveth. Plural, we love-in, ye love-in, they love-in."[8] In 1807, in the year of his death, Henshall brought out an *Etymological Organic Reasoner,* whose title revealed his conviction that "throughout *all languages* there is a resemblance in the sound, and an affinity of ideas, attached to the tones produced by the exertions of the same organic powers of human speech,"[9] a principle which he took to be his unique discovery though both de Brosses and especially Court de Gébelin had held similar opinions, which were also accepted by Henshall's contemporary Walter Whiter. Thus "*Up* is formed by emitting the voice in as *up*right a direction as the organic powers of speech will admit, by raising the lower jaw till the lips are fully closed."[10] It is doubtful whether anyone could have gone so far astray without leaning on Tooke. The violent polemic that filled many pages of Henshall's last work shows that he suffered from persecution mania, but even without such evidence it is clear that he was, in Kemble's phrase, an "irrecoverable madman."[11] Still, in 1800 he was one of the two candi-

[8] Pages 47-58. The paedagogical device of interlinear and attempted literal translation was urged and illustrated in du Marsais' *Méthode raisonnée pour apprendre la langue latine,* which derived the suggestion from Locke's *Thoughts on Education* in Coste's translation.

[9] Part I, 7-8. In all, four installments were published.

[10] Part II, 4.

[11] "Letter to Francisque Michel," p. 15.

dates for the Anglo-Saxon chair at Oxford, though he lost with 71 votes against 148.[12]

No less fantastic was Walter Whiter, who in 1782 was elected fellow of Clare College, Cambridge, "probably on account of his reputation for classical and philological knowledge."[13] His nearly three thousand pages of endless etymologies must make him one of the contenders for first prize for length in a field where the competition is severe. Dissatisfied with the state of etymology, he was determined to find a general law that would be valid for all the phenomena of language irrespective of time and place. He found this law in his conviction that the same elementary consonants convey the same fundamental ideas in every part of the globe. He put the consonants into three separate groups, within which each might pass into another, but found further—most astounding of all —that the consonants of all three groups might also under certain conditions pass into each other. The field was therefore wide open, and it was not difficult to show the complete affinity of all languages past and present in any place whatever. He next sought a ruling principle to which the total unity and coherence of all etymological phenomena could be referred. Where could he find "an agent sufficiently potent and predominating . . . but in that great object, which is ever present with us, at all times, and on all occasions. . . . This great object, so interesting—so important, which must necessarily predominate over the mind of man, is assuredly the *Earth*." The rest of the work produces the demonstration, whose essential ingredients are citation of etymological forms ad infinitum, very free association of ideas, and complete absence of even the most rudimentary common sense. One section, for instance, deals with "terms expressing what is *grating—rough—harsh—hirsute* &c., connected

[12] *Gentleman's Magazine*, LXX (November, 1800), 1,097.
[13] *DNB*, s.v. "Walter Whiter."

with the idea of *grating* upon or *scratching* upon the *Earth*, or relating to the *Earth*, as being in this *grated—scratched* state." Here we find concerning *hart*, the Old English *heort*, and the German *hirsch*, that they "denote the animal which possesses the harsh—pricking—pushing or goading horns." These belong to the earth considered in a state of agitation, while *heart* pertains to ideas of the earth in a state of rest, since *heart* expresses the ideas of something substantial. It may, however, be connected with *hart* in this fashion: "The English *heart-en* . . . may belong to the race of words, which signify to *stir up—excite*. If this should be the case, *heart* and *hart,* the animal, may belong to the same idea. The *heart* is the seat of boldness—that which is *stirred up* or *excited* to deeds of valour; and the *hart* is the *stirrer up*—the *exciter*—the annoyer,—pricker or pusher, with his horns —the animal, which *hurts*." *Hearse* falls in the same category, meaning "perhaps the clumsy carriage, which makes a *harsh grating* upon the ground." Though Tooke cannot be made responsible for all this, he had set an example with his etymology of *bark*.[14] In a review of Whiter's earlier work, Francis Jeffrey had said that he proceeded "like the pilgrim who looks for a beaten track among the moving sands of the desert, or the mariner who steers his course by the bearings of the summer clouds."[15] But one wonders how it ever found its way into print.

Another curious work used eight hundred pages in an attempt to show that Tooke was seriously wrong because

[14] See Whiter's *Etymologicon Universale or Universal Etymological Dictionary* (3 vols.; Cambridge University Press, 1822-1825); the principles are set forth in the "Preliminary Dissertation" in I, 1-142. His *Etymologicum Magnum* (1800) had advanced the same ideas. Quotations are drawn from I, 80-81 ("Preliminary Dissertation" with separate pagination); II, 627; II, 629; I, 188-189; and II, 629.

[15] *Monthly Review*, N.S., XXXVIII (1802), 134.

he had failed to pay attention to the structure of language, and because he had derived prepositions from past participles when they should in fact have been derived from present participles. The author of *Anti-Tooke*[16] was John Fearn, who considered himself a "philosophical grammarian" and set out to establish a "true or real philosophy of language," with a heavy admixture of misunderstood German idealism. He was disturbed that grammarians had not yet removed "that disparity of nature which exists between Scientific Notation and Ordinary Language." He asserted that "there exists both a generic and a specific identicalness . . . the supposed difference between the two systems having arisen entirely from a profound misconception of the Real Structure and Elements of Ordinary Speech," for algebraic notation and ordinary language are, he said, "specifically One and the Same System of Signs." This he tried to prove by considering the "category of relation" or prepositions, which in Fearn's interpretation turned out to include all verbs except the verb substantive, and "no preposition, rightly understood, is a corrupt word, or can ever have proceeded from corruption."[17] He approaches his goal— "to make the Illogical Idioms of Language conform to the unyielding Principles of a Grammar of Pure Reason"[18]—by such passages as the following: "If we say, 'the house beneath the hill,' this means 'the house neddering the hill'; or, more strictly, 'the house onning the nedder of the hill,' which finally means, the house acting upon or against (i.e. relating to) the lower side of the hill."[19] Fearn hoped he had helped mankind to the conclusion that "there is no substance and no energy in the whole universe, except the substance and the energies of mind," against "the most horrible demoralisation, the

[16] *Or an Analysis of the Principles and Structure of Language, Exemplified in the English Tongue* (2 vols.; London, 1824-1827). [17] I, 10-16.   [18] I, 436.   [19] I, 294.

fruits of an atheism founded in the belief of matter."[20] If he had, no one paid any attention; but his *Anti-Tooke* is perhaps one of the most surprising absurdities spawned by the Purleian philosopher.[21]

Much more interesting than these figures was the Scots minister Alexander Murray who, largely self-taught but with an avid passion for languages, was admitted as a free scholar to the University of Edinburgh in 1794. He became associated with the *Scots Magazine* and was soon engaged by Archibald Constable to do a second edition of Bruce's *Travels in Abyssinia*, which appeared in 1805 with his learned comments on Arabic, Ethiopian, and Coptic. In 1812 he was appointed to the chair in Oriental languages at Edinburgh, but died of consumption within a year in April 1813. Ten years later appeared his two-volume work, *A History of the European Languages; or, Researches into the Affinities of the Teutonic, Greek, Celtic, Sclavonic, and Indian Nations*, published by David Scott from an unfinished manuscript.[22] The special

[20] II, 347, 418.

[21] Equally absurd was Nicholas Salmon's *Αρχαι, or the Evenings of Southill* (London, 1806), which, like the *Diversions* and *Anti-Tooke*, was in dialogue form. One of the interlocutors is "By" who is apparently a personification of some linguistic force or entity vaguely connected with the preposition by: "BY: You have been told, I suppose, and you have yourself observed, that, in my travels, my name has undergone many changes? Salmon: Yes, yes, my dear little *By*, alias *Be*, alias *Bi*, alias *Big*, alias *Bii*" (p. 7).

[22] This work was written after 1808. See Thomas Constable, *Archibald Constable and His Literary Correspondents* (Edinburgh, 1873), I, 263-264, 331-333, in which the uncertain progress of the *History* can be followed. That there was some doubt about his qualifications for the professorship is revealed by the "Documents," etc. published in the *Scots Magazine*, LXXIV (July, 1812), 507-539, but he had the support of such eminent men as Dugald Stewart, James Gregory, Thomas Brown, John Leslie, John Playfair, Francis Jeffrey, and Sir Walter Scott, though several admitted to having neither personal acquaintance nor competence to judge the candidate's professional ability. One of the most interesting statements came from Alexander Hamilton, who

interest of Murray's work lies in its vacillation between speculation in the eighteenth-century manner on etymology and the origin of language, which dominates the first part, and the sounder principles which are set forth in the latter part, perhaps under the influence of Sir William Jones, whose work he knew, at least during the later stages of writing.[23]

Murray called his work "a philosophical history of the European languages" and prefaced his account of the "rudiments of speech" with the assurance that it depended "not on hypothetical but inductive reasonings," containing all that "investigation can now supply."[24] His work belonged to natural philosophy, to science. He acknowledged his debt to Tooke "for the recent discovery, that there are no words in language destitute of meaning" and especially admired him as "the first writer who applied the inductive philosophy to the history of speech," as well as for the spirit Tooke had "diffused through philological enquiries"[25]—he admired him for his method, in other words, rather than for his account of particular words. Unlike Tooke, however, Murray at-

---

was then professor of Oriental languages in the East India Company's college at Haileybury. He wrote to Thomas Brown: "I happened last week to meet with [Murray] in Galloway, and found his acquisitions in Oriental Literature and Languages so extensive and various, as greatly to exceed my power to appreciate them accurately. With the few languages in which I am conversant, he discovered an acquaintance that surprised me exceedingly; but the range of his studies included many of which I am completely ignorant."

[23] This may explain why the *History* proved so hard to finish on time. On August 8, 1812, Constable wrote to Murray that he anticipated publication the following spring, but Murray answered that he wished to have "about 100 or 150 pages additional on the Latin, Slavic, Persic, and Celtic," because "some learned men may perhaps dispute the truth of parts of the preliminary chapters, if they are not confirmed by the addition." See Constable, I, 333.

[24] Murray, I, 48.   [25] II, 3-4.

tempted to widen the account of the origin of language to include an explanation of the origin of speech. Speech began with the "articulation of a few short interjectional syllables . . . while the feeling, or external action, affected the mind." Thus all languages came to be based on action, for the inventors of speech like barbarians and children "imagined that the effects, produced by external objects on their senses, arose from an agency similar to that of which they were conscious in themselves." Their first deliberate attempts at speech consequently "consisted in an effort to give short expressive names to the great classes of effects which association had formed, which experience continually perceived, and judgment arranged agreeably to their characters."[26] The net result was nine short words, the ultimate raw material of all language. These words were all both nouns and verbs, and all implied "power, motion, force, ideas united in every untutored mind." The nine "words" were: *ag, bag, dwag, gwag, lag, mag, nag, rag,* and *swag,* with meanings attached on the principle that "harsh and violent action . . . was expressed by harsher articulations," whereas "variation of force in degree was not designated by a different word, but by a slight change in the pronunciation." *Ag,* for example, expressed "to strike or move with swift equable penetrating or sharp effect," but if the motion was less sudden, though still of the same kind, the pronunciation was changed to *wag,* and further, if "made with force and a great effort," to *hwag. Mag* meant "to press by strong force or impulse so as to condense, bruise, or compel." For some time these were the only words that existed, with occasional modification of the vowel to -i- to indicate diminution of the action; but in due course

[26] I, 29-31. It will be noticed that Murray, without discussion, assumed that man prior to speech possessed "the natural faculties of the human mind," which he listed as perception, memory, abstraction, and judgment (I, 28).

"the fathers of those nations, whose languages were to receive the most abstract or animated thoughts which the mind is capable of forming, began . . . to compound their words, and to multiply terms with all the fertility of arithmetical permutation."[27] At this point began the secondary stage of language, characterized by composition of self-explanatory elements, a process that was steadily repeated in the creation of new compounds. But this stage soon passed into a third as these "long harsh combinations" coalesced and decayed into "softer forms of the same produced by attenuation, aspiration, and elision of the consonants, and subsequent contraction of the vowels." According to Murray's inductive reasoning, English would then have developed in this fashion: "Our own language was once monosyllabic; then composed of monosyllables joined together; then softened into Visigothic, corrupted into Saxon; and at last, having lost many of its inflections, it supplied their place by prepositions, auxiliary verbs, and other resources of that plain rational faculty, which first compounded the elements of speech."[28]

Murray's account of the rudiments of speech forms the first part of his "philosophical history." It is accompanied by the usual profusion of etymological examples, drawn primarily from the Teutonic dialects because the "mysteries of language, in its rudest state, can be explained by the words of our own tongue to better purpose than by those of any other speech."[29] The second part presents the application of those facts and principles to the history of the Greek, Roman, Indian, Slavic, and Celtic languages and is designed to bear out his conviction that all these languages, as well as the Teutonic, are related. It is at this point that he refers to Sir William Jones, hoping that his own history would do for the European languages

[27] I, 31-34.   [28] II, 331-332.   [29] I, 17.

what his more illustrious predecessor's work had achieved concerning the affinity between Greek, Persian, and Sanskrit.[30] In this part of the work, being forced to deal with actual forms, he occasionally makes observations which are correct, adhering to his hitherto unfulfilled promise to deal only with all that investigation can now supply. He remarks for instance that "in all languages the hard consonants b, d, and g are particularly liable to be softened into p, t, and c or k. Both b and p fall into f and v, and thence into w. D softens into t, or into th, as in those or them." In the same place he observes that "in every language, g, c, d, t, before or after a slender vowel, e, i, or y; are particularly liable to be changed into j or dge; and ch or tsh; so *rig* becomes *ridge*; *kirk* becomes *church*; *nation* becomes *natyon, natsion, natshon, nashion*."[31] Perhaps he is speaking from his own observation when he says that "the philologist, as he advances in general knowledge of the European tongues, will discover, that hw, in Teutonic, is almost always ka or ca in Celtic, Latin, Greek, Sanscrit, Persic, and Slavonic. The Gothic pronoun *hwas, hwo,* and *hwata*, is *quis, quae, quod* in Latin"; he also gives the correspondence *Cutis*: *hyd* 'a covering, skin'; Caput: *heofod* 'head'; *Capio*: *haba* 'I seize'[32]—though being convinced that the Teutonic was the most original and uncorrupted of all the European languages, he took the h or hw to be the source of the k-forms.

The final chapter of Murray's history, "Principles of Philological Investigation," also reveals a strange contrast to the speculation of the first part—in fact, his own rules invalidate his earlier conclusions. He insists, for instance, that the resemblance of a few words in different languages is no proof of affinity, "even though sound and sense agree"; that "all artificial similarity in words, pro-

[30] I, 174-175.   [31] I, 169-171.   [32] I, 289-290.

duced by cutting any of them into syllables or parts; or by affirming that words in one language have such forms and senses in other languages, as it may suit our purpose to ascribe to them; must be considered as false"; and that "it is always better to leave the history of the word in doubt, than to multiply useless etymologies of it." Some parts of Murray's work have the great and unexpected virtue of showing a clear awareness that the concept of change alone—whether it is called progress or decay— is not sufficient to produce a coherent treatment of language; it must be more or less regular change. Furthermore, unlike all but a few of his predecessors and contemporaries—among them Sir William Jones—he saw that the indispensable prerequisite to the discovery of regularity is the chronological arrangement of forms;[33] however, like his contemporaries, he placed too great faith in the regularity which he derived from the principle of the association of ideas, and from the eighteenth-century axiom that "ordinary men generally feel and think in a similar way on common subjects."[34] Even if he did not pay attention to them in practice, Murray did have the barest rudiments of an historical and comparative method, a fact which, in spite of the many resemblances between the two men, sets him apart from Whiter. Murray confined himself to the European languages because he saw no justification for going beyond the area in which

[33] II, 324-328. Cf. also these passages: "No inquirer must overlook the historical, geographical, and commercial relations of the two countries in which the languages are spoken." "The history of any language and its dialects may be discovered by a series of writings or true vocabularies of these dialects, throughout successive ages. Such a series being no where preserved entire, the parts of it which exist are valuable in proportion to their united antiquity, connection, purity, and number. The philologist must consult them as the facts of his philosophy. He must carefully discover the process by which changes are effected in the sound, form, and sense of words."
[34] II, 326, 331.

material was available. He had no confidence "in works which pretend to divine the sense of words from their articulations,"[35] a remark that states the historical objection to Whiter's doctrine, against which it seems reasonable to assume that it was directed.

The striking contrast in Murray's work between the uninhibited speculation, which is so evident in the early part, and the sounder principles he laid down in the last chapter—between his own practice and the procedures he recommended—raises a question whose answer may also throw light on the reasons for Tooke's philological and philosophical reputation. In the letters to Constable, Murray often commented upon the progress of his "philosophical history," as if to whet the prospective publisher's appetite. On January 15, 1807, Murray wrote from the vicarage at Urr: "In my attempts I wish to combine etymology with the study of the human mind, and to trace the history of nations in the history of language."[36] The latter purpose was Sir William Jones's exclusive concern; the former was that of Horne Tooke, with whom Murray agreed that "so far from being debased or corrupted by their union with philological inquiries, the principles of the philosophy of the mind would receive very considerable illustration, and might be applied in practice with wider effect, by the assistance of a just, accurate, and logical account of Language."[37]

[35] I, 180. Murray had not committed this mistake in setting up his own nine primary syllables: "If I had not ascertained the existence of the above syllables, by the analysis of throwing off the parts of words, which are evidently additional, and affixed for obvious purposes, and of examining varieties, till the simplest form of the word appeared, I would neither have considered these syllables as original, nor stated them as such to the reader."

[36] Constable, I, 258.

[37] Ibid., 293 · (Murray to Constable, December 29, 1810). Turgot had also stressed both uses of etymology: "L'application la plus immédiate de l'art étymologique est la recherche des origines d'une langue en particulier," and "on voit assez jusqu'où et comment on peut faire usage des étymologies pour éclaircir les

Trying to satisfy both purposes, Murray wavered between the two—hence the inconsistencies.

Here is the key to Tooke's persistent influence. Impressed by the success of Newtonian science, his age was eagerly trying to convert mental philosophy into a branch of natural philosophy, encouraged by the simple schemata of Hartley's association of ideas, Priestley's and Bentham's pleasure-pain principle, and etymology with its exploration of the "causes of language." Furthermore, since something akin to mechanics was assumed to operate in all, analogies were freely drawn between the two disciplines and the corresponding general concepts in each. In this context, Tooke immediately came to occupy an important place. His *Letter to Mr. Dunning* and *Diversions* appeared at a time when the fortunes of materialism were at a low ebb for reasons brought out in John Stuart Mill's remark that Hartley's *Observations* failed at first to make much of an impression because its "publication so nearly coincided with the commencement of the reaction against the experience psychology, provoked by the hardy scepticism of Hume."[38] This circumstance, which was to some extent unplanned on Tooke's part, greatly enhanced the success of his work. The *Diversions* gave support to philosophic radicalism from a quarter which was least expected to produce it, language having provided what appeared to be the most cogent arguments of the opposition—as, for instance, in the work of Harris, Beattie, Monboddo, Blair, and Campbell. Tooke's system and "discovery" came as a tonic to materialist philosophy. But there was also a reason of a

---

obscurités de l'histoire"; but to him this was only an indispensable preliminary to achieving "sous son vrai point de vue, la théorie générale de la parole et de la marche de l'esprit humain dans la formation et les progrès du langage." For the historical use, he refers to the authority of Leibniz. (*Oeuvres*, I, 504-506, 516.)

[38] Preface in the 1869 edition of James Mill's *Analysis*, I, xii.

different kind which, at least from Tooke's point of view, was independent of his intentions, though there was an historical connection. Chemistry—the youngest product of natural philosophy—came into prominence during the years that elapsed between the publication of the first and second volumes of the *Diversions*. It immediately gained the strong hold both on the popular and the scientific imagination which Coleridge so greatly deplored in 1819 in his lecture on "Dogmatical Materialism." Chemistry afforded a powerful analogue to the study of language and the philosophy of mind, and it soon became their much admired model.

Chemistry had many claims on the attention of the philologist and the mental philosopher, apart from its novelty. Its history first of all provided an encouraging parallel; what alchemy was to chemistry, metaphysics was to mental science.[39] Secondly, though a separate discipline, chemistry was generally assumed to be a study of motions, its concern being with insensible motions, whereas mechanical philosophy studied sensible motions.[40] It was hoped that mental science might achieve a similar relationship to the archetypal science; indeed, Hartley's doctrine of vibrations had taken its cue from mechanics, though Priestley had dismissed the vibrations in his abridgment of the *Observations*, published in 1775 as *Hartley's Theory of the Human Mind*, which became much more influential than the original work. Thirdly, chemistry, like mental science, studied phenomena that were immediately at hand, although they had not pre-

[39] The alchemic origins of chemistry were pointed out at least as early as 1802 in the Introduction to Thomas Thomson's *System of Chemistry*, I, 4ff. and again in 1812 in Sir Humphrey Davy's *Elements of Chemical Philosophy* (see *Collected Works* [London, 1840], IV, 9ff.). Coleridge was not the first to make this point, though a note to the *Philosophical Lectures*, ed. K. Coburn, p. 440, says that this observation was "an unusual one for his time . . . supported by modern scholars."

[40] Thomson, I, 2-3.

viously been scientifically examined. Fourthly, chemistry had quickly given practical results and abundantly proved its utility—in dyeing and tanning for instance.[41] Fifthly, and perhaps most important of all, the characteristic method of chemistry was analysis. Although this method had also for some time been used in the study of mind and language, its standing was enhanced by its success in the new natural science. At the time, chemistry was an analytical rather than a theoretical science, its laws, like those of mental science, being incapable of mathematical statement—in spite of Hutcheson's and Hartley's amusing and often-quoted, though not original, attempts. For the study of language in particular, there was the consideration that the rapid progress of chemistry seemed to owe a good deal to the creation of a precise terminology, perhaps the only example in history of the deliberate and large-scale application to science of the fruits of language study, in this case of the much earlier efforts to create a philosophical language.[42] The chemical analogy made it possible for the nonmaterial sciences to accept the dogma that all mental science was also, in a very direct and almost literal fashion, amenable to the method of natural science.

This dogma found its classical statement in Thomas

[41] Davy gave an eloquent, almost enthusiastic, account of the uses of chemistry, both scientifically and practically, in the "Introductory Discourse" to his *Course of Lectures on Chemistry*, delivered and published in 1802 (see *Collected Works*, II, 311ff.).

[42] See Lavoisier's "Mémoire sur la nécessité de réformer & de perfectionner le nomenclature de la chimie," read to the Academy on April 18, 1787. In this he rests his eloquent argument on Condillac's doctrine that "l'algèbre est une véritable langue: . . . ainsi une méthode analytique est une langue; une langue est une méthode analytique." See *Méthode de nomenclature chimique* proposée par MM de Morveau, Lavoisier, Berthollet, et de Fourcroy (Paris, 1787), p. 7, as well as Davy's *Elements* (published 1812) in *Collected Works*, IV, 31-32, and Dugald Stewart in *Collected Works*, ed. Sir William Hamilton (Edinburgh, 1854-1860), II, 197, 347. Hereafter cited StH.

Brown, who very early became aware of the need to modify the principles of scientific inquiry so as to make them suitable for chemistry and thus also, as it turned out, for the philosophy of mind. In his *Observations on the Zoonomia* (1798), written when he was eighteen, he had already suggested that "to philosophize is nothing more, than to register the appearances of nature, and to mark those which each is accustomed to succeed,"[43] that is to examine the phenomena themselves, and to record their sequence, the former relating to space and the latter to time.[44] In his influential *Lectures on the Philosophy of the Human Mind*, first delivered 1810-1811, Brown developed and abundantly illustrated this doctrine, which in 1820 found axiomatic expression in his *Physiology of the Mind*. As in the mechanical and especially in the chemical branch of science, so also "in the philosophy of the other greater department of nature, the physical inquirer has the same objects in view, or objects that are at least very closely analogous,—the *analysis* of what is complex, and the arrangement of the various feelings or *successive* states of mind, in the regular order of their sequence, as causes and effects." He had unshaken faith that "almost every feeling is susceptible of . . . reflective analysis, in some greater or less degree; and inquirer after inquirer, in the field of mind, may evolve as unsuspected elements of thought and passion, as chemist after chemist, in the world of matter, presents to us elements that never had been perceived by us, in substances which may have been before us from the moment of our birth."[45] This

[43] Preface in *Observations*, pp. ix-x.

[44] This distinction was also made in Thomson's *System*, I, 15, in the opening of Part One, "Principles of Chemistry." It was likewise emphasized by James Mill in his review of that work in the *Anti-Jacobin Review*, XII (June, 1802), 164. Alexander Bain ascribes the review to James Mill in his *James Mill* (London, 1882), p. 41.

[45] *Physiology*, pp. 18-22.

conviction was fully shared by James Mill and explains Brougham's opinion that Tooke left "the science, scanty when his inquiries began, enlarged and enriched by his discoveries; for discoveries he made as incontestably as ever did the followers of physical science by the cognate methods of inductive investigation."[46]

Tooke's great and tenacious influence can be understood only in the light of these conceptions of the nature and procedures of contemporary science. He had applied the new method before it had received philosophical sanction. He had studied the elements of the matter of language and the effect that occurred when they were joined. What he called "resolution" was now "analysis," but the principle was the same, just as he—if they had been available to him—could have employed all the chemical terms which now appeared in philology both in England and abroad. "Compound," "affinity," and "verwandtschaft," had for some time had separate histories in language study and in chemistry, but their coincidence greatly strengthened the analogy for the benefit of philology. In addition to "analysis," Murray used the terms "combination," "decomposition," "element," and "compound" with the more precise meanings they had acquired in chemistry. Hazlitt merely stated a commonplace when he said that Tooke "treated words as the chemists do substances." In the opinion of the age, Tooke had made the study of language scientific and placed it in the service of the philosophy of mind. And it was for this reason that his "system" and his "discovery" hit the Utilitarians "like

[46] *Historical Sketches*, 2nd series (London, 1839), p. 114. The article on "Logic" in the *Edinburgh Encyclopedia*, by the Rev. James Esdaile of Perth, stated the interesting opinion that the astonishing advances in natural philosophy since Bacon's day were under no obligation to him except those in chemistry, which "is almost the only branch of modern science which was in a state of complete stagnation when Bacon gave his writings to the world."

a flash of light." To James Mill fell the lot of providing a scientific account of mind to support and complete the social philosophy of his friends. In fulfilling this task, he restored Hartley's psychology and combined it with the teachings of Tooke and Thomas Brown.[47]

James Mill had early become acquainted with Tooke. As the editor of the *Literary Journal,* he had in 1806 reviewed both volumes of the *Diversions,* which he found a "profound and satisfactory" investigation of language "to be ranked with the very highest discoveries which illustrate the names of speculative men." He stated that the account of conjunctions "instantly appeared to the learned so perfectly satisfactory, that it was almost universally adopted; and so remarkably ingenious as to entitle the author to some of the highest honours of literature." He disagreed, however, on two significant points, no doubt because he was still under the influence of his admired teacher Dugald Stewart, whose arguments he used. Mill found Tooke's theory of abstraction incomplete, for "unless abstract terms were formed by persons who perfectly understood abstraction, the contrivances on which they might fall, to supply themselves with those terms, afford no decisive proof of the nature of the operation." And he feared that the tenor of the work pointed toward a system of materialism "which, whether cast in the mould of Helvetius or Hartley, appears to us equally abhorrent from reason, and mischievous in tendency."[48] Ten years later, Mill had

[47] See Elie Halévy, *The Growth of Philosophic Radicalism,* tr. D. Lindsay (London, 1928), pp. 433ff.

[48] *Literary Journal,* I (January, 1806), 1-16, attributed to Mill by Bain, *James Mill,* p. 55. This review forms a very instructive parallel to Mill's review, four years earlier, of Thomson's *System of Chemistry* in the *Anti-Jacobin Review,* XII, 161-170. Mill used etymological argument drawn from Tooke in his reviews of R. E. Scott, *Elements of Intellectual Philosophy* (Edinburgh, 1805), in the *Literary Journal,* I, 572 (attributed to Mill by Bain, p. 56), and of Thomas Smith, *Essay on the Theory of Money*

abandoned those fears along with the philosophy of Stewart and was ready to begin the work which, he said, would make "the human mind as plain as the road from Charing Cross to St. Paul's." This work was written in the 1820's and appeared in 1829 as the *Analysis of the Phenomena of the Human Mind*, a title deliberately chosen to point to the chemical analogy.[49]

Mill's indebtedness to the *Diversions* is defined by the epigraph he placed at the head of his chapter on abstraction. The passage contained Tooke's basic belief that "the perfections of Language, not properly understood, have been one of the chief causes of the imperfections of our knowledge."[50] Mill, much like Locke, saw the need to include language in his mental philosophy. He introduced the subject at a very important point between the account of the "simple and elementary" states of consciousness and "the more complicated cases," for the latter involve "something of the process of Naming."[51] Naming is the essence of language as Tooke had shown by tracing all words via etymology to the names of sensible objects.[52] Hence language, though indispensable both for communication and for the inward as well as the outward preservation of our ideas, contains nothing that cannot ultimately be analyzed in terms of Mill's psychology— that is by reference to sensation and the association of ideas. The mysteries of language are dispelled by revealing what a reviewer of the *Analysis* called "the miserable cheat of words."[53] The complexities of mind are illusory

---

and Exchange (London, 1807), in the *Edinburgh Review*, XIII (October, 1808), 44-45 (attributed to Mill by Halévy, p. 447). Halévy suggests that Tooke's influence on Mill preceded that of Bentham.

[49] See J. S. Mill's Preface to the 1869 edition, I, x.

[50] *Analysis*, I, 294 (quoted from *DP*, I, 37).

[51] I, 128.   [52] I, 134.

[53] *Westminster Review*, XIII (October, 1830), 279 *et passim*. This phrase was one that Locke used on several occasions.

and have their origin in a misunderstanding of language. Though we might, for instance, have had names for all our individual sensations, most marks, or words, stand for "clusters" of sensations "because there is hence a great saving of marks," as Mill explained, using Tooke's —and for that matter Locke's—principle of economy, which is invoked over and over again in the *Analysis* with many different applications.[54] Following Tooke, Mill then explained each of the parts of speech, with the slight modification that he considered the verbs "names of action"—which is perhaps what Tooke himself would have said—to which are added the determination, and here he followed Tooke to the letter, of tense, mood, number, and person.[55] Thus James Mill succeeded in giving a complete "analysis of the phenomena of the human Mind" by combining Hartley with Tooke, a fact which clearly indicates how important Tooke was to the Utilitarians. Mill had shown, in the triumphant words of a reviewer, that "sensation, association, and naming, are the three elements which are to the constitution of the mind what the four elements, carbon, hydrogen, oxygen, and azote, are to the composition of the body."[56]

[54] *Analysis*, I, 135-137, 144, 160.

[55] If any further evidence is needed, it is easy to point to innumerable verbal echoes and direct borrowings from Tooke. Lists of words and etymologies are lifted directly from the *Diversions*. See for instance the etymologies of "with" and "and" (I, 213, cf. *DP*, I, 321-322 and *DP*, I, 135, 219); "else" (I, 218, cf. *DP*, I, 181); "although" (I, 219, cf. *DP*, I, 184); "still" (I, 220, cf. *DP*, I, 135, 179). See also Mill's treatment of abstraction (I, 294-317) and the examples given there. For the 1869 edition of the *Analysis*, Andrew Findlater added "from the rich stores of his philological knowledge, the corrections required by the somewhat obsolete philology which the author had borrowed from Horne Tooke" (J. S. Mill's Preface, I, xx). Findlater's notes, all found in the first volume, are on pp. 135, 178, 197, 209, 213, 215, 216, 218-222, and 310. It is characteristic that Findlater's notes are only corrections; the new material he offers is made to serve the argument as well as the old material from Tooke.

[56] *Westminster Review*, XIII, 284. In their view and use of

The expectations of the philosophic radicals had been fulfilled, but only just in time, for the very same year saw the publication of Macaulay's review of Mill's essay "On Government," the strongest and most effective critique of Utilitarianism that had yet appeared. Around 1830, there were many signs that the spirit of the age was in a process of complete transformation. The great heritage of the eighteenth century, philosophic radicalism, was yielding to the ideas that mark one of the essential qualities of the thought of the nineteenth century. For the study of language in England, it is an historical fact of the utmost importance that Horne Tooke was adopted by the Utilitarians. With them his reputation was secure, and language study remained philosophical rather than historical or philological much longer than on the Continent, where romanticism had found expression in a philosophic faith whose attitude toward the past fostered the new philology and provided the conditions under which it could develop into a new and independent historical discipline. Still, in England the way was prepared for the new philology by the philosophical criticism which was aimed at skepticism, materialism, and Utilitarianism.

For almost forty important years, Dugald Stewart occupied a unique position in British thought. As a Scottish philosopher and James Mill's admired teacher, he never lost the respect of the Utilitarians, but his criticism of some points basic to their system, and his moderation, secured him the regard of the Germano-Coleridgean school as well. His eloquence, the acknowledged beauty of his style, and the ease and clarity of his exposition made him a highly successful lecturer. Dugald Stewart was a follower of Thomas Reid, whose lectures he at-

---

language, Tooke and the Utilitarians had much in common with the contemporary French Ideologists. See H. B. Acton, "The Philosophy of Language in Revolutionary France" in *Proceedings of the British Academy*, XLV (1959), 199-219.

tended at Glasgow during 1771-1772; and for the rest of his long and influential life, Stewart remained true to the spirit of Reid's philosophy, sharing his teacher's critical attitude toward Humean skepticism, and toward the various forms of materialism which that skepticism implied in regard to the nature of mind.

Reid's challenge was clearly stated in the title of his first published work, the *Inquiry into the Human Mind on the Principles of Common Sense* (1764), which in outline contained his whole philosophy. According to Reid, man's descent into the abyss of skepticism began with Descartes' "ideal system"—as Reid called it—of the human understanding. Locke did not mend matters when, to retain the reality of the material world, he framed his representationist theory of knowledge on the *camera-obscura* principle—"methinks the mind is not much unlike a *closet*, wholly shut up from light," Locke had said in a passage which Dugald Stewart used as an example of the dangerous consequences of applying analogies from the material world to the mental.[57] Extending the argument, Berkeley had done away with the material world, and Hume finally had done away with mind by showing that it was "nothing but a train of ideas connected by certain relations between themselves," a flux.[58] The unrelenting pursuit of reason and the dictates of logic had produced this estrangement between philosophy and common sense. "In this division," Reid admitted, "to my great humiliation, I find myself classed with the vulgar."[59] Reid could not accept that mind was so much simpler than the body of man, that it was, if it existed at all, entirely passive, a mere puppet, "an enchanted castle, imposed upon by spectres and appari-

[57] StH. V, 168-169.
[58] Thomas Reid, *Works*, ed. William Hamilton, 2 vols. with continuous pagination (Edinburgh, 1863), p. 299. Hereafter cited as RH.
[59] RH, 302.

tions."[60] The argument that led to skepticism was unassailable; Reid therefore sought the origin of its evil in the premises. The central point in his philosophy was the rejection of the representationist theory of knowledge and of the entire "ideal system." "It would be want of candour not to own, that I think there is some merit in what you are pleased to call *my Philosophy*," Reid wrote in 1790 to his friend Dr. James Gregory in Edinburgh; "but I think it lies chiefly in having called in question the common theory of *Ideas* or *Images of things in the mind* being the only objects of thought;—a theory founded on natural prejudices, and so universally received as to be interwoven with the structure of language."[61] To support his interpretation, Reid did not put another theory in the field. The idea-theory had in fact not explained what it had been introduced to explain,[62] and Reid believed that "no man is able to explain how we perceive external objects, any more than how we are conscious of those that are internal. Perception, consciousness, memory, and imagination, are all original and simple powers of the mind, and parts of its constitution."[63] In this refusal to pretend to explain ultimate causes, Reid was, as Stewart pointed out, strictly following Newton, who similarly declined to explain the cause of gravitation. As Reid was charged with mysticism, so Newton had been accused of leaving gravitation an occult quality in the manner of the Schoolmen. The motto which Reid prefixed to his *Inquiry* must be understood in this light—"The Inspiration of the Almighty giveth them understanding."[64] Reid had avoided error and absurdity

[60] RH, 103.
[61] Quoted in Stewart's excellent "Account of the Life and Writings of Thomas Reid, D. D." in StH, X, 291-292, first read to the Royal Society of Edinburgh in 1802. It will also be found at the beginning of RH.
[62] RH, 305.   [63] RH, 309.
[64] See StH, X, 289-291 ("Life of Reid"), and I, 148 ("Disserta-

by willingly abstaining from the temptation to explain all or too much; he had brought the philosophy of mind in harmony with our natural belief in the existence of the material world. Mind was an independent entity, it was active, and we were justified in talking of its operations. First and last, he had vindicated the principles of common sense; his philosophy did not contradict the views of the common man—and the nature of the common language he spoke.

A characteristic feature of Reid's writings is, as we would expect, his frequently repeated words of caution against the dangers of the mind-body analogy. The analogy is misleading both because the basic assumption of a similarity or identity in their operations cannot be justified and because the accessibility of the evidence in question and the procedure of proof are, as a matter of practical fact, altogether different. He devoted a whole chapter of the first of his *Essays on the Intellectual Powers of Man* (1784) to "Analogy" and concluded that "in our inquiries concerning the mind and its operations, we ought never to trust to reasonings drawn from some supposed similitude of body to mind; and that we ought very much to be upon our guard that we be not imposed upon by those analogical terms and phrases, by which the operations of the mind are expressed in all languages."[65]

---

tion: Exhibiting the Progress of metaphysical, ethical and political philosophy, since the revival of letters in Europe," written for the Supplement to the *Encyclopaedia Britannica* and published in two parts in 1815 and 1821). Cf. also StH, X, 282: "Sir Isaac Newton's query concerning the causes of gravitation was certainly not *inconsistent* with his own discoveries concerning its laws; but what would have been the consequences to the world, if he had indulged himself in the prosecution of hypothetical theories with respect to the former, instead of directing his astonishing powers to an investigation of the latter?"

[65] RH, 238. Cf. also Ch. I, Sect. ii, "The Impediments to our Knowledge of Mind" in the *Inquiry* (RH, 98-99); and the *Intel-*

During the next generation, the philosophy of mind followed the very opposite path, and Dugald Stewart consequently devoted even more space than Reid to criticism of that great fallacy. In his "Life of Reid" he counted it that philosopher's greatest merit that he was the first to apply Bacon's method of induction to mental philosophy, notwithstanding the claim which Hume had made in the subtitle to his *Inquiry*—"an attempt to introduce the experimental method of reasoning into moral subjects."[66] Stewart admired Reid's soundness and saw in it a reminder that the disquisitions of scholastic pneumatology and of physiological metaphysics were both "an idle waste of time and genius on questions where our conclusions can neither be verified nor overturned by an appeal to experiment or observation."[67]

Language played an important role in Reid's argument, but he was not entirely consistent in the uses he made of it. On the one hand, he shared Locke's opinion that the ambiguity of words is one of the chief sources of philosophical error and confusion. His *Essays on the Intellectual Powers* began with a chapter on the "Explication of Words," in which he pointed out that many words are irreducible and consequently cannot be provided with a logical definition, words such as to *think*, to *apprehend*, to *will*, to *believe*, to *desire*. The job of producing meaning thus falls to usage, to the common acceptation of words, for "every man who understands the language, has some notion of the meaning of those words."[68] But Reid also made a positive use of language,

---

lectual Powers in RH, 301-302, 396-397, of which the latter passage criticizes the analogy between chemical and mental analysis.

[66] StH, X, 258ff. Both Reid and Stewart frequently refer to the authority of Bacon and the example of Newton against the quasi-a-priori method, which seemed sanctioned by the current interpretation of Newton's method. For Stewart's estimate of Bacon, see especially StH, I, 63-79 ("Dissertation I").

[67] StH, X, 282.   [68] RH, 220.

for where could he find material evidence for the views of the common man beyond his own subjective observations, in which he might after all be mistaken? Language was one of his chief sources of information on this point, an idea he borrowed from the expositors of universal grammar.[69] Reid observed that language reveals "certain common opinions of mankind," for "language is the express image and picture of human thoughts; and, from the picture, we may often draw very certain conclusions with regard to the original." We find the same parts of speech, the same modifications of the nouns and verbs, and the same syntax in languages; and we can therefore conclude that "this uniformity in the structure of language shews a certain degree of uniformity in those notions upon which the structure of language is grounded."[70] On these grounds Reid rejected Hume's notion of "impressions on the mind," because the structure of all languages shows that seeing, hearing, desiring, willing, are considered operations of the mind itself; consequently the mind cannot be passive as Hume believed. This is perilous proof, however. Harris and Monboddo had also used language to support their attack on skepticism, but in the process they had relied on speculation which Tooke, with his Lockean presuppositions, could easily prove much less reasonable and convincing than his own—and his speculation, which was also a priori, led to diametrically opposed conclusions. Was there any way out of this impasse? Could language be of any help at all to the philosophy of mind, and if so, what would its precise function be?

Stewart is generally rated a mere transmitter of Reid's philosophy rather than an originator—by Leslie Stephen, for instance, who had a heavy Utilitarian bias and who

[69] Reid several times referred to the "learned" author of *Hermes*; see, for instance, RH, 404.
[70] RH, 233.

has had considerable influence on the estimates we now form of the Utilitarians and their contemporaries. But on the question of language at least, Stewart saw the inconsistency of Reid's position and its dangerous consequences. Stewart dismissed entirely the philosophical usefulness and validity of etymological speculation. He further made it very doubtful that language in any other way—even in its structure—could give direct aid to philosophy. In regard to language, he brought back philosophy to the cautious suspicion, which had also been Locke's attitude, at least at the outset. Stewart divorced philosophy from the study of language and thus helped prepare the ground for philology proper as an autonomous discipline.

Stewart has perhaps devoted more time to language than any other British philosopher. He lectured on the *Letter to Mr. Dunning* as early as 1778-1779, when he substituted for Adam Ferguson during the latter's absence in North America, and to the end of his life he retained an active interest in the subject. He corresponded with Dr. Parr and was very grateful to him for mentioning "Michaelis on the First Language," which Parr presented to Stewart around 1820, later receiving the latter's thanks that Parr "could not possibly have thought of a more acceptable gift . . . at this moment."[71]

[71] See *Works of Samuel Parr*, ed. John Johnstone (London, 1828), VII, 547-548 (letter of August 1816 from Stewart stating his interest in the book, which Parr had, it seems, previously recommended), and page 553 (undated letter, which from internal evidence can be dated 1820 or just after). The book in question was Michaelis' prize-essay on the *Influence of Opinions on Language, and of Language on Opinions* (first English edition London, 1769). A reference in the last volume of Stewart's *Elements* (1827) shows that Stewart had not read it prior to the publication of his previous volumes (StH, IV, 55). Stewart and Michaelis agree on so many points that the possibility of earlier influence is ruled out only by our knowledge that the prize-essay came into Stewart's hands after his mind was settled on questions of language.

He read articles on Sanskrit in the *Asiatic Researches*[72] and knew of Bopp's *Conjugationssystem* through a review.[73] Toward the end of 1824 or the beginning of 1825, he wrote a treatise entitled "Conjectures Concerning the Origin of Sanscrit."[74] It presented the unfortunate theories on the origin of Sanskrit, which he included in the third volume of his *Elements of the Philosophy of the Human Mind*, published in 1827, a year before his death. His critique of contemporary language study and of the entire eighteenth-century tradition was presented in 1810 in his essay "On the Tendency of some Late Philological Speculations."[75]

The speculations he specifically had in mind were Tooke's; but the *Diversions* are not mentioned until half-way through the essay and were its occasion rather than its general subject. Stewart attacked what might be called the atomistic theory of meaning, the notion that each single word has a precise idea affixed to it and that the total meaning of a sentence is, so to speak, the sum of these meanings. In the opinion of the age, the difficulty which the "un-meaning" parts of speech had caused to this view had been removed by Tooke's etymological discovery. Stewart went to the heart of the matter, asserting that words gain meaning only in context and that many have none apart from it. Thus "our words, when examined separately, are often as completely insignificant as

[72] StH, IV, 93.
[73] StH, IV, 79-80, with reference to *Edinburgh Review*, XXXIII (May, 1820), 431-435. This review was by Alexander Hamilton.
[74] StH, IV, 115 (note by the editor Sir William Hamilton).
[75] This was one of the *Philosophical Essays* and will be found StH, V, 149-188. In the second and third volumes of the *Elements of the Philosophy of the Human Mind* (1814 and 1827), he elaborated but added nothing that was not already in that essay or clearly implied in the principles it set forth. Stewart's basic position is already clear in his critique of Adam Smith's "Considerations Concerning the First Formation of Languages" (1767), in his "Life of Adam Smith" from 1794 (see StH, X, 32-37).

the letters of which they are composed." Many words in Johnson's *Dictionary*, for instance, are listed with as many as forty, fifty, or even sixty different meanings, whose distinction it is by no means easy to grasp; yet in context the reader or listener can without the slightest effort find the right meaning—"how is this to be explained but by the light thrown upon the problematical term by the general import of the sentence?"[76] These considerations hold a fortiori for such words as "of" and "by," whose "import . . . is fully understood by children of three or four years of age," though to Adam Smith, in his "Considerations Concerning the First Formation of Languages," their invention had caused almost insuperable metaphysical difficulties, not least because he found the intellectual effort required hard to reconcile with the fact that primitive man had invented them.[77] Here the contrast between Stewart and Tooke becomes clear when we recall Tooke's statement that *from* continues "to retain invariably one and the same single meaning" in spite of the more than seventy separate meanings given by Johnson.[78]

Taken as plain observation on the manner in which words function, Stewart's statement was neither new nor startling; it was, for instance, implied in Berkeley's assertion that his servant would understand the words *time* and *place* perfectly well if told to meet his master "at such a *time*, in such a *place*," without ever having thought about their abstract and metaphysical meanings.[79] But stated as a principle in this specific context, Stewart's axiom was nothing less than revolutionary. It achieved a great many things. First of all, language cannot be the precise image of thought, as even Reid had asserted. Our words merely supply hints to our readers or suggest a train of ideas, "leaving by far the principal

[76] StH, V, 154-155. [77] StH, IV, 25-27.
[78] *DP*, I, 346-347. [79] *Principles*, par. 97.

part of the process of interpretation to be performed by the Mind itself."[80] The wonder is not so much in the mechanism of speech, which Tooke had admired, as in the "far more wonderful *mechanism* which it puts into action behind the scene." The mind is active, and language is imperfect as a vehicle of mental intercourse, two conclusions which flatly contradict Tooke's fundamental presuppositions. Again, Stewart's axiom implies that "the intellectual act, as far as we are able to trace it, is altogether simple, and incapable of analysis," which means that "the elements into which we flatter ourselves we have resolved it, are nothing more than the *grammatical elements of speech*;—the logical doctrine about the *comparison of ideas* bearing a much closer affinity to the task of a schoolboy in *parsing* his lesson, than to the researches of philosophers, able to form a just conception of the mystery to be explained."[81] Thus the role of the principles of association psychology, which had previously been used very generally and carelessly, is strictly circumscribed.

Another set of important consequences derive from Stewart's axiom. If the meaning of a sentence is produced not by the addition of the individual and fixed ideas attached to each word but by the reader's general awareness of the possible range of the meaning of some words and of the functions of others, combined with a scanning of the context, then the meaning depends entirely on what is actively present in the reader's or listener's mind in the act of grasping the meaning, or at least a meaning. Tooke's unexpressed premise that the current meaning of a word is equivalent to the product of its etymological explanation, is therefore false; first, because the etymology according to Tooke produced only a single fixed and unvarying meaning, and secondly, because the etymology

[80] StH, V, 153-154.
[81] StH, V, 156.

could never be relevant unless it was present in the mind
and, so to speak, operative in the process of understanding—a view that must assume, contrary to fact, that the
reader or listener is at all times familiar with the etymology of every single word in the discourse. This latter view
is certainly implied in Tooke's *Diversions* and contains
a supreme mysticism, which was contrary to his pro-
fessed aims. Or did he perhaps, just before his death two
years after the publication of Stewart's essay, burn all
his notes to the third volume because he saw that his system had collapsed? The source of the mysticism is in
such mechanical metaphors as the "operations of language" and the "power" or "force" of words, almost as if
language was a huge stamping machine which—to retain
the inconsistency in a mixed metaphor—put into the
hands of the mind, counters impressed with their etymological value. We are reminded of Hobbes' striking
statement: "For words are wise men's counters, they do
but reckon by them; but they are the money of fools, that
value them by the authority of an Aristotle, a Cicero, or
a Thomas, or any other doctor whatsoever, if but a
man." In this light, Tooke was in fact nothing but an
etymological doctor.

Stewart's argument was especially effective with regard
to philosophical terms. He declared: "To me, on the contrary, it appears that to appeal to etymology in a
philosophical argument . . . is altogether nugatory, and
can serve, at the best, to throw an amusing light on the
laws which regulate the operations of human fancy."[82]
After the philologer has told us, for instance, "that
imagination is borrowed from an optical *image*, and
acuteness from a Latin word, denoting the sharpness of
a material instrument, we are no more advanced in
studying the theory of the human intellect, than we should
be in our speculations concerning the functions of money,

[82] StH, V, 161.

or the political effects of the national debt, by learning from Latin etymologists, that the word *pecunia* and the phrase *aes alienum* had both a reference, in their first origin, to certain circumstances in the early state of Roman manners."[83] With keen insight, Stewart found the source of this "etymological metaphysics," as he appropriately called it, in Locke's familiar statement that "it may also lead us a little towards the original of all our notions and knowledge, if we remark how great a dependence our words have on common sensible ideas." Of this Stewart said, "Mr. Locke himself prepared the way for Mr. Tooke's researches,"[84] and in fact, as we have seen, for the entire eighteenth-century preoccupation with the origin of language. The foundation of "etymological metaphysics," however, is the acknowledged "difficulty attending the origin of words expressive of things which do not fall under the cognizance of any of our senses," and in the "disposition of the Mind, on such occasions, to have recourse to metaphors borrowed from the Material World," as the only means of achieving communication on such subjects. "The moment that the terms *attention, imagination, abstraction, sagacity, foresight, penetration, acuteness, inclination, aversion, deliberation,* are pronounced, a great step towards their interpretation is made in the mind of every person of common understanding; and although his analogical reference to the Material World adds greatly to the difficulty of analyzing, with philosophical rigour, the various faculties and principles of our nature, yet it cannot be denied, that it facilitates, to a wonderful degree, the mutual communications of mankind concerning them, in so far as such communications are necessary in the ordinary business of life."[85] But the philosophical consequences of our inability to speak about mind or its phe-

[83] StH, V, 158.   [84] StH, V, 433.   [85] StH, V, 152-153.

nomena without employing a metaphorical phraseology had caused the fatal error, against which Stewart's entire argument was directed, the error that arose when "the common analogical phraseology concerning mind [is] mistaken for its genuine philosophical theory."[86] Stewart found that a consideration of the figurative language used with regard to mind does not support the belief in the material nature of mind, but leads to a conclusion which is directly opposite. "For whence this disposition to attenuate and subtilize, to the very verge of existence, the atoms or elements supposed to produce the phenomena of thought and volition, but from the repugnance of the scheme of Materialism to our natural apprehension, and from a secret anxiety to guard against a literal interpretation of our metaphorical phraseology?"[87] Since "it is by the exclusive use of some favourite figure, that careless thinkers are gradually led to mistake a simile or distant analogy for a legitimate theory," Stewart suggested the remedy of varying the metaphors "so as to prevent any one of them from acquiring an undue ascendant over the others, either in our own minds, or in those of our readers." It was "in many cases, a fortunate circumstance, when the words we employ have lost their pedigree."[88] The last point is especially interesting, for

[86] StH, V, 157.

[87] StH, V, 165. Stewart further argued that the very variety of metaphors, which may be used with equal propriety concerning the phenomena of mind, tells against the material doctrine. He asked "whether the indiscriminate use, among all our most precise writers, of *these obviously inconsistent metaphors*, does not justify us in concluding, that none of them has any connexion with the true theory of the phenomena which he ['the Materialist'] conceives them to explain; and that they deserve the attention of the metaphysician, merely as familiar illustrations of the mighty influence exerted over our most abstracted thoughts, by *language* and by *early associations*" (p. 170).

[88] StH, V, 173-174. On his suggestion to vary the metaphors, Stewart remarked that "obvious as it may appear, I do not recollect to have met with it in the writings of any of my predecessors,"

there is no telling what eighteenth-century philosophy would have been like if the word "mind" had been etymologically transparent. Even Tooke never attempted an etymology of that word and would no doubt have been surprised to find that the best present-day etymological dictionaries do not trace it beyond "the principle of thinking," "thought," and the like.

Stewart, of course, did not wish to disparage philological scholarship and had considerable admiration for Tooke's achievement in that department. But he did wish to make it very clear that philology was purely an historical discipline, which must avoid speculation and instead work with ascertainable facts. The "captivating researches" of the philologer and his discoveries "belong to the same branch of literature with that which furnishes a large proportion of the materials in our common lexicons and etymological dictionaries."[89] Toward the end of the essay "On the Tendency of some Late Philological Speculations," Stewart said that his purpose was "only to mark out the limits of [the philologers'] legitimate and very ample province. As long as the philologer confines himself to discussions of grammar and of etymology, his

---

though he admitted "it is very possible, that in this my memory may deceive me." For fuller illustration, he referred to Vols. I (1792) and II (1814) of his *Elements of the Philosophy of the Human Mind* (in StH, II, 355, and III, 57ff.). But he could have met a similar observation in Robert Boyle's *Origin of Forms and Qualities* (1666). Having remarked that scholastic writers "do not always mean the same things by the same terms, but some imploy them in one sense, others in another, and sometimes the same writer uses them in very different senses," Boyle continued: "And this put me in mind of intimating, that whereas, on the contrary, I sometimes imployed variety of terms and phrases to express the same thing, I did it purposely . . . both I and others having observed, that the same unobvious notions being several ways expressed, some readers, even among the ingeniouser sort of them, will take it up much better in one of these expressions, and some in another" (Thomas Birch, ed., *Works* [1772], III, 6).
[89] StH, V, 158.

labours, while they are peculiarly calculated to gratify the natural and liberal curiosity of men of erudition, may often furnish important data for illustrating the progress of laws, of arts, and of manners;—for clearing up obscure passages in ancient writers;—or for tracing the migrations of mankind, in ages of which we have no historical records."[90] This was a philological program to which Sir William Jones would have had nothing to add. Indeed, it seems that Stewart may be indebted to Jones, whom he read and elsewhere quoted at length on the deceptions of etymology "in the hope of guarding my younger readers against lending too easy a faith to the seducing theories of etymologists."[91]

There can be little doubt that Stewart's analysis demonstrated that the "philologers" had committed two fundamental errors. The first was "the error of confounding the historical progress of an art with its theoretical principles when advanced to maturity"; and the second, "that of considering language as a much more exact and complete picture of thought, than it is in any state of society, whether barbarous or refined."[92] The former point is especially important since it implies Stewart's notion of theoretical or conjectural history, which he first developed in this context, that is, with regard to the origin of language. If Adam Smith in his essay on the origin of language had shown that common nouns had gradually developed by a transformation of proper names, that demonstration did not warrant the assertion that the two are now "radically and essentially the same" and even less that the present distinction between proper names and common nouns is not significant.[93] Theoretical his-

---

[90] StH, V, 176.

[91] StH, IV, 66n; this is in the third volume of the *Elements* (1827), but Stewart had already referred to Jones in the *Philosophical Essays* (1810) and in the second volume of the *Elements* (1814).

[92] StH, V, 166.   [93] StH, V, 167.

tory is conjectural because it must eke out the paucity of facts with a priori reasoning based on assumptions concerning the constancy of human nature and the influence, for instance, of climate and society on man. It can show how things *may* have been, but cannot establish how things were. Consequently the "findings" of theoretical history have no legitimate place in our study of how things *are*.

In language study Stewart adhered to the great respect for inductive—or, as we would say today, empirical—procedures which Reid had taught him were the most effective weapons against skepticism, materialism, and the philosophical confusion he observed around him: "In order to succeed, it is necessary to ascertain facts before we begin to reason, and to avoid generalizing, in any instance, till we have completely secured the ground that we have gained."[94] It is this critical and empirical temper that explains his wise counsel that in order "to render the study of the affinity of languages a solid foundation for our conclusions, it is necessary that those who devote themselves to it . . . should guard against the danger of rendering their labours fruitless, by aiming at what is wholly beyond the comprehension of our faculties. A few languages, grammatically and critically possessed, would enable them to add more usefully to the mass of philological knowledge, than the almost miraculous gift of tongues displayed in the labours of Adelung and some of his successors."[95] In language study no change of attitude was more essential than the one for which Stewart argued when, in defending Reid, he called it "a very mis-

[94] StH, II, 344 (Volume One of the *Elements* [1792]).

[95] StH, IV, 65. In a footnote Stewart adds: "I call it an *almost miraculous gift*, because in looking over such tables as that exhibited in the Supplement to the *Encyclopaedia Britannica*, (See Article *Languages*,) I can only wonder and admire at faculties to which I am unconscious of possessing in myself anything at all analogous."

taken idea, that the formation of a hypothetical system is a stronger proof of inventive genius, than the patient investigation of nature in the way of induction. To form a system, appears to the young and inexperienced understanding a species of creation; to ascend slowly to general conclusions, from the observation and comparison of particular facts, is to comment servilely on the works of another."[96] Stewart's words agree entirely with those of Johann David Michaelis, the great orientalist and theologian at Göttingen. He was one of the soundest philologists of the eigthteenth century and exercised through Herder a strong influence on philology in Germany before Schlegel, Bopp, and Grimm. Toward the end of his dissertation on the *Influence of Opinions on Language and of Language on Opinions,* he had said: "Languages, generally speaking, would deserve that philosophy should devote a particular science to them; but let not this science, by any means be reduced to a system, till experience had collected and arranged every particular of it."[97] The new philology owes its origin to a scholar who fully shared the opinion of Michaelis, Sir William Jones.

Stewart's critique helped clear the way for new views of language, but the deplorable state of philology in England did not become cause for national reproach and shame until the 1830's, with Horne Tooke as the chief culprit. To the notion that "all rational and philosophical English etymology must be founded on his system," Richard Garnett gave a clear answer in 1835: "We think

[96] StH, X, 287 ("Life of Reid"). Many of Stewart's points were cited against Tooke by John Barclay in his *Sequel to the Diversions of Purley* "containing an essay on English verbs with remarks on Mr. Tooke's work, and on some terms employed to denote soul or spirit" (London, 1826). It is a measure of what had happened since Tooke's time that Barclay still hoped that "the works of Horne Tooke will have some effect in checking the license of etymological conjecture" (p. 6).

[97] Michaelis, p. 76.

there are no sufficient grounds for this persuasion, and
that the general prevalence of it would be more likely to
impede the improvement of sound philology than to promote it."[98] Four years later, John William Donaldson
made opposition to Tooke the purpose of his *New
Cratylus*, and the next year *Blackwood's Magazine* strongly
attacked Tooke in a review of the third edition of the
Diversions:

> It is with a mixture of mirth and amazement that we
> look back to the position it used to occupy; when even
> those who felt it to be wrong and ridiculous, could only
> qualify themselves to appear as its opponents by first
> paying homage to its ingenuity and learning. It reflects
> little credit on English philology that it should have
> been so regarded then; and it is not much to our praise
> now, that it should still be named in works of science
> of a respectable character, and named without censure,
> or even with eulogium and deference. Its authority and
> influence have done much harm to us as philologists,
> both in our reputation and in our progress. It has
> lowered the high name which England once could
> boast in Teutonic philology. It has blinded us to better
> guides—it has led us upon a false track, and lulled us
> into a delusive security. It has palsied our better efforts
> and aspirations, like a nightmare upon our breasts.
> Let us escape from the slavish fear or silly supersti-
> tion that has tyrannized over us; let us shake the
> incubus from his hold, and hail with gladness the
> beaming of a better day, in which, under fairer aus-
> pices, we shall pursue, with reverential zeal and hum-
> ble diligence, some of the worthiest and most mys-

[98] "English Lexicography" in the *Quarterly Review*, LIV (September, 1835), 311. Reprinted in the *Philological Essays of the
Late Rev. Richard Garnett* (London, 1859), pp. 1-40 (with this
passage on p. 18).

terious subjects of knowledge that the study of man can open to our understandings.[99]

Garnett, Donaldson, and the anonymous reviewer in *Blackwood's* wrote during the years when the new philology was gaining acceptance in England.

[99] XLVII (April, 1840), 496.

CHAPTER IV

Sir William Jones and the New Philology

Sir William Jones sailed for India in April 1783, to take
up his duties as a judge of the supreme court of judica-
ture at Fort William in Calcutta, where he landed after a
pleasant voyage with his bride Anna Maria Shipley, the
daughter of the Bishop of St. Asaph.[1] Behind him lay a
distinguished career as an orientalist which brought him
membership in the Royal Society in 1772, at the age of
twenty-six, and an equally distinguished record as a
lawyer. Before him lay ten years of incredibly hard work
in both capacities and achievements which were to make
him famous and admired among the learned both in
Europe and in India. He died in India on April 27, 1794,
six years before he had planned to return to England to
enjoy the intellectual and the modest material fruits of
his unequaled industry and devotion. In 1787 he wrote
to a friend: "I was never unhappy in England; it was not
in my nature to be so; but I was never happy till I was
settled in India."[2] While he was still a child, his mother
had admonished him: "Read, and you will know."[3] With
his age, he believed that the greatest man is the best, and
that the best is "he that has deserved most of his fellow-
creatures."[4] Unlike many of his learned contemporaries,
however, he believed that "curious or important information might be gained even from the illiterate."[5] It was on
the foundation of these precepts and beliefs that he became the greatest Indian scholar the world had yet seen.

---

[1] Lord Teignmouth (John Shore), *Memoirs of the Life, Writings,
and Correspondence of Sir William Jones* in *The Works of Sir
William Jones* (London, 1807), I, 402 and II, 11. The *Life* was
first published in 1804; it occupies Vols. I and II in the *Works*.
  [2] II, 129-130.   [3] I, 21.   [4] I, 206.
  [5] II, 300-301.

Jones's career as an orientalist began shortly after he had come to Oxford in 1764. In that year he began the study of Arabic to which he soon added Persian. The result, within the next ten years, was the publication of a number of works which greatly stimulated interest in Oriental literature at the same time as they added to the precise knowledge of the subject. Jones himself had both purposes in mind. He wanted to refute the critical opinion that Oriental poetry was inane and wished to encourage its translation, with notes and explanations, to provide English poets with new sources of imagery, reference, and allusion. Among the works of this period are the translation of the *Histoire de Nader Chah* (1770), at the request of the Danish king;[6] a *Dissertation sur la littérature orientale* which was appended to the *Histoire* and separately issued the next year; and finally, during the same year, a *Grammar of the Persian Language* which by 1828 had seen nine London editions plus a French translation in 1772. His studies were made possible by the leisure and security he enjoyed as tutor to Lord Althorp, later the second Earl Spencer, a position which on several occasions took him to France, Italy, and Germany. But Jones admitted that he was ambitious and ready to accept the advice of his friends to "banish poetry and Oriental literature for a time," take up the study of law, and "pursue the track of ambition."[7] He was admitted to the Temple in September 1770,[8] and was called to the bar in January of 1774.[9] The following ten years he devoted almost entirely to his legal career, in 1781 publishing his *Essay on the Law of Bailments,* which established his legal reputation.

[6] See Hertha Kirketerp-Møller, "Nadir Shah, Christian VII, og William Jones" in *Fund og Forskning i det Kongelige Biblioteks Samlinger*, IX (1962), 114-127.

[7] I, 163 (Jones to Count Reviczki, March 1771).

[8] I, 161.

[9] I, 207.

"The die is cast," Jones wrote in 1774, "and I have no longer a choice; all my books and manuscripts, with an exception of those only which relate to law and oratory, are locked up at Oxford, and I have determined, for the next twenty years at least, to renounce all studies but those which are connected with my profession."[10] He was in fact very eager to let the world know that he had entirely abandoned his previous studies, "for a man who wishes to rise in the law, must be supposed to have no other object."[11] He was aiming toward political or public office at home—hence the exception of books on oratory—but his lack of sympathy for the British cause in the American war did not help the preferment he hoped for, least of all when he came under suspicion because he had secured a passport to America to look after the interests of a client.[12] Under these circumstances, he found it difficult to forget his Oriental studies, and in 1779 he was already hoping for a post in Bengal, "where the vacations will give me leisure to renew my acquaintance, which I am now obliged to intermit, with the Persian and Arabian classics."[13] But he had to wait with patience, for the fact of the matter was that Lord North did not wish to appoint him, and he had to bide his time another two years before the appointment came in March 1783, thanks to the friendship of Lord Ashburton. His expectation had at last been fulfilled, and he would again, with a good conscience, be able to devote part of his time to his favorite study. In the meantime, he had early that

[10] I, 217 (letter to the Dutch orientalist H. A. Schultens, October 1774).

[11] I, 176 (Jones to Hawkins, November 5, 1771).

[12] I, 355. He also wrote a classical "Ode to Liberty" (I, 309) and planned an impartial history of the war (I, 339). The passport was issued by Benjamin Franklin.

[13] I, 298 (Jones to Prince Adam Czartoryski, February 17, 1779); two years later he wrote in a similar vein to Gibbon (I, 365).

year published *The Moallakat, or Seven Arabian Poems, which were suspended on the Temple at Mecca, with a Translation and Arguments,* a work that greatly enhanced his reputation as a poet and scholar. It established Jones's name on the Continent, a preparation for the even greater fame gained by his work during the next ten years.[14]

Jones was always very methodical in his habits. At the age of thirty-three, he drew up a plan of study for the future in which he made the resolution to "learn no more rudiments of any kind," but instead to perfect himself in the subjects he already knew, including twelve languages of which four were Eastern: Hebrew, Arabic, Persian, and Turkish.[15] If he had not abandoned this plan by the time or shortly after he arrived in India, Sanskrit studies in Europe would have taken a different course. The reason for the change is found in a sketch for an "Essay on Education," written when he was twenty-two, in which he had pointed to the necessity of knowing the languages of all people who in any period have been distinguished by superior knowledge; for he felt that man's life is too short for him to attain sufficient knowledge and

[14] The *Moallakat* had already come to Goethe's attention on November 14, 1783, when he wrote to Carl von Knebel that these poems were "im Ganzen sehr merckwürdig, und einzelne allerliebste Stellen drinne. Wir haben uns vorgenommen sie in Gesellschafft zu übersezen, und also wirst du sie auch bald zu sehen kriegen." *Briefe 1764-1786* in *Gedenkausgabe* (Zürich: Artemis Verlag, 1950-1960), XVIII, 752.

[15] Teignmouth, I, 344. Cf. the list he drew up later in life which includes altogether 28 languages arranged in three groups according to his proficiency in them (II, 264). An even more curious example of Jones's adherence to system is the Andrometer or "scale of human attainments and enjoyment," which he invented around 1775. The first year of life is devoted to "ideas received through the senses" (I, 239-244). Jones was a great admirer of Bacon and Locke, and he was much annoyed to discover that the only logic in fashion at Oxford was that of the Schools, while the passages in Locke that were derisive of the old logic were carefully passed over without comment and discussion (I, 54-55).

the improvement of reason unless his own endeavors are supplemented by "the accumulated experience and wisdom of all ages and all nations."[16] But there was also another, more immediate and urgent reason for learning the ancient language of India. As a judge, he could not perform his duties without firsthand acquaintance with native law, having realized that he could place "no reliance . . . on the opinions or interpretations of the professors of the Hindu law, unless he were qualified to examine their authorities and quotations, and detect their errors and misrepresentations."[17] To meet this practical need, Jones planned a digest of Indian law, which was begun under his direction though not finished until after his death. The first part of this digest was his own translation of the ordinances of Manu, published as *Institutes of Hindu Law* at Calcutta in 1794, the year of his death.[18] Thus an ancient language once more became the object of learned attention because it contained the law that still governed the present. The Elizabethans had turned to the study of Anglo-Saxon for the same reason, and the Grimm brothers would soon concentrate on the early dialects of Germany, thanks to the study of legal history, which they pursued under Savigny.[19]

But naturally Jones also studied Sanskrit for the same reasons which twenty years earlier had guided him toward Arabic and Persian. To satisfy his literary interests, he

---

[16] I, 155.   [17] II, 27.

[18] See Garland H. Cannon, Jr., *Sir William Jones, An annotated Bibliography of his Works* (Honolulu, 1952), pp. 61-66. It was reissued at London in 1796 and a German translation appeared in 1797. It became widely used for information about Indian cosmogony, religion, and manners, e.g. by Friedrich Schlegel.

[19] Wilhelm Schoof, *Briefe der Brüder Grimm an Savigny* (Berlin, 1953), p. 6. Savigny brought Jacob Grimm to Paris, as his amanuensis from January to September 1805. During these months, Jacob wrote to Wilhelm: "Ich habe daran gedacht, ob du nicht in Paris einmal unter den Manuskripten nach alten deutschen Gedichten und Poesien suchen könntest."

translated Calidas' drama *Sakontala*, first published in Calcutta in 1789 and soon reissued in England in several editions. Through Georg Forster's translation into German two years later, it became one of the most influential translations of all time and probably did more than any other single work or event to arouse that profound interest in Indian religion, literature, and language which was so characteristic of German Romanticism and without which the intensive study of Indian languages would hardly have developed with such amazing speed. In 1791, Herder sent the translation to Goethe, who was immediately captivated by it and never ceased to admire it, as he showed by borrowing the idea for the "Vorspiel" to *Faust* from the opening of *Sakontala*.[20] It is against this background of scholarly and literary achievement, reputation, and authority that we must understand the impact of Jones's statements on the principles of language study and the affinity of Sanskrit to other languages.

Jones did not begin the study of Sanskrit until late in the summer of 1785, almost two years after his arrival in India.[21] On September 8, he wrote to a friend that he was now at the ancient university of Nadeya, "where I hope to learn the rudiments of that venerable and interesting language which was once vernacular in all India,"[22] and in October, after his return to Calcutta, he said: "I would rather be a valetudinarian, all my life, than leave unexplored the Sanscrit mine which I have just opened."[23]

[20] See also Herder in *Sämmtliche Werke*, ed. B. Suphan, XVI, 84-106, "Ueber ein morgenländisches Drama, einzige Briefe," and XXIV, 576-580, "Vorrede" to the 2nd edn. (1803), in which he said: "Dem reich- und vielverdienten W. Jones war dieser glückliche Fund beschieden; sein Name wird mit der Sakontala blühen, wenn manche seiner andern Bestrebungen vergessen seyn werden." Cf. Goethe's words to de Chézy on October 9, 1830, in *Gedenkausgabe*, XXI, 937.

[21] A list of his daily studies for the long vacation of that year includes Sanskrit grammar. Teignmouth, II, 29.

[22] II, 66.   [23] II, 68.

In February of 1786, he was reducing his correspondence to allow more time for study,[24] and in November he gained time for Sanskrit by rising an hour before the sun and was "charmed with knowing so beautiful a sister of Latin and Greek."[25] A year later, he had advanced sufficiently to make it "an impossibility for the Mohammedan or Hindu lawyers to impose upon us with erroneous opinions."[26] In the autumn of 1790, he wrote to a friend: "I jabber Sanscrit every day with the pundits, and hope, before I leave India, to understand it as well as I do Latin."[27] Yet, his aim was never "mere philology," but the knowledge toward which it was a means,[28] a knowledge he naturally wished to make as widely shared as possible.

To extend and promote the study of the Orient beyond his own private study, Jones instituted the "Asiatick Society," later known as the Asiatic Society of Bengal, which was formed at Calcutta on January 15, 1784.[29] The presidency was first offered to the Governor General, Warren Hastings, as "the first liberal promoter of useful knowledge in Bengal, and especially as the great encourager of Persian and Sanscrit literature,"[30] but he declined and Sir William Jones was instead nominated to the post which he retained until his death. He had planned the society, brought it into being, and was chiefly responsible for the fame it gained within a few years. "When I was at sea last August," Jones explained, calling to mind a famous letter, "on my voyage to this country, which I had long and ardently desired to visit, I found one evening, on inspecting the observations of the day, that *India* lay before us, and *Persia* on our left, whilst a breeze from *Arabia* blew nearly on our stern. . . . It gave me inexpressible pleasure to find myself in the midst of so

[24] II, 78.   [25] II, 107.   [26] II, 120.
[27] II, 206.   [28] II, 265.   [29] II, 14.
[30] *Asiatic Researches*, printed verbatim from the Calcutta Edition, I (London, 1799), vii.

noble an amphitheatre, almost encircled by the vast regions of *Asia*, which has ever been esteemed the nurse of sciences, the inventress of delightful and useful arts, the scene of glorious actions, fertile in the productions of human genius, abounding in natural wonders, and infinitely diversified in the forms of religion and government, in the laws, manners, customs, and languages, as well as in the features and complexions, of men."[31] Only by a united effort would it be possible to undertake all the pressing "inquiries and improvements" relating to India. His model was the Royal Society. Geographically the scope of the society's investigations was to include all of Asia and the neighboring parts of Africa. Intellectually the ultimate aim of the inquiries was "MAN and NATURE," divided according to the three faculties of the mind—memory, reason, and imagination—into history, science, and art. Languages were omitted as an end, for in conformance with the belief he emphatically stated on many occasions, he had always, with Dr. Johnson, "considered languages as the mere instruments of real learning," and thought them "improperly confounded with learning itself," a statement which was undoubtedly— in the spirit of Bacon, Locke, and the Royal Society— designed to strike directly at universal grammar and etymological metaphysics. This belief was the very foundation of what we might call his empirical attitude and procedures in the study of language.[32] The *Asiatic Re-*

[31] III, 1-2 in his "Discourse on the Institution of a Society, for inquiring into the History, civil and natural, the Antiquities, Arts, Sciences, and Literature, of Asia."

[32] III, 7. In the "Preface" to the *Dictionary*, Johnson had said: "I am not yet so lost in lexicography, as to forget that words are the daughters of the earth, and that things are the sons of heaven. Language is only the instrument of science, and words are but the signs of ideas." Jacob Grimm held a similar belief: "Sprachforschung, der ich anhänge und von der ich ausgehe, hat mich doch nie in der weise befriedigen können, dass ich nicht immer gern von den wörtern zu den sachen gelangt wäre."

searches began to appear in print as soon as there was enough of value to make a volume. The first volume was ready early in 1789, though it bore the date 1788, and other volumes soon followed regularly. It is doubtful whether any learned journal has ever achieved such success and exercised so wide an influence on European thought and scholarship, with the possible exception of the *Transactions* of the Royal Society. On the Continent, the demand immediately became so great that reissues and even translations were soon made from the original edition published at Calcutta.[33]

By far the most important items in the *Researches* were Sir William Jones's own "Anniversary Discourses," eleven in all, delivered each year in February, the last within a few months of his death. In these addresses he outlined the progress of his own rapidly accumulating knowledge in all fields—from literature, religion, history, and mythology to Indian chronology, botany, and chess. They are all full of penetrating remarks on methodology, reflecting his keen mind and suspicion of all conclusions arrived at by speculation rather than by careful examination of the evidence and acceptance of the limitations it imposed. Applied to such subject matter, this scientific and critical attitude was a rare quality at the time, though it brings to mind Thomas Reid's and Dugald Stewart's insistence on careful induction.[34] His importance to language study extends far beyond the familiar statement

[33] A pirated edition began to appear in London in 1799, and during the next five or six years two other editions came out in octavo. A translation of the first seven volumes appeared in Paris in 1805 in two volumes as *Recherches Asiatiques* with notes by Langlès, Cuvier, Delambre, and Lamarck. Four volumes of selected articles were published at Riga (1795-1797) as *Abhandlungen über die Geschichte und Alterthümer, Künste, und Literatur Asiens.*

[34] In 1789 he wrote to his biographer: "If you can spare *Reid*, we are now ready for him, and will restore his two volumes on our return from Crishna-nagur" (II, 175).

on the affinities of Sanskrit. To Friedrich Schlegel has gone the credit for introducing the views that created comparative philology, especially for rejecting careless and speculative etymology, for fixing attention on structure and the organic nature of language rather than the atomistic mechanism of words, and for making language study an historical rather than a philosophical discipline. But this credit belongs to Jones, from whom Schlegel borrowed so heavily—on occasion even textually—that his indebtedness is easy to demonstrate; further, in his treatment of language, Jones adhered to evidence. He did not put his philology—which was the word he used[35]— in the service of the sort of philosophy that made Schlegel fully as fantastic as Horne Tooke, though on the opposite side of the question. I shall return to this matter near the end of this chapter. The origin of Jones's method is no doubt to be found in part in the careful and precise Greek and Latin scholarship, which he had learned from Robert Sumner at Harrow; but it has its foundation also in Jones's own systematic and critical bent of mind. He was said to be good enough in mathematics to read and understand Newton's *Principia*;[36] in Linnaeus he found "system, truth, and science, which never failed to captivate and engage his attention";[37] and he attended some of his friend John Hunter's lectures on comparative anatomy.[38]

[35] In 1780, shortly after his return from Paris where he had found time to examine an Arabian manuscript, Jones wrote to Lord Althorp: "How little soever I may value mere *philology*, considered apart from the knowledge to which it leads, yet I shall ever set a high price on those branches of learning, which make us acquainted with the human species in all its varieties" I, 338.

[36] I, 409. His father, who died when Jones was three, was a mathematician, a friend of Halley and Newton, whose small tracts on the higher mathematics he edited "in a mode which obtained the approbation, and increased the esteem, of the author for him" (I, 7).

[37] II, 296.

[38] I, 409 and II, 296: "I have heard him assert, that his admiration of the structure of the human frame, induced him to attend

Jones's most important statements on languages and philological method are contained in the seven discourses he delivered between 1785 and 1792. The first five of these (actually, the third through the seventh of the "Anniversary Discourses") were devoted to the principal nations of Asia, to the Hindus, the Arabs, the Tartars, the Persians, while the last two dealt with the "Borderers, Mountaineers, and Islanders of Asia" and "The Origin and Families of Nations." They all followed a similar plan, announced in "On the Hindus" and most consistently followed in the first four. It was, he explained, the purpose of his enquiries "to extend them upwards, as high as possible, to the earliest authentick records of the human species," in order to find out who the five nations "severally were, *whence* and *when* they came, *where* they now are settled, and *what* advantage a more perfect knowledge of them all may bring to our *European* world." In the fifth "Discourse," "On the Chinese," he would attempt to "demonstrate the connexion or diversity between them, and solve the great problem, whether they had *any* common origin, and whether that origin was *the same*, which we generally ascribe to them."[39] But realizing that the available historical accounts would not be sufficient for the earliest history, he found that "we seem to possess only *four* general media of satisfying our curiosity concerning it; namely, first, their *Languages* and *Letters*; secondly, their *Philosophy* and *Religion*; thirdly, the actual remains of their old *Sculpture* and *Architecture*; and fourthly, the written memorials of their *Sciences* and *Arts*."[40] Following this plan, he closely examined

---

for a season, to a course of anatomical lectures delivered by his friend, the celebrated Hunter." These were the six Croonian lectures given to the Royal Society (1776-1782). In the "Anniversary Discourses," Jones several times refers to Hunter.

[39] III, 27-28.
[40] III, 32.

the evidence of all four media in regard to the Hindus, the Arabs, the Persians, and the Tartars. The scope and precision of the examination made it clear that there was nothing casual about the method. The last three media had long been accepted as legitimate sources of knowledge in Greek and Roman antiquities. The first source, languages, had been mentioned before, but Jones was the first to use it with care when he knew the relevant languages and to abstain from guesswork when he did not. In the opening passage of "On the Tartars," he explained that he entered with extreme diffidence on his subject, "because I have little knowledge of the *Tartarian* dialects; and the gross errours of *European* writers on *Asiatick* literature have long convinced me, that no satisfactory account can be given of any nation, with whose language we are not perfectly acquainted."[41] It was in this manner that languages found a place in his scheme, as a means toward historical knowledge but not themselves the end.

No subject matter and no method of investigation could have excited greater curiosity among the learned in Europe, and no scholar raised higher expectations concerning the outcome of the inquiry. At last the West might hope to find reliable answers to its millennial fascination with the mystery of the East. It might, as Jones had earlier suggested and as Friedrich Schlegel was to hope after him, lead to an Oriental Renaissance.[42] It was

[41] Cf. III, 84: "The only *Tartarian* language, of which I have any knowledge, is the *Turkish* of *Constantinople*."

[42] XII, 308-309 in "Dissertation sur la littérature orientale." Here, addressing the princes of Europe, Jones had said: "Elevez des collèges, des imprimeries; n'épargnez pas les récompenses, les médailles, les lauriers; faites en sorte que les beaux jours des Médicis renaissent en ce siècle; que vos cours soient les sanctuaires des Mirandoles, des Politiens, des Giraldes; ouvrez ainsi les sources cachées de l'érudition, et triomphez de l'Asie en la couronnant." I have heard it said in all seriousness that "Jones was a bit of a communist, you know." Cf. *ibid.*, 304-305.

Jones's great merit not to try to answer mystery with more mystery and speculation. He was fully aware of the dangers of what Dugald Stewart called conjectural history.

It is universally agreed that the decisive turn in language study occurred when the philosophical, a priori method of the eighteenth century was abandoned in favor of the historical, a posteriori method of the nineteenth. The former began with the mental categories and sought their exemplification in language, as in universal grammar, and based etymology on conjectures about the origin of language. The latter sought only facts, evidence, and demonstration; it divorced the study of language from the study of mind. This method was first introduced, clearly explained, and fully argued by Sir William Jones. To him there were two ways of knowing: history and science or philosophy. Science, he said, meant "an assemblage of transcendental propositions discoverable by human reason, and reducible to first principles, axioms, or maxims, from which they may all be derived in a regular succession."[43] To science belonged "metaphysicks and logick," and to metaphysics he referred "the curious and important science of *universal grammar*."[44] History, on the other hand, was exclusively concerned with "the observation and remembrance of *mere facts*, independently of *ratiocination*, which belongs to philosophy, or of *imitations* and *substitutions*, which are the province of art."[45] To history, he said, belonged what the French called the sciences, such as "philology, chymistry,

[43] III, 230, in the eleventh discourse "On the Philosophy of the Asiaticks." Philosophy here pertains to reason and contains all the "abstract sciences."

[44] III, 236. In the Preface to the *Persian Grammar*, he said that he had "even refrained from making any enquiries into general grammar" (V, 175).

[45] III, 207, in the tenth discourse "On Asiatick History, Civil and Natural."

physicks, anatomy, and even metaphysicks, when we barely relate the phenomena of the human mind; for, in all branches of knowledge, we are only historians, when we announce facts, and philosophers, only when we reason on them."[46] Thus to Jones, universal grammar formed no part of the study of language, and etymology must strictly adhere to the given facts and altogether avoid conjecture.

It was on these grounds that Jones criticized Jacob Bryant's *Analysis of Ancient Mythology*, whose title suggested a procedure which Bryant had failed to follow. Synthesis might be the proper mode in pure science, but not in history, "where every postulatum will perhaps be refused, and every definition controverted." It would be much better to discuss theory "in a method purely analytical, and, after beginning with facts of general notoriety or undisputed evidence, to investigate such truths, as are at first unknown or very imperfectly discerned."[47] The fallacy of mixing history with science was especially evident in Bryant's derivation of words, in etymology.

Etymology has, no doubt, some use in historical researches; but it is a medium of proof so very fallacious, that, where it elucidates one fact, it obscures a thousand, and more frequently borders on the ridiculous, than leads to any solid conclusion: it rarely carries with it any *internal* power of conviction from a resemblance of sounds or similarity of letters; yet often, where it is wholly unassisted by those advantages, it may be indisputably proved by *extrinsick* evidence. We know *a posteriori*, that both *fitz* and *hijo*, by the nature of two several dialects, are derived from *filius*; that *uncle* comes from *avus*, and *stranger* from *extra*; that *jour* is reducible, through the *Italian*, from *dies*;

and *rossignol* from *luscinia*, or the *singer in groves*;
. . . which etymologies, though they could not have
been demonstrated *a priori*, might serve to confirm, if
any such confirmation were necessary, the proofs of a
connection between the members of one great Empire;
but, when we derive our *hanger*, or *short pendent
sword*, from the *Persian*, because ignorant travellers
thus misspell the word *khanjar*, which in truth means
a different weapon, or *sandal-wood* from the Greek,
because we suppose, that *sandals* were sometimes
made of it, we gain no ground in proving the affinity
of nations, and only weaken arguments, which might
otherwise be firmly supported.[48]

This passage makes two very significant observations
which had never before been so clearly stated: that
etymological postulates must begin with demonstrable
facts and proceed a posteriori, which is Jones's word for
what we might call "empirical," a word which in his language did not assume its present meaning until around
1840. And secondly, that etymology pursued in this manner may give reliable information about the affinity of
languages and thus of nations.[49] On a later occasion,

[48] III, 25-26.
[49] The ethnological uses of etymology had occasionally been
mentioned, most clearly by Turgot, but without examples and
Jones's careful principles. The only predecessor who comes close to
Jones is Leibniz, especially in the *Nouveaux Essais*, III, ii, 1: "Les
langues en general estant les plus anciens monumens des peuples,
avant l'ecriture et les arts, en marquent le mieux l'origine, cogna-
tions et migrations. C'est pourquoy les Etymologies bien entendues
seroient curieuses et de consequence. . . . En general l'on ne doit
donner quelque creance aux etymologies que lors qu'il y a
quantité d'indices concourans." This was not published until 1765,
but Leibniz had made the same points in his "Brevis designatio
meditationum de originibus gentium, ductis potissimum ex indicio
linguarum," in *Miscellanea Berolinensia*, I (1710), 1-16, which is a
restatement, with some amplification, of the former passage. The
"Brevis designatio" had some influence, chiefly in Germany, before
1765, but without ever leading to statements as clear as Jones's.

Jones demonstrated the absurdities that were the inevitable result of the current etymological mode:

> I beg leave, as a philologer, to enter my protest against conjectural etymology in historical researches, · and principally against the licentiousness of etymologists in transposing and inserting letters, in substituting at pleasure any consonant for another of the same order, and in totally disregarding the vowels: for such permutations few radical words would be more convenient than *cus* or *cush*, since, dentals being exchanged for dentals, and palatials for palatials, it instantly becomes *coot*, *goose*, and, by transposition, *duck*, all waterbirds, and *evidently* symbolical; it next is the *goat* worshipped in *Egypt*, and, by a metathesis, the *dog* adored as an emblem of *Sirius*, or, more obviously, a *cat*, not the domestick animal, but a sort of ship, and, the *Catos*, or great sea-fish, of the *Dorians*.[50]

Jones added an apology that he did not wish to give the effect of ridicule; but the apology was unnecessary, for his example was not an extravagant specimen of eighteenth-century etymology. It was the context that damned it.

But the arbitrary transposition of letters was not the only factor that made it possible to demonstrate almost any kinship among languages and nations. An equally

---

To Jones, Leibniz' exposition would have been vitiated by the nonphilological doctrine "qu'il y a quelque chose de naturel dans l'origine des mots" and by the examples Leibniz adduced in favor of that doctrine. But there is no evidence whatever that Leibniz' writings on language exercised any influence on or were even known to Jones, who mentioned Leibniz only once and very generally; in the abstract sciences we have the valuable volumes "de Newton, de Leibnitz, de Wallis, de Halley, de Bernouilli, et de plusieurs autres" XII, 279, in "Dissertation sur la littérature orientale."

[50] III, 199-200 in the ninth discourse "On the Origin and Families of Nations."

productive source of error was the failure to recognize loan-words; on this basis, Tooke had argued that Latin and Greek were derived from the northern languages. Jones, however, was fully aware that no kinship can be established by etymology until loan-words have been recognized and put aside and further, that the basic words of any language are the most stable and therefore offer the most reliable evidence. If it was true that Hindu merchants had heard Sanskrit spoken in Saudi Arabia, "we might be confirmed in our opinion, that an intercourse formerly subsisted between the two nations of opposite coasts, but should have no reason to believe, that they sprang from the same immediate stock."[51] Similarly, since Persian shows "no trace of any *Arabian* tongue, except what proceeded from the known intercourse between the *Persians* and *Arabs*," it follows that one is not derived from the other.[52] The possibility that political or commercial intercourse may account for the similarity of words in different nations can only be ruled out when those words are "in the first place, too numerous to have been introduced by such means, and, secondly, are not the names of exotick animals, commodities, or arts, but those of material elements, parts of the body, natural objects and relations, affections of the mind, and other ideas common to the whole race of man."[53]

[51] III, 56, in "On the Arabs."
[52] III, 114, in "On the Persians."
[53] III, 119-120. Jones's friend at Oxford, N. B. Halhed, whom Jones had encouraged to study Arabic, had in his *Bengal Grammar* (1778) made a similar observation: "I have been astonished to find the similitude of Sanskrit words with those of Persian and Arabic, and even Latin and Greek, and these not in technical and metaphorical terms, which the mutation of refined arts and improved manners might have occasionally introduced; but in the main ground-work of language, in monosyllables, in the names of numbers, and the appellations of such things as would be first discriminated on the immediate dawn of civilization."

Still, Jones would not have postulated kinship even on these grounds. Grammatical structure was the final factor which by its concurrence raised high probability to certainty: "That the written *Abyssinian* language, which we call *Ethiopick*, is a dialect of old *Chaldean*, and a sister of *Arabick* and *Hebrew*, we know with certainty, not only from the great multitude of identical words, but (which is a far stronger proof) from the similar grammatical arrangement of the several idioms."[54] Similarly, since he could assure his audience "that very many *Persian* imperatives are the roots of *Sanscrit* verbs; and that even the moods and tenses of the *Persian* verb substantive, which is the model of all the rest, are deducible from the *Sanscrit* by an easy and clear analogy: we may hence conclude, that the *Parsi* was derived, like the various *Indian* dialects, from the language of the *Brahmans*."[55] This criterion was especially useful in demonstrating lack of kinship; Arabic, for instance, did not bear "the least resemblance, either in words or the structure of them, to the *Sanscrit*," because "*Sanscrit*, like the *Greek*, *Persian*, and *German*, delights in compounds . . . while the *Arabick*, on the other hand, and all its sister dialects, abhor the composition of words, . . . so that, if a compound word be found in any genuine language of the *Arabian* Peninsula . . . it may at once be pronounced an exotick."[56] There is no need to look to later writers for this principle that became the cornerstone of the new comparative philology, for it could hardly have been more emphatically stated than in Jones's own words.

The famous statement about the affinities of Sanskrit must be understood in the light of these principles. It must be read as it was read by Jones's contemporaries and followers, in the total context of the "Anniversary

[54] III, 166, in "On the Borderers, Mountaineers, and Islanders of Asia."
[55] III, 114.   [56] III, 53.

Discourses," not in isolated quotation as has now universally been the case for more than a hundred years. Paradoxically, its clarity and succinctness have had the unfortunate consequence of making it so eminently quotable that the context which alone makes it significant has been altogether forgotten. The statement occurred in the discourse "On the Hindus," delivered on February 2, 1786, in the same year Horne Tooke published the first volume of the *Diversions*. Jones said:

> The *Sanscrit* language, whatever be its antiquity, is of a wonderful structure; more perfect than the *Greek*, more copious than the *Latin*, and more exquisitely refined than either, yet bearing to both of them a stronger affinity, both in the roots of verbs and in the forms of grammar, than could possibly have been produced by accident; so strong indeed, that no philologer could examine them all three, without believing them to have sprung from some common source, which, perhaps, no longer exists: there is a similar reason, though not quite so forcible, for supposing that both the *Gothick* and the *Celtick*, though blended with a very different idiom, had the same origin with the *Sanscrit*; and the old *Persian* might be added to the same family, if this were the place for discussing any question concerning the antiquities of *Persia*.[57]

These words were spoken less than six months after Jones had begun the study of Sanskrit in which he did not, of course, have the help of the grammars and chrestomathies we take for granted. It may be suggested that the observation has a freshness and immediacy about it, which is likely to come from a mind which in learning the grammar and vocabulary of a new language has created its own mnemonic devices with reference to the languages

[57] III, 34-35.

it has already mastered, in this case especially Latin, Greek, and Persian. By making it strictly historical, comparative, and structural, Jones caused a revolution in the study of language. His famous statement should be read only as a reminder but not as an adequate summary of the contents of the discourses.

It has been said that Jones "did little by way of systematization beyond the pronouncement of a tentative genetic hypothesis, which in any case was given no prominence in immediately subsequent work." This is not true, for the work that has generally been considered the initiator of comparative philology, F. Schlegel's *Ueber die Sprache und Weisheit der Indier*, opened with a paragraph that was a complete restatement, in fact almost a translation, of Jones's words. And no one who has read the "Anniversary Discourses" can fairly say that Jones did not systematize and that he gave no more than a "tentative genetic hypothesis." Nor is it true to say, as the same source does, that "as it stood, Jones' observation was impressionistic only; and it is the essence of the comparative discipline that it seeks to replace the intuitive recognition of similarities by a systematic analysis of their nature."[58] The observation may have been impressionistic and intuitive when first made in the third discourse, but it was a brilliant insight that was borne out by the systematic analysis presented in the ensuing eight discourses. It has been said elsewhere that Jones's statement brought "no demonstration whatever,"[59] to which one can only reply that neither did Newton's statement of the law of gravity, but the *Principia* did; and so did the discourses in relation to Jones's hypothesis. No one could reasonably

[58] W. S. Allen, "Relationship in Comparative Linguistics" in *Transactions of the Philological Society 1953*, pp. 56-57.

[59] Giuliano Bonfante, "Ideas of the Kinship of the European Languages from 1200 to 1800" in *Cahiers d'histoire mondiale*, I (1954), 696-697.

ask for more unless he expected to see the results of the first fifty years of comparative philology put into a single paragraph. Jones did in fact give a good number of examples, but he realized that oral delivery did not permit full citation of all the forms that would be necessary for conclusive proof. Here he could only appeal to the good sense and trust of his listeners:

> I am sensible, that you must give me credit for many assertions, which on this occasion it is impossible to prove; for I should ill deserve your indulgent attention, if I were to abuse it by repeating a dry list of detached words, and presenting you with a vocabulary instead of a dissertation; but, since I have no system to maintain, and have not suffered imagination to delude my judgement; since I have habituated myself to form opinions of men and things from *evidence*, which is the only solid basis of *civil*, as *experiment* is of *natural*, knowledge; and since I have maturely considered the questions which I mean to discuss; you will not, I am persuaded, suspect my testimony, or think that I go too far, when I assure you, that I will assert nothing positively, which I am not able satisfactorily to demonstrate.[60]

It is therefore hardly fair to suggest that Jones had little more to offer than a tentative hypothesis, especially when such suggestions are offered in contexts that give not the slightest hint that the writers have read beyond the conventionally quoted statement.

Jones can undoubtedly be criticized for a number of mistaken views, but it is worth noting that the most obvious of these occurred when he was not familiar with the

---

[60] III, 111-112. In *Ueber die Sprache*, Schlegel borrowed a phrase from this passage: "Wollten wir auf die Untersuchung der Wurzeln eingehen . . . so würden wir statt einer Abhandlung ein vergleichendes Wörterbuch entwerfen." *Sämmtliche Werke*, zweite Original-Ausgabe (Wien, 1846), VIII, 289.

relevant languages and had to depend on quite unreliable information about arts, manners, and religion. These cases, therefore, cannot be said to invalidate or weaken the principles he advocated in the study of languages. He also seems to have changed his mind on some points as his knowledge grew from year to year. In 1790 he had argued, in "On the Chinese," that both the Chinese and the Japanese ultimately belonged to the same family as the Hindus, though without using any evidence from language. Two years later, however, he was more cautious, stating that this opinion was "no more than highly probable."[61] Unlike F. Schlegel, he never said that all the languages related to Sanskrit were also derived from it, but he did believe that the three original stems—from the Hindus, the Tartars, and the Arabs—might be traced to Iran, "as to a common centre, from which it is highly probable, that they diverged in various directions about four thousand years ago."[62] This belief, however, found no demonstration in language, being prompted entirely by a desire to satisfy the scriptural account of the single origin of mankind, which he found supported by a consideration of "the rapid increase of numbers in geometrical progression." And if his adherence to traditional, scriptural chronology caused some errors and distortions, then he must share the blame with a number of people, including Cuvier, who as late as 1826 cited Jones on this point.[63] Finally, Jones never related Sanskrit to the question of the origin of language.

In his opening address and on frequent other occasions, Sir William Jones had expressed the hope that his countrymen would find time from their professional duties to apply

[61] III, 186.   [62] III, 161.

[63] *Recherches sur les ossemens fossiles*, I (Paris, 1821), lxxvi-lxxvii ("Discours préliminaire"). Also separately as *Discours sur les révolutions de la surface du globe* (Paris, 1826), pp. 88-89, in a section entitled "L'antiquité excessive attribuée à certains peuples n'a rien d'historique."

themselves to the exploration of all aspects of oriental knowledge so that the Asiatic Society might become a veritable Royal Society. His expectation was well founded, for many of his fellows and followers also became distinguished scholars, of whom the most important were Charles Wilkins, Henry Thomas Colebrooke, the Baptist missionary William Carey, G. C. Haughton, and H. H. Wilson, who in 1819 published a *Dictionary, Sanskrit and English*, which remained the standard reference work for scholars until late in the century. Wilson was the first to occupy the Boden chair of Sanskrit studies in Oxford, and with his encouragement, Bopp's *Comparative Grammar* first appeared in English in 1845. Wilkins had preceded Jones's *Sakontala* by a few years, with translations of the *Bhagavadgita* and the *Hitopadeca*; later, after his return to London, he published the first major *Grammar of the Sanskrita Language* in 1808. Colebrooke was active in many subjects, but he gained fame and influence chiefly from his "Essay on the Vedas" of 1805, which twenty years later appeared with several of his other essays on related subjects as *On the Philosophy of the Hindus*. Through the French translation in 1833, it exercised an enormous influence on the European image of Indian philosophy.[64] No less important to scholarship was the large collection of manuscripts which he gave to the East India Company's office in London in 1819, where they were studied by the first generation of great Continental scholars. Carey translated the Bible into several Indian dialects and also wrote a number of grammars of these same dialects. All his works were issued at the Mission Press at Serampore, a Danish colony previously called Frederiksnagor. With the encouragement of the Danish governor, Serampore became the center of missionary

[64] See Raymond Schwab, *La renaissance orientale* (Paris, 1950), pp. 103-107. This book offers a spirited and well-informed treatment of its subject.

work and publication, since the East India Company for political reasons did not wish to encourage missions.

For none of these men was their scholarship their profession, but several taught both at the Company's college of Fort William and, upon their return, at the college it established at Haileybury in 1805 for the training of its civil servants. One of these was a young man who had come to India as a naval officer, Alexander Hamilton. He was a member of the Asiatic Society from the beginning, later pursued Sanskrit studies in London and Paris, which, after the peace of Amiens, became the learned center of Oriental studies on the Continent, chiefly owing to the large store of manuscripts which Jesuit missionaries had brought back during the eighteenth century. When the war again broke out in May of 1803, he was retained as a hostage but released a few years later because of the services he had rendered by drawing up a catalogue of the Oriental manuscripts in the Bibliothèque Royale.[65] Since he was the only person on the Continent with a knowledge of Sanskrit, he was in great demand as a teacher. He not only taught Schlegel, but also de Chézy, the first professor of Persian and later of Sanskrit at the Collège de France, as well as Claude Fauriel and Langlès.[66] On his return to England, Hamilton became fellow of the Royal Society in 1808 and professor at Haileybury College. During the years when the original Calcutta publications were very scarce, at times even

[65] *Catalogue des manuscrits samskrits de la Bibliothèque Impériale*. It contained Hamilton's brief summaries of the contents of most of the manuscripts and was translated into French by Langlès. De Chézy wrote a notice of it, with a romantic eulogy on Sanskrit language and literature, in the *Moniteur universel* for May 31 and June 25, 1808 (XXXVI, 596-597, 694-696).

[66] S. Lefmann, *Franz Bopp, sein Leben und seine Wissenschaft* (Berlin, 1891), p. 18. This is one of the most important sources of knowledge about the early history of Sanskrit studies, not least owing to the 400 pages of letters communicated in the *Anhang* and the *Nachtrag*.

unobtainable, on the Continent, Hamilton may have exercised a greater influence than is readily apparent. Without the work of these men, Continental—and especially German—scholars would never have been able to satisfy their lust for knowledge of India.

Yet, in England the knowledge of Indian languages and literature failed to have any appreciable impact. Outside its practical utility to the conduct of business in the East, it remained largely the affair of a few scholars; and to judge by the results alone, there was no tendency to enter upon a comparative study of languages as a separate branch of learning. In a negative way, this aspect of the history of the study of language owes a great deal to the Utilitarians, who with Bentham still believed that "of the nature of language no clear, correct, and instructive account can be given but with reference to thought," and who shared his low opinion of Oriental writers.[67] Macaulay believed that all Oriental literature would not in value equal one shelf of English classics. Nor were the English likely to be impressed by the wisdom of India, for the common chorus spoke of the treachery and deviousness of the Hindus and the effeminacy, languid habits, and deceit of the Bengalee—Macaulay again could be quite eloquent on the subject: "What the horns are to the buffalo, what the paw is to the tiger, what the sting is to the bee, what beauty, according to the old Greek song, is to woman, deceit is to the Bengalee."[68] This reputed deceitfulness was one of the chief props to Dugald Stewart's attempt to argue that Sanskrit—"this so much vaunted language"—was a sort of kitchen-Greek concocted by the Brahmans as a secret language of religion after Alexander's conquests had brought India into contact with the Greeks. But Stewart may also, not un-

[67] *Works*, ed. Bowring, VIII, 186, 331.
[68] Essay on "Warren Hastings."

reasonably, have been afraid that Sanskrit would be used to support the philosophy of language and mind he opposed.[69]

This attitude was not likely to be passed over, for it was ardently embraced by James Mill, who presented it forcefully and at great length in his *History of British India*, most strongly in Book Two "Of the Hindus."[70] His description of their form of government, their laws, religion, manners, art, and literature forms a long list of Utilitarian nightmares—a despotically ruled, priest-ridden, superstitious, deceitful, barbarous, rude, ignorant, and unrefined people. Their cultural level did not bear comparison to that of our own rude Northern forefathers, for the Hindus were ignorant "that air is the great agent in the conveyance of sound," as well as of all other facts relating to the science of matter and the phenomena of mind. *Sakontala* contained nothing that was "above the powers of the imagination in an uncultivated age."[71] It was largely to correct Mill's distortions that H. H. Wilson undertook a new edition. In the Preface he remarked of the *History*, that "in the effects which it is likely to exercise upon the connexion between the people of England and the people of India, it is chargeable with

[69] See StH, IV, 78-115 (*Elements*, III [1827]). His point of departure was Gibbon's suggestion that "some, *perhaps much*, of the Indian science was derived from the Greeks of Bactriana." His authority for the deceit practised by the Brahmans was F. Wilford's "Essay on the Sacred Isles of the West," whose thesis was that the British Isles were the Sacred Isles of the Hindus (*Asiatic Researches*, octavo edition [London, 1808], VIII, 245-375). But the tradition was much older, having been given wide currency in an article on "Samskret" first inserted in the *Encyclopédie méthodique* (1786), which for authority cited Alexander Dow in the translation of *Dissertation sur la religion des brahmines* (1769).

[70] *History of British India*, ed. H. H. Wilson, 5th edn. (London, 1858), I, 107-342, and II, 1-164. Mill began the *History* in 1806 and completed it in 1818.

[71] II, 66 and 39.

more than literary demerit: its tendency is evil; it is calculated to destroy all sympathy between the rulers and the ruled . . . to substitute for those generous and benevolent feelings, which the situation of the younger servants of the Company in India naturally suggests, sentiments of disdain, suspicion, and dislike. . . . There is reason to fear that these consequences are not imaginary, and that a harsh and illiberal spirit has of late years prevailed in the conduct and councils of the rising service in India, which owes its origin to impressions imbibed in early life from the History of Mr. Mill." He had good reason to fear. In 1828 the demolition of the Taj Mahal was seriously proposed in order to profit from the sale of its marble, a plan that was abandoned only because "the test auction of materials from the Agra palace proved unsatisfactory."[72]

To the study of Indian languages, Mill's *History* was perhaps especially harmful, partly because Sanskrit did not escape his fulminations—"that which is a defect and deformity in language is . . . celebrated as a perfection."[73] Furthermore, Mill in his Preface felt obliged to argue that far from being disabilities, both his ignorance of the language and his never having been to India made it possible for him to write an impartial and true history of the country; for was it not true that the "mental habits which are acquired in mere observing, and in the acquisition of languages, are almost as different as any mental habits can be, from the powers of combination, discrimination, classification, judgment, comparison, weighing, inferring, inducting, philosophizing in short: which are the powers of most importance for extracting the precious ore from a great mine of rude historical materials?" And

[72] See Duncan Forbes, "James Mill and India" in the *Cambridge Journal*, V (October, 1961), 22. This article gives a good analysis of the motives for Mill's harsh treatment of the Hindus.
[73] II, 63.

did it not follow that "a man who is duly qualified may obtain more knowledge of India in one year in his closet in England, than he could obtain during the course of the longest life, by the use of his eyes and ears in India?"[74] Nothing could be more directly opposed to Jones's "unremitted application, during the vacations, to a vast and interesting study, *a complete knowledge of India*, which I can only attain in the country itself."[75] Mill's defense sounds like a prospectus for the *Analysis of the Phenomena of the Human Mind*, which indeed was begun as soon as the *History* was finished. His arguments clearly cast suspicion on Jones and his successors. He missed no opportunity to ridicule Jones, whose translations he occasionally corrected because he found it reasonable to suppose "from other instances, that [Jones] endeavoured to cloak a most absurd idea under an equivocal translation."[76] His final judgment was that "Sir William, when he had a theory, seems to have had eyes to see nothing but what made in its favour,"[77] and Jones was not the only Indian scholar who was subjected to Mill's "weighing, inferring, inducting, philosophizing in short." Held by a man of no consequence, these opinions would merely have been curious, but in his double capacity as high administrative officer in the East India Company—a post he gained by the *History*—and Utilitarian philosopher, Mill occupied a unique position of influence, both practical and intellectual. With regard to language, as we have seen, he held beliefs which were as little designed as any to accept and further the new study of languages, which was just becoming known, though not practiced, in England—"a science so new as to be yet

[74] I, xxiii.
[75] Teignmouth, II, 184 (Jones to John Wilmot, September 20, 1789).
[76] II, 66.
[77] II, 130.

without a name."[78] For a sympathetic, even enthusiastic, absorption of the new knowledge and the developments it occasioned, we must turn to the Continent, and especially to Germany.

The philosophical study of language that was characteristic of the eighteenth century never gained a strong hold in Germany. After 1760 it became known through a number of translations, from French and especially from English, or adaptations such as Meiner's influential *Sprachlehre* (1781), which was heavily indebted to Harris' *Hermes*. But the most important and original works did not follow this tradition. When Court de Gébelin, for instance, late in 1768 asked Johann David Michaelis at Göttingen for information about "tout ce, que les Savans de la Germanie ont publié, pour éclaircir l'origine des langues et de l'écriture, et sur la comparaison des langues, à commencer par le célèbre *Leibnitz*," he was told that this question had received little attention in Germany.[79] Largely owing to the influence of its French members, but due also in part to the memory of Leibniz, the Berlin Academy began to debate questions of language during the 1750's. This debate resulted in a prize-essay topic, occasioned by a specific philosophical problem and set for 1759: "Quelle est l'influence réciproque des opinions du peuple sur le langage et du langage sur les opinions?" Michaelis won the prize for an answer in German, published in Berlin in 1760 and soon translated into French, English, and Dutch.[80] This essay had raised another ques-

[78] Sir James Mackintosh in a review of "Stewart's Introduction to the Encyclopaedia" in the *Edinburgh Review*, XXXVI (October, 1821), 264, distinguishing between the "philosophy of language" and the new "philosophy of languages."

[79] *Literarischer Briefwechsel von Johann David Michaelis*, ed. J. G. Buhle, II (Leipzig, 1795), 492, 496.

[80] The title of the Berlin edition was *Beantwortung der Frage von dem Einfluss der Meinungen in die Sprache und der Sprache in die Meinungen*. The answer greatly impressed d'Alembert, who in 1763 recommended Michaelis to the king for a high position

tion which was set as the prize topic for 1771: "En supposant les hommes abandonnés à leurs facultés naturelles, sont-ils en état d'inventer le langage? Et par quels moyens parviendront-ils d'eux-mêmes à cette invention? On demanderoit une hypothèse qui expliquât le chose clairement, et qui satisfît à toutes les difficultés." This topic received no less than thirty-one answers, of which six gained *accessit*, but the prize was won by Herder, who like his predecessor gave his answer in German. Both answers were unorthodox in their context and helped focus attention on forms of study other than those that pertained exclusively to the philosophical questions of universal grammar and the origin of language. Both were familiar with the literature on the subject, but placed their emphasis on the opinion expressed by Condillac: "Tout confirme donc que chaque langue exprime le caractère du peuple qui la parle."[81] It is an historical commonplace that one of the chief marks of romanticism is its interest in the expression of the spirit of the folk in languages, dialects, and early poetry, an interest that was in large measure sustained by the same motives that had guided the eighteenth century to its interest in universal grammar and the origin of language.

---

in Prussia. The French edition appeared in 1762, the English in 1769 and 1771, the Dutch in 1771. I am using the London edition of 1769: *A Dissertation on the Influence of Opinions on Language and of Language on Opinions*, which was based on the French edition. In the early 1740's, Michaelis had lived in London and visited Oxford, where he attended the second of Lowth's lectures *De Sacra Poesi Hebraeorum*, all of which he later published in Germany with extensive notes. For his English contacts, see the Buhle edition of the correspondence and Hans Hecht, *T. Percy, R. Wood und J. D. Michaelis, ein Beitrag zur Literaturgeschichte der Genieperiode* (Stuttgart, 1933). The prize topics and the winners for the years 1745-1785 are listed in Adolf Harnack, *Geschichte der Königlich Preussischen Akademie der Wissenschaften zu Berlin* (Berlin, 1900), II, 305-309.

[81] *Oeuvres*, I, 98b (*Essai*, II, i, xv, par. 143).

Michaelis' treatise is remarkable in a number of ways; it contains, for instance, the best and fullest argument against a universal learned language to be found anywhere. But its chief interest lies in its respect for the vernacular, in its hard common sense, adherence to fact and observation, clear understanding of etymology and its limitations, and in its disinclination to engage in philosophical system-building and wide generalizations. To Michaelis, "language is a democracy where use or custom is decided by the majority," and it is "from the opinions of the people and the point of view, in which objects appear to them, that language received its form." The right to add to it belongs only "to classic authors, the fair sex, and the people, who are indeed the supreme legislators,"[82] and to children because they are free of prejudice and full of bold associations of ideas. The occasions for the making of new expressions are especially "cheerfulness, which utters truths unknowingly, sprightly company, wine which expands the genius, poetry which, in its enthusiasm, brings forth so many novelties, medlies of truth and fiction." The learned on the other hand, have only a negligible share in language because they often have "but a narrow genius," are "blinded by pre-possession," and "after all scarce make the hundredth part of mankind."[83] These observations are so plain and straightforward that no one would question their truth. Yet this is perhaps the first time that language is seen entirely as a product of usage by generation after generation of speakers, illiterate as well as literate. Previously, the nature of language had not been conceived in this fashion since the object of inquiry was most frequently some aspect of the language of the learned, with emphasis on Greek and Latin terms, whose etymologies were transparent and in any case likely to be known. The dead lan-

[82] Michaelis, pp. 2-3.
[83] Michaelis, pp. 12-13.

guages being a branch of literature, we were "apt to think their etymologies more significant, and their nomenclature more proper; in short, to give them the preference above living languages, which perhaps is more than they can absolutely claim."[84]

More important, however, than the democratic conception of language is Michaelis' use of that notion, for he sees that the authority and limitations of etymology are determined by it. Languages being an immense heap of the truths and errors of the people,[85] it follows that "etymology is the voice of the people."[86] In a metaphor he uses several times, he compares language to a kind of archive or library, "where the discoveries of men are safe from any accidents, archives which are proof against fire, and which cannot be destroyed, but with the total ruin of the people."[87] Language is an historical record, but—like a library—it carries no guarantee that its contents conform to philosophical truth. Wrongly understood, etymology may therefore lead to great error: "It is incredible what a proneness there is in us to account whatever propositions we imagine to have discovered in etymology infallible truths, as if people, for it is they who make languages, could never be mistaken." Grammarians no less than other people commit this error, for they are all "ready to take for a proof a word of which they do not so much as know the inventor, and often will beat their brains to forge a specious proof, purely for upholding the authority of the word."[88] From another direction, Michaelis was approaching the same view of language that

---

[84] Michaelis, p. 18. Michaelis deplored the use of Latin in botany because it loaded the mind with a "crabbed nomenclature." If the terms had been an integral part of the vernacular, botanical knowledge would have been much more widely disseminated, whereas now, without words, people wandered blind through the fields (p. 23).

[85] Michaelis, p. 3.   [86] Michaelis, p. 73.
[87] Michaelis, p. 13.   [88] Michaelis, p. 59.

Reid adopted to support his common-sense philosophy. More strongly than Condillac, Reid had implied that the vernacular expresses the national character of its speakers and deserves study for that reason rather than for any philosophical truth it may contain or be made to yield. Neither universal grammar nor the search for the origin of language can be accommodated to this conception of language. The man who above all was responsible for spreading this view in Germany was Herder, who owed a very large debt to Michaelis.

In his treatise Michaelis deliberately avoided the question of the origin of language,[89] but toward the end he had suggested that the Academy might some day set this topic for a prize-essay: "How can language be introduced among men, who as yet have no language, and by what means may it attain among them to the perfection in which we see it?"[90] His own opinion seems clear, for the suggestion immediately followed his wish that a particular science may be devoted to languages, and he clearly saw that this would never come about until the contemporary fashion in dealing with the origin of language had been abandoned; after all, he himself had very close and scholarly firsthand knowledge of a number of remote languages.

Herder's answer to Michaelis' question was written after decades of speculation on the origin of language had failed to produce any generally accepted answers or even agreement on the method to be followed or the basic principles to be admitted initially. On the contrary, the answers had steadily become more and more irreconcilable, with the orthodox view of divine origin on the one side and a variety of naturalist and rationalist theories on the other. Herder seems to have been aware that the Academy expected an answer that avoided the extremes.

[89] Michaelis, p. 35.
[90] Michaelis, p. 76.

He wrote his essay very hastily at Strassburg, during the last month before it was due on January 1, 1771, in a manner full of irony and enthusiasm both in style and argument.

There is no need here to retrace the entire argument of Herder's essay, of which Edward Sapir has given a masterly exposition;[91] but we must single out those qualities which determined its influence. Even before the topic was set in 1769, Herder had come to believe that "der Genius der Sprache ist . . . auch der Genius von der Litteratur einer Nation,"[92] but in the essay, he was to make more comprehensive assumptions concerning the nature and role of language. First of all, the phrasing of the prize-topic implied that language might be of natural origin, a product of man's natural faculties; and secondly, that its creation could be a matter of invention, a notion which implied that language is a tool—of reason and thought—that could be created on purpose just as a machine is made to perform a certain job. The most radical aspect of the essay bears on those two assumptions, for Herder showed that the whole question was meaningless, and he consequently provided neither an answer nor an alternative hypothesis, an act of disobedience which he frankly admitted in the final paragraph.[93]

Thus the chief subject of the essay was not the origin of language but the nature of language and the manner in which it may have developed, an essay in fact on the evolution of language and the factors that have determined that evolution. To Herder, language was so intimately

[91] "Herder's 'Ursprung der Sprache'" in *Modern Philology*, V (July, 1907), 109-142.

[92] "Ueber die neuere Deutsche Literatur" (1766-1767) in *Werke*, ed. Suphan, I (Berlin, 1877), 148.

[93] *Werke*, ed. Suphan, V (Berlin, 1891), 147. Herder's *Abhandlung über den Ursprung der Sprache* will be found in this volume, pp. 1-147. Herder's essay came out in English translation as *Treatise upon the Origin of Language* (London, 1827).

bound up with the nature of man that the two were altogether inseparable. Language was an imminent quality,
whose existence was dependent neither on oral expression
nor on society. Language even lay in the soul of the mute
who had never been able to speak, just as "der Wilde,
der Einsame im Walde hätte Sprache für sich selbst
erfinden müssen; hätte er sie auch nie geredet. Sie war
Einverständniss seiner Seele mit sich, und ein so noth-
wendiges Einverständniss, als der Mensch Mensch war.
Wenns andern unbegreiflich war, wie eine Menschliche
Seele hat Sprache erfinden können; so ists mir unbegreiflich, wie eine Menschliche Seele, was sie ist, seyn konnte,
ohne eben dadurch, schon ohne Mund und Gesellschaft,
sich Sprache erfinden zu müssen"[94]—that is Herder's
explanation of the invention of language, "Erfindung der
Sprache ist ihm also so natürlich, als er ein Mensch
ist."[95] Elsewhere Herder used the metaphor of organism,
which was soon to become one of the chief factors in
determining the influence exercised by his view of the
nature of language: "Die Genesis der Sprache [ist] ein so
inneres Dringniss, wie der Drang des Embryons zur
Geburt bei dem Moment seiner Reise. Die ganze Natur
stürmt auf den Menschen, um seine Kräfte, um seine Sinne
zu entwickeln, bis er Mensch sei. Und wie von diesem
Zustande die Sprache anfängt, so ist die ganze Kette von
Zuständen in der Menschlichen Seele von der Art, dass
jeder die Sprache fortbildet."[96]

The outward development of language is conditioned
by man's unique capacity for *Besonnenheit* or *Reflexion,*
a word deliberately chosen to escape from the confusion
which the word *Vernunft* would have caused. *Besonnenheit,* however, embraces reason, which sets man apart
from the animals—it was the German word for one of
Plato's four cardinal virtues and is perhaps in English
best rendered by a literal understanding of "thoughtful-

[94] *Werke,* V, 38.   [95] *Werke,* V, 34.   [96] *Werke,* V, 96.

ness." Herder does not think of it in logical terms, but rather as the capacity for thinking which is linked to or conditioned by a certain organization of the body. The animal only has instinct; but man, thanks to reason, has freedom.[97] *Besonnenheit* enabled man not only to become clearly aware of the many appearances and qualities of things, but also to single out those which could be used as distinguishing characteristics. Here Herder believed that the sense of hearing had priority; a sheep, for instance, among all its characteristics became known first as a bleating animal—a doctrine which had for long been especially popular in Germany. It followed that the first words were verbs, viz. the "innerlichen Merkwörter" or "tönenden Interjektionen," which took their cue from the sound, whether of animals, wind, water, or anything whatever.[98] The ear became the first teacher of language as nature met man halfway and supplied through the sense of hearing the sounds that became the models of expression for the inner language, which was already in *his* nature, by a sort of harmony existing between the two—Leibniz had seen the question in a similar fashion. Thus the outward language corresponds to speech. Herder assigned this important role to sound and hearing for a number of reasons, but especially because "das Gefühl liegt dem Gehör so nahe: seine Bezeichnungen z. E. hart, rauh, weich, wolligt, sammet, haarigt,

[97] *Werke*, V, 28-32. *Reflexion* was, of course, also Condillac's term.

[98] *Werke*, V, 35-37; cf. also p. 52: "Tönende *Verba* sind die Ersten Machtelemente. Tönende Verba? Handlungen, und noch nichts, was da handelt? Prädikate und noch kein Subject?" And further: "Das erste Wörterbuch war also aus den Lauten aller Welt gesammelt. Von jedem tönenden Wesen Klang sein Name: die Menschliche Seele prägte ihr Bild drauf, dachte sie als Merkzeichen—wie anders, als dass diese tönenden Interjektionen die ersten wurden, und so sind z. E. die Morgenländischen Sprachen voll *Verba* als Grundwurzeln der Sprache." The contrast to Tooke is noteworthy.

starr, glatt, schlicht, borstig u. s. w. die doch alle nur Oberflächen betreffen, und nicht einmal tief einwürken, tönen alle, als ob mans fühlte," and he added "das Wort: Duft, Ton, süss, bitter, sauer u. s. w. tönen alle, als ob man fühlte: denn was sind ursprünglich alle Sinne anders, als Gefühl."[99] The first language was a natural language, a collection of imitated sound-pictures, a fact that gave truth to the old observation that poetry is older than prose, "denn was war diese erste Sprache als eine Sammlung von Elementen der Poesie? . . . Ein Wörterbuch der Seele, was zugleich Mythologie und eine wunderbare Epopee von den Handlungen und Reden aller Wesen ist! Also eine beständige Fabeldichtung mit Leidenschaft und Interesse!—Was ist Poesie anders?"[100] Much like Condillac and some English writers, he further maintained that this first "tönende Sprache" was song, so that early language, poetry, music, and song are intimately connected—an idea that exercised a wide influence, since it was to become one of the chief motives for the study of early literature and language. In 1778 Herder himself published the first part of the collection that was later given the title *Stimmen der Völker in Liedern*, which was a truly international compilation of folk songs. Its popularity made it a forerunner of Grimm's collection of fairy tales, just as it indirectly had a share in determining the emphasis of modern philology. In this fashion, speech began, with metaphors—as in Locke and Condillac—supplying words for what was not open to the senses as language evolved from its original, purely emotional, and spontaneous nature. Language and culture went hand in hand, for "was ist also die ganze Bauart der Sprache anders, als eine Entwickelungsweise seines Geistes, eine Geschichte seiner Entdeckungen!"[101] or "eine Schatzkammer Menschlicher Gedanken, wo

[99] *Werke*, V, 63. [100] *Werke*, V, 56-57.
[101] *Werke*, V, 52.

jeder auf seine Art etwas beitrug! eine Summe der Würksamkeit aller Menschlichen Seelen."[102] Man in nature had cooperated with nature in man to create language, which in its continuous development left traces of the history of early man and the folk.

There is finally one aspect of Herder's conception of language which requires emphasis, though it has been implied above. That the history of a race or nation follows the same course as a human being from birth to old age was not a new idea; but it was new that language itself and its development not only could be conceived in terms of that metaphor, but actually in a real sense had a life of its own as if it were an organism. This shift in point of view had the important consequence that language not only could, but ought to be studied as an entity that had independent existence without reference to thought and logical categories. It could be studied as any other natural being; and since language also showed development, it should be studied historically. This tendency in Herder's thought is, apart from the often-repeated organic metaphors, evident in his habit of setting up natural laws—*naturgesetze*—for language. The older and more original a language is, for instance, the more clearly will the emotions dominate in the roots of words, and the fewer the abstractions.[103] Thus the study of language became a branch of natural history. In this new approach to language lies the great historical importance of Herder's *Ueber den Ursprung der Sprache*. It flowed into the stream of German romantic thought, and together their influence is everywhere evident in the outlook and activities of the· Schlegel brothers, Wilhelm von Humboldt, and Jacob Grimm. It was with Herder that the spirit of

[102] *Werke*, V, 136.
[103] *Werke*, V, 71, 78. These observations were not new, but it was new to set them up as "laws of language." See also *ibid.*, pp. 93, 112, 123-124, 134.

language came alive as the highest expression of man's nature.

Herder's importance extends to another, related area: he seems to have been largely responsible for giving new currency, in eighteenth-century terms, to the age-old belief that the Orient—and especially India—was the original home of mankind, its cradle. All wisdom and knowledge could be traced to India, including the foundation of it all, language. Bengalese, he believed, formed all its verbs, nouns, and other parts of speech out of seven hundred basic roots, corresponding to the elements of reason, though unfortunately it was hard to learn for the European who would have to discard the useless copiousness of his own language before he could enter the carefully reasoned, regular system of the invisible language of thought.[104] An early and often-quoted source of information on this point was a letter written by a French Jesuit missionary in 1740. He described Sanskrit in terms of universal grammar as a language of the highest perfection in which each of the limited number of roots had reference only to a single idea, from which other ideas and their words could be formed by simple and regular modification. To de Brosses, who quoted this passage, Sanskrit illustrated his principle, now no longer apparent in any other language, that the basic roots of all languages were abstract signs. Beauzée, who also referred to this passage, believed that Sanskrit actually was an artificial, universal language of the sort John Wilkins had attempted and Leibniz imagined.[105] The contrast between

---

[104] *Werke*, XIII, 407-408, in *Ideen zur Philosophie der Geschichte der Menschheit*, Pt. 2 (1785). See also *ibid.*, XIV, 25-32 on "Indostan." For the subject in general, A. Leslie Willson, "Herder and India: The Genesis of a Mythical Image," in *PMLA*, LXX (1955), 1,049-1,058.

[105] The letter was written by le P. Pons and published in the *Lettres édifiantes*, Vol. XXV, from which it was quoted by de Brosses in *Traité*, II, 372-374. It was again quoted by Beauzée

rationalism and romanticism—if it is permissible to use those vague and much abused terms—is nowhere more clearly defined than in their views of Sanskrit. Both saw it as the perfection of their philosophy, but with a difference. To one it was simple, regular, mechanical, a product of the most perfect philosophical invention. To the other it was profound, spiritual, organic, the work of the Godhead. To Novalis, who with his contemporaries was much influenced by Boehme's mystical doctrine of the language of nature, language was "ein so wunderbares und fruchtbares Geheimnis, indem, wenn einer bloss spricht, um zu sprechen, er gerade die herrlichsten, originellsten Wahrheiten ausspricht." Still, he believed, like Condillac, that "denken ist sprechen" and that the first language was musical; in this "allegemeine Sprache der Musik," he said, "der Geist wird frei, unbestimmt angeregt; das tut ihm so wohl, das dünkt ihm so bekannt, so vaterländisch—er ist auf diese kurzen Augenblicke in seiner indischen Heimat."[106] Add to this Friedrich Schlegel's belief that "Der Historiker ist ein rückwärts gekehrter Prophet,"[107] and the role of the Sanskrit historian becomes evident. The prophet was Schlegel himself.

Friedrich Schlegel left Germany for Paris in the spring of 1802. He had a number of reasons for going, but his

---

in the new article on Sanskrit in the *Encyclopédie méthodique*, where he took occasion to argue for the adoption of a universal language in Europe, the existence of Sanskrit proving that such a language was not a chimera. Herder elsewhere quoted both de Brosses and the *Lettres édifiantes*, though not on this particular point.

[106] *Gesammelte Werke*, ed. Carl Seelig (Zürich, 1945), V, 43-44 ("Monolog über die Sprache"), and III, 266 (*Fragmente* No. 1709).

[107] In *Athenaeum*, I (1798), Pt. ii, 20. According to the new *Kritische Friedrich-Schlegel-Ausgabe*, ed. Ernst Behler, XVIII (München, 1963), 85, these words can be identified as F. Schlegel's.

chief aim was the study of Oriental languages, especially Persian and Sanskrit.[108] He soon began to concentrate on Sanskrit, however, having now met Alexander Hamilton, who had become his teacher by May of 1803. In November, Hamilton had already shared the Schlegels' household for several months, and he stayed throughout the winter, though he did not eat at their table.[109] Early in this period he wrote to Tieck that "alles, ja alles ohne Ausnahme seinen Ursprung in Indien hat," and made a note that Cook and Jones were the greatest men of the century.[110] It was during these years while Schlegel was receiving instruction from the young Englishman that he prepared the book which appeared in the spring of 1808 as *Ueber die Sprache und Weisheit der Indier*, almost simultaneously with his conversion to the Church of Rome in the Cathedral of Cologne. This act had a close connection with the subject and the tenor of the book, as Goethe immediately saw—with the result that he became very suspicious of Sanskrit studies.[111]

[108] On the other reasons see Josef Körner (ed.), *Krisenjahre der Frühromantik, Briefe aus dem Schlegelkreis*, III, "Kommentar" (Bern, 1958), 52; in the fall of 1802, Schlegel had secured a letter of recommendation from Cuvier.

[109] Oskar F. Walzel (ed.), *Friedrich Schlegels Briefe an seinen Bruder August Wilhelm* (Berlin, 1890), pp. 511, 523. *Krisenjahre*, I, 72. On July 21, 1804, F. Schlegel wrote to his brother from Cologne that he did not know the pronunciation of Sanskrit, "denn in Frankreich kennt man sie nicht, und Hamilton liest schon so viel Indisch mit mir, dass ich ihm nicht damit beschwerlich fallen konnte, da ich für ihm zuweit zurück war, als dass ich ihm hätte Vergnügen machen können" (*Krisenjahre*, I, 126-127). On Hamilton, see also R. W. Chambers and F. Norman, "Alexander Hamilton and the Beginnings of Comparative Philology" in *Studies in English Philology, a Miscellany in Honor of Frederick Klaeber*, eds. Kemp Malone and Martin B. Ruud (Minneapolis, 1929), pp. 457-466.

[110] *Kritische Ausgabe*, XIV, xxxi (letter of September 15, 1803), and XVIII, 500 (philosophical notes, October 1803).

[111] In September 1804, Schlegel wrote from Cologne to the Berlin publisher Georg Reimer: "Der wichtigste Ertrag meiner Pariser Reise sind meine *indischen* Studien, Uebersetzungen,

It is a curious fact that all commentators still agree that Schlegel's *Ueber die Sprache und Weisheit der Indier* deserves the entire credit for introducing the method and the views that became the foundation of the new comparative and historical study of languages, although they also agree that the work does not display a very profound knowledge of Sanskrit. One of them has said that it was as if a curtain had suddenly been torn aside to reveal the new at a single stroke.[112] But curtains rarely fall so suddenly in history except in men's imaginations. These accounts would have been much more believable if they had shown acquaintance with Jones's "Anniversary Discourses," apart from isolated quotation of the statement on the affinities of Sanskrit, and if they had noted the very questionable doctrines which Schlegel's book also contains. We are told that his epoch-making contributions were his warning against "etymologischen Künsteleien,"[113] his emphasis on the structure of words, and his insistence on the historical and comparative study of languages—even the word "empirical" has been used, without discussion that Schlegel in the same work specifically rejected "der blos empirischen Denkart" as a fatal lapse from idealism.[114] But on all three counts, the

---

Materialien usw. Ich möchte jetzt gerne was ich in Paris gesammelt und gearbeitet habe, nun hier in Ruhe in den Druck und die Welt befördern" (Körner, ed., *Briefe von und an Friedrich und Dorothea Schlegel* [Berlin, 1926], p. 464).

[112] Hans Arens, *Sprachwissenschaft* (München, 1955), p. 145. Similarly Walter Porzig, *Das Wunder der Sprache* (Bern, 1950), pp. 263ff., and Heinrich Nüsse, *Die Sprachtheorie Friedrich Schlegels* (Heidelberg, 1962), pp. 40-49. This dogma goes back to Theodor Benfey, *Geschichte der Sprachwissenschaft und Orientalischen Philologie in Deutschland* (Müchen, 1869), pp. 357-369. They were anticipated by Max Müller, who said of Schlegel's book that it "became the foundation of the science of language" (*Lectures on the Science of Language* [London, 1862], I, 164).

[113] *Sämmtliche Werke*, VIII, 279.

[114] *Sämmtliche Werke*, VIII, 375.

priority, as has already been shown, belongs to Jones. Quite apart from what he may have heard from Hamilton—who may have attended the meetings at which the discourses were delivered—Schlegel had the benefit of having the discourses at hand when he prepared his work. The most admired and quoted statement is perhaps the following: "Jener entscheidende Punkt aber, der hier alles aufhellen wird, ist die innre Structur der Sprachen oder die vergleichende Grammatik, welche uns ganz neue Aufschlüsse über die Genealogie der Sprachen auf ähnliche Weise geben wird, wie die vergleichende Anatomie über die höhere Naturgeschichte Licht verbreitet hat."[115] It is true that Jones did not, at least in words, mention comparative grammar and anatomy, but he had strongly argued that grammatical structure was the safest guide in these matters, and he clearly did talk of derivation and genealogy, not merely about affinity. In his treatment of language, Jones adhered to his analytical and historical a posteriori procedures. He was empirical, whereas the same claim cannot rightfully be made for Schlegel.

Read in its entirety—a reasonable expectation with so short a work—Schlegel's book presents a strange mixture of attitudes. On the one hand, we find a nearly mystical idealism combined with a personal religious program that led him into a number of very doubtful and certainly not

---

[115] *Sämmtliche Werke*, VIII, 291. We are told that F. Schlegel was the first to use the term "vergleichende Grammatik." (See, e.g. the authorities cited in Nüsse, p. 42, n. 10. It is a remarkable fact that Jones is not once mentioned in Nüsse's book. It is also worth noting that the phrase had occurred in Court de Gébelin's *Grammaire universelle et comparative*.) But this is not so. It first appeared in print in the autumn of 1803 in A. W. Schlegel's review of A. F. Bernhardi's *Reine Sprachlehre*, in Friedrich Schlegel's journal *Europa*, II, Pt. i, 193-204. The term will be found on p. 203, in spaced type. A few lines earlier, in the same context, A. W. Schlegel used the phrase "Organismus der Sprache."

productive doctrines, and on the other, the observations which were fruitful but not original. His spiritual longings conflicted with the desire to make the same work a qualification for the academic post he so eagerly sought in those years.[116] He divided all languages in two categories. Some languages formed all modification by mechanical composition of elements, by prefixes, suffixes, prepositions, auxiliary verbs, and the like. He made it plain that these languages were bound up with materialist philosophy, with apostasy, or with native imperfection outside the divine dispensation. They had their origin in sense and the imitation of nature, in the brutish stupidity of their first speakers. But Sanskrit, which he calls the *Ursprache* and the common source of what we call the Indo-European languages, is "durchaus organisch gebildet." The organic languages, which were all derived from Sanskrit, form their modifications by inward *Flexion* in the root itself. In Indian and Greek, each root is like an organism, "ein lebendiger Keim," but "in Sprachen . . . die statt der Flexion nur Affixa haben, sind die Wurzeln nicht eigentlich das; kein fruchtbarer Same, sondern nur wie ein Haufen Atome, die jeder Wind des Zufalls leicht aus einander treiben oder zusammenführen kann."[117] The organic languages did not begin with the mere physical cry; they had a higher origin and did not take their spiritual terms from the sensible, for they expressed "in ihren ersten und einfachsten Bestandtheilen die höchsten Begriffe der reinen Gedankenwelt, gleichsam den ganzen Grundriss des Bewusstseins nicht bildlich, sondern in unmittelbarer Klarheit." Sanskrit is "eine philosophische oder vielmehr religiöse Terminologie . . . es [ist] kein veränderliches Combinations-Spiel willkührlicher Abstractionen sondern ein bleibendes System, wo die ein-

---

[116] The latter purpose is abundantly evident in the correspondence in the collections cited above.
[117] VIII, 302.

mahl geheiligten tiefbedeutenden Ausdrücke und Worte sich gegenseitig erhellen, bestimmen und tragen." At this point he abstains from going beyond history, but he clearly wishes to suggest that Sanskrit is of divine origin.[118] It is only within this nonempirical, mystical context that Jones's sound observations find their place. Schlegel could safely insist on the historical study of Sanskrit, for he had started with the conviction that history could reach that far toward the Godhead, which was close enough for truth and conversion. It is very interesting, at times beautiful, and certainly romantic, but it can hardly be called an empirical program for the study of language. Jones was the source of the parts that were of value, and it is a good question whether language study would not have taken the same course without the philosophy and mysticism of *Ueber die Sprache und Weisheit der Indier*. The discourses were widely read. Schlegel's book caused excitement, but no person who took all of it seriously would ever have arrived at what came to be called comparative philology.

In the fall of 1812, shortly after his twenty-first birthday, Franz Bopp set out on the long walk from Aschaffenburg to Paris, excited by Schlegel's—and Sir William Jones's—vision of an Oriental Renaissance. For the next three years he studied Sanskrit on his own and prepared his first work, *Über das Conjugationssystem*, which appeared in 1816, the year which best serves to mark the beginning of comparative philology. In the latter part of 1818, he arrived in London where he spent a year and a half studying the rich collection of manuscripts in the East India Company's library. He did not find it the most convenient place to work—too many interruptions—but he was grateful to Colebrooke for his interest in his work and his kind permission to take manuscripts home, and

[118] VIII, 308, 310.

to Hamilton for other favors. Still, he found that "den Engländern liegt das Sanskrit sehr wenig an, überhaupt stehen sie an wissenschaftlichem Eifer den Franzosen weit nach."[119] While in London, he prepared a new version of his first work. It was written in English under the title *Analytical Comparison of the Sanskrit, Greek, Latin, and Teutonic Languages, shewing the original Identity of their Grammatical Structure*, and was published in the first volume of *Annals of Oriental Literature*, which soon ceased publication for lack of interest.[120] In the opening pages, Bopp wrote that it was "chiefly by comparison that we determine as far as our sensible and intellectual faculties reach, the nature of things. Frederic Schlegel justly expects, that comparative grammar will give us quite new explications of the genealogy of languages, in a similar way as comparative anatomy has thrown light on natural philosophy." But he did not agree with Schlegel's notion of *Flexion* or internal modification, opposing to it his own conviction that "in this family of languages the principle of compounding words will extend to the first rudiments of speech, as to the persons, tenses of verbs, and cases of the nouns, &c."[121] In the Preface to the English edition of Bopp's *Comparative Grammar*, the translator remarked that the work had "created a new epoch in the science of Comparative Philology . . . corresponding to that of Newton's Principia in Mathematics, Bacon's Novum Organum in Mental Science, or Blumenbach in

[119] Lefmann, *Anhang*, pp. 57-63.

[120] The *Analytical Comparison* has been reprinted in Techmer's *Internationale Zeitschrift für Allgemeine Sprachwissenschaft*, IV (1889), 14-60. The full title of the original German work was: *Ueber das Conjugationssystem der Sanskritsprache in Vergleichung mit jenem der griechischen, lateinischen, persischen und germanischen Sprache* . . . herausgegeben und mit Vorerinnerungen begleitet von K. J. Windischmann (Frankfurt a. M., 1816).

[121] See pp. 20-21 for Bopp's critique of Schlegel.

Physiology."[122] In his own Preface, Bopp had said that his purpose was "eine vergleichende, alles Verwandte zusammenfassende Beschreibung des Organismus der auf dem Titel genannten Sprachen, eine Erforschung ihrer physischen und mechanischen Gesetze und des Ursprungs der die grammatischen Verhältnisse bezeichnenden Formen," and he had stressed that he would deal with languages for their own sake, "als Gegenstand und nicht als Mittel der Erkenntniss."[123]

The two other founders of the new philology were Rasmus Kristian Rask and Jacob Grimm. In 1814 Rask's *Undersøgelse om det gamle Nordiske eller Islandske Sprogs Oprindelse* won the prize of the Royal Danish Society of Science, but it was not published until 1818, too late to influence the first edition of the first volume of Grimm's *Deutsche Grammatik* in 1819, but early enough to cause some important changes in the second in 1822.[124] The *Grammatik* was the first large-scale historical examination of the old vernacular and its cognates. Rask and Grimm were both visited at home by the two Anglo-Saxon scholars Benjamin Thorpe and John Mitchell Kemble. They brought the new philology to England in the 1830's, some fifty years after Sir William Jones had laid the foundation.

[122] The translator was Edward B. Eastwick, here quoted from the Preface to the 2nd edition of Vol. I (London, 1856; 1st edn. London, 1845). He was quoting from a review in the *Calcutta Review*, XII (1849), 472.

[123] "Vorrede zur ersten Ausgabe" (1833) in *Vergleichende Grammatik*, 3rd edn. (Berlin, 1868), I, iii.

[124] On Rask, see Paul Diderichsen, *Rasmus Rask og den Grammatiske Tradition, Studier over Vendepunktet i Sprogvidenskabens Historie* (*Historisk-filologiske Meddelelser udgivet af Det Kongelige Danske Videnskabernes Selskab*, Vol. 38, No. 2 (1960). This stimulating monograph explores Rask's intellectual background.

CHAPTER V

The New Philology in England to 1842

In March 1830, the *Foreign Review* carried a review of Grimm's *Deutsche Grammatik*. The reviewer was Rasmus Rask, and he began with a few reflections on the history of philology. He said: "The Continental nations, especially the Germans and the Danes, have been for a long time very industriously, and we think successfully, engaged in illustrating their ancient languages and remnants of literature." Then, confining himself to the Danes, he continued:

> It is a curious observation, that so small a nation as the Danes should take the lead in researches of such interest to every people, aspiring to the honour of a continuity of literature and mental cultivation. This, however, seems in reality to have been the case in the north of Europe; for though we have no wish to depreciate the labours of Peringschöld, Hadoroph, etc. in Sweden; of Palthen, Schilter, Scherz in Germany; nor of our own justly celebrated Hickes, Wilkins, etc., etc. yet their labours were not only comparatively imperfect, but even discontinued, and in all probability, would never have been resumed with such ardour and success, but for the emulation excited by the learned men of Denmark.

Is this statement merely an expression of patriotic sentiment, or is it also a sound judgment on the early Danish interest in the literature and the language of the past? It is certainly both, for as Rask pointed out in the same passage: "We think we may with truth affirm that it was the great Danish historiographer Suhm, together with the royal Arna-magnean Institution for publishing the ancient

Scandinavian or Icelandic manuscripts, who gave the first impulse to the labour, now carried on so eagerly both in the north and south of Gothic Europe."[1] The unique collection of manuscripts gathered by Arni Magnusson (1663-1730) and the fund he established for its care and publication, acted as incentives to scholarly work and led to the publication of several good editions beginning as early as the middle of the eighteenth century. The Codex Argenteus at Uppsala had a similar effect in Sweden. But Danish scholarship was especially fortunate in having a man like Peter Frederik Suhm (1728-1798), whose great wealth, acquired by marriage in Trondhjem, was almost entirely spent within his lifetime on scholarship, publication, and a remarkable library of 100,000 volumes, which were incorporated in the Royal Library at Copenhagen. He undertook the cost of publication of Langebek's *Scriptores rerum Danicarum* (1772), and between 1772 and 1787, he supported publication of several Icelandic manuscripts, including *Landnamabok, Viga-Glums Saga*, and *Eyrbyggja Saga*. Suhm himself produced the monumental and scholarly *Historie af Danmark* (up to 1400), in fourteen volumes, of which the first seven were published before his death and the rest from his notes during the next thirty years. One significant result of all this activity was that G. J. Thorkelin (1752-1829) received public support for a trip to England and Scotland to search for historical material bearing on relations between those two countries and Denmark and Norway. He spent the years from 1786 to 1790 abroad, meeting among others John Jamieson, to whom

[1] *Foreign Review*, V (March, 1830), 493; the review was reprinted in H. K. Rask (ed.), *Samlede tildels forhen utrykte Afhandlinger*, med bidrag til Forfatterens Levned af N. M. Petersen (3 vols.; Copenhagen, 1834-1838), II, 442-462. The attribution is also accepted in Louis Hjelmslev (ed.), *Rasmus Rask, Ausgewählte Abhandlungen* (3 vols.; Copenhagen, 1932-1937), III, 392.

he suggested the work which appeared in 1808 as an *Etymological Dictionary of the Scottish Language*, a book of considerable value and the first independent lexicographical effort in Britain after Johnson's *Dictionary*.[2] But the chief result of Thorkelin's visit to England was, of course, his transcription of the *Beowulf* manuscript, which he undertook in the belief that the poem was about the wars between a Danish hero and the Swedish kings. From this transcription followed in 1815 the publication, delayed eight years by the British bombardment of Copenhagen in 1807, of the first edition of *Beowulf* in the original under the title: *De Danorum rebus gestis seculo III. et IV. Poëma Danicum dialecto Anglo-Saxonica.* A Latin translation and critical commentary accompanied the text. Five years later appeared the first translation of *Beowulf* into a modern language. Its title was *Bjowulfs Drape*, and it was the work of N.F.S. Grundtvig, who was later to take an active part in Old-English scholarship during his visits to England between 1829 and 1831. Thus Rask's statement had ample support in the history of recent Danish scholarship, a tradition which reached a climax with Rask's own contributions.

Considering that Rask was reviewing, for an English journal, a German work whose philological importance had already been recognized, it is impossible not to notice the implication that English scholarship had not as yet produced anything that was at all comparable to dozens of works that had been published on the Continent. During the early twenties, Murray's *History of the European Languages* appeared, and the Cambridge Press published

[2] N.F.S. Grundtvig, *Bjowulfs Drape* (Copenhagen, 1820) points out in the Preface that Jacob Langebek had made reference to *Beowulf* in his *Scriptores rerum Danicarum*, where Thorkelin may have come across the reference; Grundtvig surmises in the same place that Thorkelin's trip to England was arranged with the generous assistance of Suhm (p. xxix). The best-known reference to *Beowulf* occurred in Wanley's Catalogue.

the three massive volumes of Walter Whiter's *Etymolog-icon Universale*, both works which were out of tune with contemporary Continental philology. It was to guard against their mistakes and the tradition behind them that Bopp wrote in the Preface (1833) to his *Vergleichende Grammatik*: "Nur das Geheimniss der Wurzeln oder des Benennungsgrundes der Urbegriffe lassen wir unange-tastet; wir untersuchen nicht, warum z. B. die Wurzel *I gehen* und nicht *stehen*, oder warum die Laut-Gruppirung *STHA* oder *STA stehen* und nicht *gehen* bedeute." But 1830 was also very nearly the last year when a statement like Rask's could go unchallenged, for the following decade witnessed very lively philological activity in England, thanks largely to the two Old-English scholars Benjamin Thorpe (1782-1870) and John Mitchell Kemble (1807-1857), who studied abroad under Rask and Grimm respectively. Soon, in 1842, the Philological Society of London was formed, and among its members originated the project for a new English dictionary; by 1860, the plans had been laid and agreed upon, and the work had begun toward the *New English Dictionary*, which still stands as one of the most impres-sive monuments to the philological learning and scholarly cooperation of the nineteenth century.

The new dictionary is unthinkable without the rapid absorption of Continental scholarship by English philol-ogists and their intensive study after 1830 of early Eng-lish language and literature; and, equally important, with-out the complete departure from the powerful Tooke tradition, from philological speculation, from random etymologizing, and from the notion that the chief end of language study is the knowledge of mind. Bopp, Rask, and Grimm never tired of pointing out that the success of language study depended on the dismissal of questions which it could never be expected to answer, quite in agreement with Dugald Stewart. Their method was careful observation and comparison guided by historical sense. In Grimm's words: "Allgemeinlogischen begriffen bin ich in den grammatik feind; sie führen scheinbare strenge und geschlossenheit der bestimmungen mit sich, hemmen aber die beobachtung, welche ich als die seele der sprachforschung betrachte."[3] But this was a method which did not easily gain acceptance in England, where the pioneering work of Junius and Hickes had been almost forgotten. The introduction of the new philology into England can be exactly dated. It occurred in 1830 with Thorpe's translation of Rask's *Grammar of the Anglo-Saxon Tongue* and Grundtvig's prospectus for the publication of texts, for a *Bibliotheca Anglo-Saxonica.* But the ground had already been prepared.

It seems that philology can only prosper under two conditions. One is genuine interest in the early literature of the country; the other is proper provisions for its study by others than dilettantes, mere antiquaries, and amateurs. In England the former condition was soon fulfilled; with the second it took much longer, partly because English universities, unlike the German, were very slow to welcome the new philology within their walls. During the decisive years, all the work was done outside the universities, though the situation was somewhat remedied by the formation of learned societies.

An adequate motive being the prerequisite for any serious effort, it seems natural that philology could get nowhere without respect for early literature and eagerness to study every aspect of it. Grimm left no doubt about his motive: "Das einladende studium mittelhochdeutscher poesie führte mich zuerst auf grammatische untersuchungen."[4] In England there was one work which prepared the way: Bishop Percy's *Northern Antiquities,* a translation of Paul-Henri Mallet's *Introduction à l'his-*

[3] *Deutsche Grammatik*, I (2nd edn., 1822), vi.
[4] *Ibid.*, viii.

toire de Dannemarc, où l'on traite de la religion, des loix, des moeurs et des usages des anciens Danois (1755). It was, perhaps more than any other single work, responsible for the Gothic revival. In the Preface, Mallet had quoted Montesquieu's *De l'esprit des lois* on the importance of the northern nations because they had forged "those instruments which broke the fetters manufactured in the south" and "left their native climes to destroy tyrants and slaves, and to teach men that nature having made them equal, no reason could be assigned for their becoming dependent, but their mutual happiness."[5] To his translation, Bishop Percy added material drawn from his own extensive knowledge, his most important contribution being the Preface, which corrected the widely held misconception, shared by Mallet, that the Gauls and the Germans, the Britons and the Saxons, were one and the same people—a view that was detrimental to the study of "Gothic" antiquities as long as the Ossianic poems held the imagination captive. Percy's correction is of considerable significance because it cleared up a muddle that was very harmful to the serious study of Anglo-Saxon, especially in England, where the misconception was most widespread.[6]

In England the revival of interest in early English history, culture, language, and literature was reserved for Sharon Turner's *History of the Anglo-Saxons from the Earliest Period to the Norman Conquest*, whose three

[5] I. A. Blackwell (ed.), *Northern Antiquities; or, an Historical Account of the Manners, Customs, Religion and Laws, Maritime Expeditions and Discoveries, Language and Literature of the Ancient Scandinavians (Danes, Swedes, Norwegians and Icelanders) with Incidental Notices respecting our Saxon Ancestors.* Translated from the French of M. Mallet, by Bishop Percy (London: Bohn, 1847), p. 58. The original edition, in 2 volumes, had appeared in 1770.

[6] Bede's detailed account of the early inhabitants and languages of Britain made it especially difficult to overcome this misconception.

volumes appeared between 1799 and 1805. It soon gained great popularity and was regularly reissued until the seventh edition of 1852, when it had been superseded by Thorpe's translation of Lappenberg's *History of England under the Anglo-Saxon Kings* (1845) and Kemble's *The Saxons in England, a History of the English Commonwealth* (1849). Turner's *History* was a pioneering work in spite of its faults and inaccuracies and its unsuccessful attempt to emulate Gibbon's style. It was the first historical work to make extensive use of the Anglo-Saxon manuscripts in the Cottonian collection, which it cited together with other sources, mostly Latin, in its very copious footnotes. Unlike Hume's *History,* Turner's work took a sympathetic, if somewhat idealized, view of the Anglo-Saxons, at least after their conversion. This tendency is nowhere so evident as in the more than two hundred pages devoted to King Alfred, who, according to a tradition already found in Hume, is seen as one of the greatest rulers of all time, greater than Charlemagne because Alfred was a better man. He was a philosopher-king, whose greatness was the result of his steady pursuit of intellectual improvement, a poet, a moral essayist, a metaphysician, a patron of the arts and sciences, a wise legislator, a benevolent protector of his people, a good father; and first and last, he was a good ruler and a pious man, constantly striving for morality and enlightenment in the midst of barbaric invasions and the "twilight of mind" that reigned around him—in short as near as any to the eighteenth-century image of the ideal king. The picture may lack accuracy and be deficient in historical sense, but the exaggerations helped stimulate interest. Turner also devoted separate sections to Anglo-Saxon "Poetry, Literature, Arts and Sciences" and to the language. The former contained summaries, paraphrases, and quotations from individual works and thus for the first time made a rudimentary knowledge of Anglo-Saxon literature readily available, though here also Turner made many mistakes, believing for instance that the subject of *Beowulf* was the hero's attempt to seek revenge on Hrothgar for a murder committed by the latter.[7] Turner's credulity is most apparent in the section on the language, to which he added—and in the fifth edition (1828) greatly expanded—long lists of words showing the affinities between Anglo-Saxon and such remote languages as Arabic, Chinese, Malay, Japanese, Turkish, and Tonga. But for all its obvious faults, the *History of the Anglo-Saxons* abundantly fulfilled Turner's wish to arouse a taste for Anglo-Saxon history and literature.

But interest in the language and literature of the past is not enough and may indeed lead to mere dilettantism if the study is not pursued under conditions which insure a certain scholarly standard. These conditions one would normally expect to find in the universities, but the general state of the English universities between 1750 and 1850 was not such that the new philology could hope to prosper within their walls, or even gain admission. Philology was left to shift for itself in the hands of people who had more enthusiasm than scholarly acumen. This situation could even become a hindrance to the progress of scholarship, as in the case of the Antiquarian Society, about which Kemble said that, "were it not mischievous by fostering all the mediocrities, [it] would be merely childish."[8] The Anglo-Saxon lectureship which Sir Henry Spelman had established at Cambridge in 1640 was soon discontinued, and Cambridge did not again have an Anglo-Saxon chair until Bosworth in 1867 gave ten thousand pounds for the purpose. Oxford was seemingly better off, due to the Rawlinsonian bequest which took

[7] In the third edition (1820) Turner added a more correct chapter on *Beowulf*, drawn from Thorkelin's edition.

[8] "The English Historical Society" in the *British and Foreign Review*, VII (July, 1838), 178; for ascription to Kemble, see below, note 55.

effect in 1795, each holder to occupy the chair for a term of five years. But when the thirteenth incumbent John Earle was appointed in 1849, the chair was, according to Charles Plummer, "little more than an elegant sinecure," which Earle was the first to raise to a position of real usefulness.[9] Of the previous professors only three had published on Anglo-Saxon before 1830: James Ingram (1803-1808), John Josias Conybeare (1808-1812), and Thomas Silver (1817-1822).

James Ingram's *Inaugural Lecture on the Utility of Anglo-Saxon Literature* (1807) is, as the title indicates, a plea for the study of Anglo-Saxon. Ingram rests his argument on three points. The first bears on the continuity of scholarship, for "if we diligently examine the whole history and progress of Saxon literature in this country, we shall find that, so far from having been totally neglected at any time, it has been uninterruptedly cultivated and continued to this day amongst us by the public-spirited exertions of illustrious and learned men, who suffered no obstacles to overcome their sense of its utility."[10] He concluded that through the efforts of these men, the Anglo-Saxon language "has become an object of relative importance even in this age of fastidious refinement."[11]

His second argument is more cogent and draws its inspiration from the patriotic feelings which were the natural outcome of the events of European history since 1789. Hume's opinion that the rise of English culture and institutions began with the Norman Conquest was no longer attractive. The study of Anglo-Saxon literature is,

[9] S.v. "John Earle" in *DNB* (2nd Supplement).
[10] Ingram, p. 3.
[11] Ingram, p. 12. At this point he surmised that "if the 'Diversions of Purley' had been written without any studious intermixture of political sentiments . . . it might have produced the desirable effect of making us better acquainted and satisfied with our own language, and at the same time have extended the bounds of philological science."

Ingram explains, of the greatest importance to Englishmen because "it is intimately connected with the original introduction and establishment of their present language and laws, their liberty, and their religion."[12] Of these, the arguments drawn from legal history and religion were old, but the other two were, at the time, new and powerful arguments. With regard to liberty, "what are our present *Parliaments*, but the revival of the free and simple *witena-gemotes* of our Saxon ancestors?" Saxon freedom began with the destruction of Norman tyranny, "for, however historians may differ with respect to the precise æra of the first assembling of a *Parliament*, we may well rest assured, that there is nothing French or Norman in it but the name."[13]

But it is in his view of the language that Ingram shows his greatest originality. Asserting that the "great mass of the people of this country are still of Saxon origin,"[14] Ingram argues that the present language is "completely Anglo-Saxon in its whole idiom and construction" and not, as was commonly believed, a "heterogeneous compound . . . compiled from the jarring and corrupted elements of Hebrew, Greek, Latin, French, Spanish, and Italian"[15]—a notion that was just as stultifying to the progress of philology as the identification of Celtic and Germanic antiquities. Ingram, however, did not stop there, but argued further that the present language was the outcome of "the *gradual changes* which have taken place according to the natural course of events," a slow but not imperceptible process, as must be apparent to those "who have compared the language of the Saxon Chronicle, and other ancient specimens, with that of Robert of Gloucester, Chaucer, Spenser, Milton," and others.[16] Ingram himself announced his intention to de-

[12] Ingram, p. 2. [13] Ingram, p. 24.
[14] Ingram, p. 3. [15] Ingram, p. 13.
[16] Ingram, p. 18.

liver a lecture on "the formation of the English language on the foundation of the Anglo-Saxon."[17] He also saw that the Saxon Chronicle, "having been compiled at different intervals of time . . . may be considered, independently of its merits as a faithful register of historical facts, as a kind of chronological memorial of the progress of our national language."[18] Before Friedrich Schlegel and Bopp had made the idea a commonplace, Ingram stated that "we must study, if I may use the expression, the *comparative anatomy* of human language."[19] The study of Anglo-Saxon was useful not only for its particular importance to Englishmen, but was "also capable of being made a subject of *general* interest in the pursuit of universal knowledge, and may serve as a medium of illustration to those, who are disposed to study and investigate the philosophical principles of grammar, and the true theory of language."[20] The suggestion is a typical reflection of contemporary opinion, but Ingram did not seem to include himself among those who would carry their studies forward in that direction. However, he did find a new implication in the *Diversions of Purley* by citing that work to support his opinion that some acquaintance with the northern languages, not least Anglo-Saxon, "is absolutely necessary to those European scholars, who are desirous of acquiring *a scientific synopsis of universal Grammar*, as well as an accurate perception of their own vernacular idiom."[21] The exclusive attention to the learned languages had "too frequently beguiled men

[17] Ingram, p. 4. [18] Ingram, p. 32.

[19] Ingram, p. 30. The context shows, however, that Ingram did not quite have the same thing in mind as Schlegel.

[20] Ingram, pp. 2-3. To the word "grammar," Ingram adds this footnote: "The word *grammar* is here used in that enlarged, comprehensive and *proper* sense, in which it was originally understood, when it was a subject of scientific investigation to philosophers," and he adds: "A *Grammaire Raisonnée* is still a desideratum."

[21] Ingram, p. 29.

of the greatest talents and erudition into very erroneous conclusions on philological subjects."[22]

But Oxford does not seem to have taken much interest in Ingram's program. A prize-essay by J. T. Coleridge on "Etymology" in 1813 began with a quotation from Locke on the close connection between ideas and words, referred to Adam Smith and de Brosses frequently, and ended with acceptance of Horne Tooke's "excellent theory of language."[23] Ingram himself provided no illustration of the sort of study he suggested, and he laid himself open to the ridicule of posterity by his etymology of "barbarian," which "signifies nothing more than a son of the North, a North-born man, *bor-bairn!* Hence Boreas for the North wind."[24] He is remembered, however, for producing the first critical edition of the entire Saxon Chronicle (1823); but its philological apparatus was confined to a very brief survey of Anglo-Saxon grammar, at the end of which he referred to Bosworth's forthcoming *Elements of Anglo-Saxon Grammar* (also 1823), a work which itself was marked by very skimpy use of Rask's greatly superior *Angelsaksisk Sproglaere*, published at Stockholm in 1817 and by complete ignorance of Grimm's *Deutsche Grammatik*.

Thomas Silver's *Lecture on the Study of Anglo-Saxon* (Oxford, 1822) shows that there was as yet little hope for philology at Oxford. The lecture was delivered in 1822—the last lecture he gave during his five-year term. It is inferior to Ingram's lecture, being a curious mixture of all sorts of information loosely organized on the pattern of the fourfold division of grammar into Gothic, High German, Icelandic, and Anglo-Saxon found in Hickes' *Thesaurus*. He lamented the loss of the genitive plural, for "could this very melodious termination have

22 Ingram, p. 30.
23 *Oxford English Prize Essays*, III (Oxford, 1830), pp. 53-80.
24 Ingram, p. 15.

been retained, it would have given the English poet nearly all the advantages of classic rhythm."[25] But the level of scholarship represented by Silver is most strikingly illustrated in his brief account of Grimm's grammar, which brings Silver to the safer ground of Hickes. He makes no attempt whatever to give a systematic survey of recent scholarship and seems totally ignorant of Rask. "When the Anglo-Saxon student is somewhat advanced in his knowledge," we are told, "he should undertake to learn the German language, which is in a great measure little more than a continuation of that dialect, increased by time." Furthermore, "the German language is so rich in works of laborious research, that incalculable advantages might be derived from them,"[26] a knowledge of Grimm's "indispensable" grammar, for instance; but the description Silver gives of it shows that he failed to see how greatly superior it was to all previous grammars. He seems most impressed by the complete tables of inflections and conjugations, and concludes that the work was a "Gothic Polyglot Grammar"—in other words, a sort of prolegomenon to the "scientific synopsis of universal grammar" envisioned by Ingram. Silver could, of course, only be familiar with the first edition of the first volume of Grimm's work, which is very different from the much more original and influential second edition of 1822. It is true that the first edition is full of paradigms, but it also differs radically from previous grammars in a number of respects which Silver might have brought to the attention of his audience—in completeness and accuracy, in the wealth of references and citations of examples, and especially in a number of passages devoted to general observations, such as those on the strong and weak verbs.

[25] Silver, p. 22. It would seem to be this sort of thing Dugald Stewart had in mind when he scornfully talked of deciding on matters of style by appealing "from the authority of Addison and Swift to the woods of Germany." See StH, V, 182.
[26] Silver, p. 4.

Instead, Silver repeats the facts about Hickes' *Thesaurus,* which had been adequately known for a long time. The philological quality of the lecture is measured by the amusing erratum: "The word *Deutsch* should have been printed throughout with the *s*." Still, Thomas Silver deserves credit for his strong advocacy of the publication of early manuscripts as the prerequisite to a better knowledge of the language and its history, and for the suggestion that philological study must depend on "societies, who can act collectively, and in which each member taking his allotted part, the whole body of language may be easily investigated."[27] Whether owing to his advice or not, the learned society and text publication are the two features that characterize English philology in the nineteenth century.

John Josias Conybeare was Rawlinsonian professor from 1807 until 1812, when he became professor of poetry, also at Oxford. His *Illustrations of Anglo-Saxon Poetry* was published in 1826, two years after his death, and was edited, with many additions, by his brother William Daniel Conybeare. The introductory essay on Anglo-Saxon meter rightly stressed the importance of alliteration and rhythm, but the exposition was vitiated by an attempt to use the terminology of classical versification. The body of the work contained some specimens that had never before been published, from the Exeter Book for instance. In this respect the work had considerable value, but philologically the text was inadequate, partly, it seems, because Conybeare was more interested in the translations which accompanied the selections.[28]

[27] Silver, pp. 31, 7.
[28] It was in this volume that Jacob Grimm first read "Widsith" or "The Song of the Traveller," as Conybeare called it. Grimm immediately saw its importance and wrote to Karl Lachmann on April 20, 1827: "In Conybeare's *illustrations,* London 1826, stehet ein zwar schlecht behandeltes aber höchst wichtiges ags lied, worin ausser merkwürdigen anspielungen aufs alte epos neue

As yet, the universities had nothing to offer, not even the new London University where Thomas Dale in 1828 became the first man in England to hold a chair in English language and literature. But he was not familiar with the new philology and told his classes that he would "invariably aim to impart moral, as well as intellectual instruction," perhaps because he was aware that language study might otherwise, in the tradition of Tooke and the Utilitarians, become an exercise in materialist philosophy.[29] By 1830, no English scholar had yet appeared who was well acquainted with the new philology and ready to study his own language in the manner of Rask and Grimm. Sanskrit studies were not much better off, except in the closed world of Haileybury College.

Bopp's stay in London had some effect, but it did not last. In 1819, Bopp had dedicated his edition of the story of Nala and Damayanti from the Mahabharata, the so-called *Nalus*, to the East India Company, which bought six copies for its college, where Alexander Hamilton was eager to use it; but this was forty-four copies less than they had promised to buy, which caused Bopp financial embarrassment and some hardship.[30] In May of 1820, Hamilton wrote a very favorable review of the *Conjugationssystem* and the *Nalus* for the *Edinburgh Review* in which he admitted that the importance of the former would have entitled it to an earlier review had he not "despaired of rendering a grammatical disquisition interesting to the general reader."[31] The *Conjugationssys-*

ungehörte völkernamen neben bekannteren." Albert Leitzmann (ed.), *Briefwechsel der Brüder Jacob und Wilhelm Grimm mit Karl Lachmann* (2 vols.; Jena, 1927), II, 511.

[29] R. W. Chambers, "Philologists at University College, London. I. The Beginnings: 1828-1889," in *Man's Unconquerable Mind* (London, 1939) p. 347.

[30] S. Lefmann, *Franz Bopp, Anhang*, p. 59.

[31] *Edinburgh Review*, XXXIII, 432. A reference on the same page to "our review of that truly admirable work, the Sanscrit grammar of Mr. Wilkins," which is known to be Hamilton's,

tem had also received favorable mention in the *London Magazine*. The affinity between Sanskrit and the European languages was strange but true and, "tending to throw some light on the history of mankind, deserves to be developed, by laborious researches, to the utmost extent of which it is susceptible." But the same reviewer did not find that "England, with all her peculiar advantages, has done so much as was to be anticipated of her in this way."[32] The fate of the *Annals of Oriental Literature* shows that the reviewer's estimate was correct.

The career of Friedrich August Rosen tells the same story. Born at Göttingen in 1805, he first took up Oriental studies at Leipzig, but transferred to Berlin in 1824 to attend Bopp's lectures and later studied Semitic under Silvestre de Sacy in Paris. As Bopp's best student, he was in 1828 invited to fill the chair of Oriental languages in the London University—a few years later to become University College—where he taught elementary lessons in Hindustani, Arabic, Persian, and Sanskrit for sixteen hours a week at a guaranteed salary of one hundred pounds a year. He gave up his post to have time for research, trying instead to eke out an existence by writing articles on philology for the *Penny Cyclopedia*, whose editor was his friend George Long. He later returned to his family in Germany, having had little opportunity to accomplish his own scholarly work. Still, he exercised a lasting influence on a small group of colleagues who

---

makes it almost certain, given the other circumstances, that he also wrote this review. See R. W. Chambers and F. Norman, "Alexander Hamilton and the Beginnings of Comparative Philology" in *Studies in English Philology, a Miscellany in Honor of Frederick Klaeber*, eds. Martin B. Ruud and Kemp Malone (Minneapolis, 1929), pp. 457-466.

[32] *London Magazine*, I (January, 1820), 72-73. This review made Bopp decide to do his English version, which appeared during the summer as *Analytical Comparison*. See Lefmann, *Anhang*, p. 66.

learned the new philology from him.[33] Including Thomas Key, George Long, and Henry Malden, this group was organized as an informal philological society, which ten years later had some share in the formation of the Philological Society of London. With the establishment of the Boden chair at Oxford and the appointment of H. H. Wilson, Sanskrit studies gained a permanent home in England.[34]

In spite of their superiority in these years and their traditional contact with centers of learning on the Continent, the Scottish universities did not advance the fortunes of philology, though Edinburgh twice made a serious effort. In 1820, the Advocates' Library was seeking a new librarian, but when the applications were in the Faculty found no one "who combined with the other requisite attainments, a practical experience in the conduct of a well-ordered library." A qualified man had to be found elsewhere, and "many of the members who were most interested in the subject were disposed to look only to Germany for a librarian, and the library of Göttingen was the model to which they especially wished our own institution to be conformed." The salary was raised from less than two hundred pounds to not below four hundred, and the position offered to the eminent German philologist G. F. Benecke, who was then assistant librarian in the Göttingen University Library, in anticipation of "the great advantages which a Librarian so eminently qualified" would confer on the institution. Sir William Hamilton, who conducted the correspondence, assured Benecke that in case he accepted, there could be no doubt about

[33] Chambers, op.cit., pp. 345-346, and John William Donaldson, The New Cratylus, 2nd edn. (London, 1850), pp. 45-46.

[34] It was the founder's belief that "the knowledge of Sanskrit was best calculated to promote the extension of Christianity in the East." Rosen's letters to Bopp in Lefmann, Anhang, pp. 181-208, give interesting information on Sanskrit studies in England, especially pp. 202-205 on the first appointment to the Boden chair.

his appointment, which would also make him "at once acquainted with the best society of Edinburgh and Scotland; and while in this country, we greatly admire literary and learned men, a Göttingen professor (I am sorry to say it) would find almost no rivals in the extent and depth of his erudition." Benecke might find himself a bit out of his element, but Hamilton could assure him that "a feeling is . . . now beginning to prevail in favour of the literature of your country; and it will probably soon be as keenly studied as it has hitherto been shamefully neglected. In our library there is by far the best and most numerous collection of German books that exists in Britain." Benecke did not accept, but David Irving, who received the appointment, was sent to Göttingen to learn from Benecke, and though he did not as yet understand the German language, he was introduced to Benecke as "an enthusiastic admirer of the learning and classical literature of your countrymen."[35] Five years later, the same position was again offered to a European scholar and philologist of the highest qualifications, Rasmus Rask, who for several years had been assistant librarian in the University of Copenhagen. Rask had not at home received the advancement he could reasonably have expected, but he did not accept the offer, though the new position would have placed him in financial circumstances he could never hope to attain in Denmark. The offer did, however, induce the authorities to make Rask professor of literary history with special emphasis on Asiatic literature.[36]

In Germany the state of the universities was very different. Here, after the middle of the eighteenth century, a rising feeling of national identity as well as accel-

[35] Rudolf Baier (ed.), *Briefe aus der Frühzeit der deutschen Philologie an Georg Friedrich Benecke* (Leipzig, 1901), pp. 28-38.
[36] N. M. Petersen, "Bidrag til Forfatterens Levned" in H. K. Rask (ed.), *Samlede tildels forhen utrykte Afhandlinger*, I, 99 and 85.

erated activity in all fields of thought and learning brought about a renaissance of academic endeavor such as no country had seen for centuries. The leader was the great Hanoverian institution, the University of Göttingen, whose recent foundation in 1736 had left it unencumbered by tradition. Guided by such men as Albrecht von Haller, Lichtenberg, Michaelis, and Heyne, it quickly achieved a position of eminence both in research and teaching, its chief strength being its almost unprecedented liberality of thought, high standards of exact and critical scholarship, and the scientific and historical realism to which it was committed from the outset. Here and at Halle, the seminar first came into being under the classical philologists C. G. Heyne and F. A. Wolf.[37] Modeled on the theological seminar, which trained its students for the active duties of the ministry, the philological seminar was designed to prepare the students for advanced teaching and independent scholarship. Placing the burden of work on the participants, it emphasized critical independence and precision rather than the mere absorption of secondhand knowledge, an innovation of such obvious importance that it was soon copied in other branches of learning. In Germany philology became the central academic discipline—"philology" in the German sense as the historical knowledge of human nature or in August Boeckh's comprehensive definition "die Erkenntniss des Erkannten," i.e. no less than the study of the history and knowledge of all human thought and activity.

This system, both academic and social, greatly benefited the new Oriental, comparative, and Germanic philologies, which readily found a place in the universities as soon as they could satisfy the same high standards of exact and comprehensive scholarship as those that already obtained in classical philology. Nothing was left to

---

[37] See "F. A. Wolf" in *Essays of the Late Mark Pattison*, ed. Henry Nettleship (Oxford, 1889), I, 362ff.

the dilettantes and the amateurs; science and learning
became a profession—a development which in retrospect
has perhaps turned out to be not altogether a good thing.
The German universities became the wonder of Europe,
which could learn about them from Madame de Staël's
memorable commonplaces. "Tout le nord de l'Allemagne
est rempli d'universités les plus savantes de l'Europe.
Dans aucun pays, pas même en Angleterre, il n'y a autant
de moyens de s'instruire et de perfectionner ses facultés."
The professors, she said, were not only "des hommes
d'une instruction étonnante, mais ce qui les distingue
surtout, c'est un enseignement très-scrupuleux. En Allemagne on met de la conscience en tout, et rien en effet
ne peut s'en passer." But she also observed that "une
distance immense sépare les esprits du premier et du
second ordre, parce qu'il n'y a point d'intérêt, ni d'objet
d'activité, pour les hommes qui ne s'èlevent pas à la hau-
teur des conceptions les plus vastes. Celui qui ne s'occupe
de l'univers, en Allemagne, n'a vraiment rien à faire.
. . . L'éducation intellectuelle est parfaite en Allemagne,
mais tout s'y passe en théorie."[38] It was this enthusiasm
for learning, this drive toward commanding views, that
almost overnight transformed the new philology into a
science. In Germanic, and especially Anglo-Saxon, philology the Germans were soon so far ahead that the craft
had to be learned from them for almost the next hundred
years, if not in the quiet atmosphere of the University of
Copenhagen.[39] In those two places Kemble and Thorpe

[38] De L'Allemagne (Nouvelle édition, Paris, 1844), Part I, Ch.
xviii "Des Universités Allemandes."

[39] The great emphasis on Anglo-Saxon studies in Germany continued throughout the nineteenth century. In his Encyklopaedie
und Methodologie der Englischen Philologie (Heilbronn, 1888),
Gustav Körting gave a list of German university teachers of English philology, 35 altogether at 21 different universities, including
such names as Zupitza (Berlin), Sievers (Halle), Kluge (Jena),
Wülker (Leipzig), Vietor (Marburg), Einenkel (Münster),
Brandl (Prague), and ten Brink (Strassburg) (pp. 25-30). Only

sought philological training before they established the new philology on a secure foundation in England in the 1830's.

About Benjamin Thorpe's long life (1782-1870) little appears to be known before 1826, when he went to Copenhagen, chiefly to study under Rask. What exactly induced Thorpe to seek learning in Copenhagen is not clear, but he must have known of its good school of historical studies. If he did not as yet have firsthand knowledge of Rask's work, he could have read about it in Grimm's eloquent tribute to Rask in the foreword to the first edition of his *Grammatik*.[40] Interrupted by a few trips back to London, Thorpe's stay lasted until 1830. In that year he returned to London and also published at Copenhagen his highly influential translation of Rask's *Sproglaere* as a *Grammar of the Anglo-Saxon Tongue,* about which it has rightly been said that it founded the "scientific study of Anglo-Saxon."[41] With this translation and the other publications that soon followed, Thorpe established himself as the first professional English philologist.

Rask's *Grammar* in Thorpe's translation was remarkable for a number of reasons, but first of all because a model work by a great philologist now became available to English readers. Even if they could not judge its philology, they would see at a glance that it was superior, both in clarity and arrangement, to Bosworth's *Elements,*

---

5 English names came to mind: Morris, Sweet, Skeat, Ellis, and Furnivall (pp. 25-32).

40 *Deutsche Grammatik,* I (1st edn., 1819), xviii-xix, with mention of Rask's *Undersøgelse,* which had then just come into Grimm's hands, too late to have any influence on the 1st edition. He may also have been guided by references to Rask's *Sproglaere* in Bosworth's *Elements* (London, 1823), e.g. pp. 80-81, 140, 144, 154, 156.

41 See Vilhelm Thomsen, "Rasmus Kristian Rask" in Thomsen's *Samlede Afhandlinger* (Copenhagen, 1919), I, 134.

which brought Thomas Jefferson to despair. "If, indeed, this be the true genius of the Anglo-Saxon language," he said, "then its difficulties go beyond its worth, and render a knowledge of it no longer a compensation for the time and labor its acquisition will require; and, in that case, I would recommend its abandonment in our University, as an unattainable and unprofitable pursuit."[42] The *Elements* demonstrated the impossibility of producing a philological work of Continental standards on the basis of the English tradition. Still, Rask's sources were also at Bosworth's disposal: Hickes' *Thesaurus,* Lye's *Dictionarium Saxonico et Gothico-Latinum,* and Somner's *Dictionarium Saxonico-Latino-Anglicum.* He had used these auxiliaries, he said, to the utmost of his power, but he had also—and this made a vast difference—"followed my own course throughout, in which the Icelandic has been my surest guide."[43] It was not lack of material but lack of method that made the difference. Bosworth's use of the old Anglo-Saxon characters made the book typographically forbidding, and on doubtful points, as he said, he made continued reference "to our best philological writers and grammarians, Wallis, Wilkins, Harris, Monboddo, Tooke, Crombie, Grant, and others."[44] His section on "Prosody" and Rask's "Of Versification" offer a good example of the difference. Bosworth found it "probable that Anglo-Saxon poetry arose from the desire of the people to greet their chieftains," and that "when the style of the nation had been improved into a easy and accurate prose, the ancient style may have been preserved by the bards, from interest and design, and by the people from habit and veneration."[45] Rask did not spec-

[42] "Postscript, January, 1825" to his *Essay Towards Facilitating Instruction in the Anglo-Saxon . . . for the Use of the University of Virginia* (New York, 1851), p. 23.

[43] *Grammar,* pp. xlix-lii.

[44] Bosworth, p. xxxiii.   [45] *Ibid.,* pp. 210-211.

ulate on origins, but opened with a plain statement: "The Anglo-Saxon versification, like the Icelandic, and that of the other ancient Gothic nations, has a peculiar construction, the chief characteristic of which does not, as in the Phrygian tongues, consist in syllabic quantity, but in *Alliterative Rime,* or *Alliteration.*"[46]

The Preface gave a good example of Rask's method. At the time, it was widely believed that Anglo-Saxon and the Scandinavian languages were intimately related and that the former was the source of Danish. To refute this belief, Rask showed for the first time that the two groups are distinct branches of Germanic, what we now call West and North Germanic. Referring to structural differences, Rask conducted a brilliant argument, steadily proceeding through parallel passages of increasing age, to the conclusion that the old hypothesis "would be at variance with all historical accounts, and against all internal evidence derived from the structure of language itself."[47] In practical matters, the *Grammar* also had an important effect. In the Danish edition he had already abandoned Anglo-Saxon letters in favor of the Roman alphabet, retaining only þ and ð, whose "rejection from the English alphabet is much to be regretted." The importance of this innovation will appear later, but his reasons may be stated here. He gave them succinctly in a single paragraph at the end of his Preface:

> The adoption of the Roman alphabet, in the present work, is the result of mature deliberation. The written Anglo-Saxon characters, as they appear in the MSS, being themselves a barbarous, monkish, corruption of

[46] *Grammar,* p. 135. "Phrygian" was the current term for Greek and Latin, following Adelung's and Vater's *Mithridates.*

[47] *Grammar,* p. xxiii. The argument begins on p. iii, and is followed by an equally remarkable refutation of Rühs's thesis that all Icelandic meters are derived from the Anglo-Saxon; he was referring to Chr. Fr. Rühs, *Ueber den Ausgang der Isländischen Poesie aus der Angelsächsischen* (Berlin, 1813).

the Roman, and the printed ones, a very imperfect imitation of the MSS, to persist . . . in the use of them (however venerable their appearance) seems to be without good reason; for though called Anglo-Saxon, they are no other than those employed, at the same time, in the writing of Latin; if therefore we would be consistent, we ought to employ types to represent every variation of the monkish characters, throughout the middle ages; as the handwriting underwent many changes, before the discovery of printing, and the restoration of the Roman alphabet.[48]

During the fall and winter following the publication of Rask's *Grammar*, Thorpe was very busy with a matter which, if it was not entirely a credit to his moral character, led to what can only be called a "crash program" for the publication of Anglo-Saxon texts. N.F.S. Grundtvig was then undoubtedly the greatest Old-Norse and Anglo-Saxon scholar. He had translated Snorre, Saxo Grammaticus, and *Beowulf*. In 1815 he had written a very critical review of Thorkelin's edition, in which he had identified the Chochilaicus mentioned in Gregory of Tours' *Historia Francorum* with the Hygelac of the poem, Beowulf's uncle and the king of the Geats who fell in the raid on the Frisian coast.[49] In the summers of 1829,

---

[48] *Grammar*, p. lv. In his *Inaugural Lecture*, James Ingram had "purposely printed the few specimens here given of the Saxon languages with common types, because there is only one Saxon character, þ, which is not represented equally well by the Roman" (p. 45), but in his edition of the Saxon Chronicle (1823), he had reverted to the Saxon characters though it delayed publication (Preface, p. xvi). Rask was not following Ingram but well-established practice in Danish text publication, and Ingram's use of the Roman type was not referred to in the future.

[49] He repeated the identification two years later in an eighty-page examination of the poem which appeared in another Danish journal, and restated it with full references in the introduction to his translation. See R. W. Chambers, *Beowulf, an Introduction*, 3rd edn. (Cambridge, 1959), p. 4. Chambers calls this

1830, and 1831, he visited England to read and copy Anglo-Saxon manuscripts in the libraries. He caused surprise and embarrassment in the British Museum by asking for the transcription of the Exeter Book which he assumed they had. They promised to procure a copy, but in the meantime Grundtvig went to Exeter and copied it himself. He appeared in so many libraries—in the Inner Temple, the Althorp Library, in university and college libraries in Oxford and Cambridge—that his hosts began to wonder whether Anglo-Saxon manuscripts perhaps were more interesting than they realized. It was still widely believed that the contents of these remains of antiquity were "insipid and tedious" and that their publication could only be justified by "the important lights which may be thrown on the history and operations of the human mind by researches into the origin and formation of languages," a view which even to those who did not wish to accept it may have appeared sufficiently plausible for them to prefer not to open that Pandora's box.[50] Early in July of 1830, during his second visit, Grundtvig dined with "some *Radicals* who decided, if possible, to found a society for the publication of Anglo-Saxon MSS, and considering both the statements of the Archbishop (with whom I had an audience yesterday after a brief exchange of letters) and the sentiments of other people, I have no doubt that a large society for medieval history could be formed, if only the matter was approached in the right way." At that time he had apparently already made a sketch for such a proposal. Late

---

identification "the most important discovery ever made in the study of *Beowulf*." For Grundtvig's literary insights, see Kemp Malone, "Grundtvig as Beowulf Critic" in *Review of English Studies*, XVII (April, 1941), pp. 129-138, which offers extensive quotations.

[50] *Literary Journal*, I (1806), 194, in a review of George Ellis's *Specimens of Early English Metrical Romances* (3 vols.; London, 1805). The reviewer may have been James Mill.

in the summer, after his return to London from Exeter and Oxford, Mr. Black of the publishers Black, Young and Young made him "a sort of proposal for the publication of Anglo-Saxon poems."[51] The fall saw the appearance of Grundtvig's *Bibliotheca Anglo-Saxonica. Prospectus for the Publication of the most valuable Anglo-Saxon Manuscripts.* The library was to comprise ten volumes and include *Beowulf,* Caedmon, the Exeter Book, Layamon, and a collection of Homilies. Grundtvig planned to return the next summer to begin the work.

But he met an unpleasant surprise when he returned to London late in June of 1831. Benjamin Thorpe had managed to get a look at the manuscript of the *Prospectus* in the offices of Black, Young and Young, and when it

[51] See L. Schrøder (ed.), *Christian Molbech og Nikolai Frederik Severin Grundtvig, En Brevvexling* (Copenhagen, 1888), pp. 170-171 (letter of July 6, 1830); the same work reprints, pp. 213-218, Grundtvig's own account of the events, written after his third visit in 1831. See also *N.F.S. Grundtvigs Breve til hans Hustru under Englandsrejserne 1829-1831* (Copenhagen, 1920), p. 134 (letter of September 9, 1830). Grundtvig uses the English word "Radicals," which, judging by other uses of the word in the correspondence, must refer to political radicals. He elsewhere talks of the "radical printer," Richard Taylor. The description "radical" would fit Kemble, but Grundtvig did not make his acquaintance until late in July of 1831, when Kemble took a seat at the same table in the British Museum and spoke to Grundtvig in German— "a handsome young man whom I think I also saw here last year." Next day they met and talked about Anglo-Saxon, walking around Regent's Park and later returning to the Kemble residence for tea and coffee. He does not seem to have met Kemble again, and later passed somewhat adverse judgment on his philology. See *Grundtvigs Breve,* pp. 166-170, and Grundtvig, *Mands Minde* (Copenhagen, 1877), p. 463. John Bowring, whom Grundtvig did not much care for, may have had a hand in promoting the project for text publication. He spent a month at Exeter while Grundtvig was there, annoying the latter by his indiscriminate snooping in the contents of the Chapter Library while Grundtvig was copying the Exeter Book. See Schrøder, pp. 173-174 (letter of July 25, 1830). Some other relevant facts and correspondence are available in Elias Bredsdorff, "Grundtvig in Cambridge" in the *Norseman,* X (1952), 114-123.

came out he voiced amazement that Grundtvig should have taken up his own plan, an allegation Mr. Black could fortunately reject since he had himself made the proposal.[52] The new subscription list was a little longer, but contained most of the names which had also appeared in Grundtvig's list. By the end of the summer, Grundtvig's plan had finally passed into other hands. He was happy that he had after all achieved his objective; the manuscripts would now be published, but he was sorry that it came about under those circumstances, and he later spoke of Thorpe's theft. If Grundtvig had read the *Gentleman's Magazine*, he would much sooner have known what was afoot. He would then have seen that the Society of Antiquaries, in its meeting on March 17, 1831, had passed a resolution "for the publication of Anglo-Saxon and early English writers." He would have found no mention of his own name, but he would perhaps have

[52] Georg Christensen and Stener Grundtvig (eds.), *Breve fra og til N.F.S. Grundtvig* (2 vols.; Copenhagen, 1924-1926), II, 193-195 (letter of June 26, 1831). For a full discussion of Grundtvig's philological work in England and of the circumstances surrounding the project for a *Bibliotheca Anglo-Saxonica*, see Helge Toldberg, "Grundtvig og de Engelske Antikvarer" in *Orbis Litterarum*, V (1947), pp. 258-311 (with English summary, though most of the cited material is also in English), esp. pp. 284-306. This highly informative article is primarily based on unprinted material, of which the most important is Sir Frederic Madden's Diary, now in the Bodleian Library. Late in August 1830, Madden noted that Grundtvig intended "to have a transcript made of Layamon with the intention of depositing it in the Royal Library at Copenhagen, & perhaps of publishing it. This will be a disgrace to England" (p. 281). During the same days, Thorpe was already busy taking over Grundtvig's plan. Meetings were held, and by the middle of December, Madden noted in his Diary: "Agreed to join some gentlemen in forming a Society for the purpose of publishing Saxon & Early English MSS. in opposition to Grundtvig's plan, which is a reproach to English scholars. I am to undertake Layamon" (289-291). By March 1831, it had been agreed that the Society of Antiquaries, rather than a new society, would undertake the publication. On Grundtvig as philologist, see Helge Toldberg, *Grundtvig som Filolog* (Copenhagen, 1946).

been amused to discover that the Society had been moved by the reflection, that "while in France, Germany, Denmark, and Sweden, much has been done of late for the cultivation of ancient native literature, it has been a source of mortification to the English antiquary and philologist, that in this country few have been the steps taken, during the last century, towards communicating to the world the literary treasures preserved among us, from the times of our Saxon and Anglo-Norman forefathers." They proposed the publication of Caedmon, Layamon, Ormulum, *Beowulf*, the Exeter Book, Apollonius of Tyre, Aelfric's Grammar, and the Gospels. An Anglo-Saxon committee having been formed at the next meeting, it was decided that "the works shall be printed in the ancient Characters, and be accompanied, in every case, with an English translation," and that Richard Taylor would be the printer.[53] The crash program had begun.

During the next two decades, Thorpe and Kemble published an unprecedented number of texts from the original manuscripts. Thorpe brought out his *Caedmon* in 1832 under the auspices of the Society of Antiquaries. It was followed in 1834 by *Apollonius of Tyre*, next year by the *Libri Psalmorum*, and in 1842 by the *Anglo-Saxon Version of the Holy Gospels* and, again for the Society of Antiquaries, the *Codex Exoniensis*. A few

[53] *Gentleman's Magazine*, CI (March, 1831), 253-254, and advertisement at back of Thorpe's *Analecta Anglo-Saxonica* (London, 1834). (Cf. Toldberg in *Orbis Litt.*, p. 293.) It seems apparent that the matter, in addition to national rivalry, also involved competition between Black, Young and Young, and Richard Taylor, who had the Anglo-Saxon type which was, for instance, used in his edition of the *Diversions of Purley* in 1829. Black, Young and Young had reissued Grundtvig's *Prospectus* with a list of subscribers in April of 1831, no doubt because they knew what was happening. In May, the *Gentleman's Magazine* carried a full notice of Grundtvig's *Bibliotheca* under their name in the "Literary and Scientific Intelligence" (*ibid.*, pp. 450-451).

years later came the *Homilies of the Anglo-Saxon Church*, published for the Aelfric Society, for which Kemble did the *Poetry of the Codex Vercellensis* and the *Dialogue of Salomon and Saturnus*. Kemble had in the meantime brought out the text of *Beowulf* in 1833, and four years later the translation, both dedicated to Grimm, along with their amusingly conflicting prefaces—neither Kemble nor Thorpe ever knew, or acknowledged, Grundtvig's identification of Hygelac, and Thorpe in his edition later attributed it to someone else. All these editions, except the *Caedmon*, followed Rask's use of Roman type and most of them were supplied with translations and complete, or nearly complete, glossaries. One significant result was that Thorpe became the first English Germanic philologist to attract attention abroad. Kemble had already in May of 1833 written to Jacob Grimm about Thorpe's *Caedmon* and his own *Beowulf*, then being printed; and early the next year he sent copies of both. Grimm wrote a review of the former for the *Göttingische Gelehrte Anzeigen* which in England was used to advertise the edition: "Our chief hope is now placed in the uncommon zeal and productive activity of two scholars in England, for whom the honour seems reserved of rescuing the study of the Anglo-Saxon tongue (which for every genuine Englishman should indeed be a patriotic object) from the long debasement into which it has hitherto been sunk. . . . When such rich sources are once laid open, it will be our care in Germany to avail ourselves of the manifold advantages which must infallibly arise from them for the investigation of our language and literature."[54]

But the work which was most in the public eye was Thorpe's *Analecta Anglo-Saxonica* or "a selection in prose and verse from Anglo-Saxon authors of various

[54] Advertisement at end of Thorpe's *Analecta*.

ages, with a glossary, designed chiefly as a first book for students." It was an original work and contained many excerpts which had never been published. As a reader it held its ground, with a reissue in 1846, until it was replaced by Sweet's *Reader* in 1876, though others had in the meantime appeared both in the United States and in Germany. The Preface had expressed the hope that by its publication "the study of the old vernacular tongue of England, so much neglected at home, and so successfully cultivated by foreign philologists, shall be promoted in the land where it once flourished." It was printed in Roman type and gave rise to the bitter Anglo-Saxon controversy, which was the last battle between the old and the new. The leader in the fight was the young man from Cambridge, John Mitchell Kemble, who was more aggressive than Thorpe, more so, in fact, than most men.[55]

Kemble was born in 1807 into the well-known family of actors. He was sent to school at Clapham under Charles Richardson, the disciple of Horne Tooke and known for his lexicography, on which he is said to have employed his more intelligent pupils. As a boy, Kemble took a strong interest in chemistry, an interest he retained for the rest of his life. He went into residence at Trinity College, Cambridge, in 1825. He sat for his examinations in 1829, but the examiners were not satisfied with his performance, and the degree was deferred to give him a chance to improve his knowledge of Paley and Locke and to adopt a more sympathetic attitude toward them—in the examination he had called the former a "miserable sophist" and talked of the latter's "loathsome infidelity," opinions which are interesting in the light of his religious outlook and later philological endeavors. At Cambridge

[55] On Kemble and his publications, see Bruce Dickins' informative monograph "John Mitchell Kemble and Old English Scholarship" in *Proceedings of the British Academy 1939*, pp. 51-84. I have followed its ascriptions.

he was a member of the group of young men who were known as the Apostles, though the official title of their little group was the "Cambridge Conversazione Society," a discussion club limited to twelve members. Here Kemble formed close friendships with Richard Chenevix Trench, F. D. Maurice, Richard Monckton Milnes (the first Lord Houghton), Alfred and Frederick Tennyson, and William Bodham Donne.[56] In poetry the group was devoted to Shelley, Keats, Wordsworth, and Coleridge; in politics they were liberal followers of Bentham and Mill; in theology they were opposed to the Oxford movement. Kemble was one of the most prominent among them and summed up their outlook in the sentence: "The world is one great thought, and I am thinking in it." During his student years, Kemble was also a frequent speaker in the Union Society. His ardent spirit and constitutional fervor found expression in an ill-fated expedition to Spain in support of General Torrijos and the Spanish Constitutionalists. He went to Spain in the fall of 1830, where he joined Trench and other liberal-minded young men who took up residence at Gibraltar in a house they called Constitution Hall; they vowed to let their beards grow till the hour of freedom had come and listened to Kemble's disquisitions on German metaphysics, his favorite subject. But things did not turn out well; Trench left in February 1831, while Kemble held out three months longer. The end came on December 1, 1831, when Torrijos and his men were forced to surrender and all were executed on the esplanade at Malaga, including the one remaining Englishman. The events had an important effect on Kemble's life because they barred his hope of obtaining a living in the Church of England, for which he had already begun to prepare before the Spanish adventure.

[56] Frances M. Brookfield, *The Cambridge 'Apostles'* (New York, 1906), pp. 4ff.

From then on he was free to devote all his energies to the subject he loved best: philology.

It was natural for Kemble to seek to think his thoughts in Germany, and thither he resorted for the first time in the long vacation of 1829. He went to Heidelberg, where he saw Trench, and later to Munich, where he read Kant and attended lectures on philology. He was much impressed by the German universities and wrote home to Milnes "that the depth of the knowledge of the young men there is something he could hardly have conceived; they studied everything, and everything well."[57] His friend Donne called Germany Kemble's "spiritual cradle,"[58] and Trench was so concerned that Kemble might not return to England that he exhorted him in these words to come back: "I am sure you could do much more good for yourself and others here."[59] He did return, and from 1832 to 1835 he studied assiduously at Cambridge, where he used the Anglo-Saxon manuscripts in the Parker Collection. In 1834 he also lectured on the subject of the "history of the English language in the Anglo-Saxon period," but according to one source at least, the lectures were not a success and a second course, though planned, was never given.[60] In the late summer and early

[57] T. Wemyss Reid, *The Life, Letters, and Friendships of Richard Monckton Milnes, First Lord Houghton* (New York, 1891), I, 90.

[58] Brookfield, p. 168.

[59] *Ibid.*, p. 163.

[60] Dickins, p. 59. There is some disagreement on this point. "Our Weekly Gossip" in the *Athenaeum*, No. 1536 (April 4, 1857), p. 439, says: "After making a good deal to do about [the lectures], he obtained the use of the Divinity School to lecture in, and it was pretty well crowded at the first lecture, but the lecture itself was such a sickener and so unintelligible, that at the second myself and I think two others formed the whole audience." Then Kemble suggested that the lectures be held in his private quarters, but the lectures ended after the third meeting. His friend W. B. Donne, however, writing Kemble's obituary in *Fraser's Magazine*, LV (May, 1857), 614, did not support that account. Though the

autumn of the same year he visited Göttingen for the first time and spent all his spare time with the Grimms, with whom he formed a warm and lasting friendship.[61] From now on, Kemble devoted the rest of his life to philology in the German sense, embracing literature, language, ancient law, history, and archaeology. From 1835 to 1844, its entire lifetime, Kemble was also editor of the *British and Foreign Review; or European Quarterly Journal,* in which he published many articles of general interest on subjects that occupied him outside his chief scholarly work. Kemble was more often right than wrong; he was tough-minded and alert and always ready to take strong action against the things and people he disliked. English philology would have been very different without his powerful personality.

In August 1834, Kemble wrote to Trench: "I cut politics, and stick to Teutonics, which progress bravely. I have carried the point of getting people to take an interest in their own language, have shown them the system, and, even more, have created a school which will take up my work when I cease from labour. Who says that this is nothing to have achieved?"[62] Today no one would ques-

---

audience thinned, the lectures continued to be attended by some of the most distinguished members of the university and established Kemble's reputation as the first of living Anglo-Saxon scholars. There is good reason to believe that Kemble's lectures were difficult to follow, at least for an English audience, for a 51-page review of Grimm's *Deutsche Grammatik,* written and set in type for the *Foreign Quarterly Review* in 1833, was never printed because it was considered too technical, but he sent a copy of it to Grimm next year along with his own *Beowulf* and Thorpe's *Caedmon.* (See Dickins, pp. 59, 61.)

[61] Dickins, p. 61. Jacob Grimm's letters to Kemble, spanning the years from July 13, 1833 to May 15, 1846, will be found in Hans Gürtler and Albert Leitzmann (eds.), *Briefe der Brüder Grimm* (Jena, 1923), pp. 76-102. They are mainly concerned with philological matters and contain interesting and frank opinions of other philologists and their work. Thorpe's name is often favorably mentioned.

[62] Dickins, p. 73.

tion Kemble's confident appraisal of his own achievement. But at the time of writing, he was already engaged in the Anglo-Saxon controversy, which perhaps, measured by its consequences, was as important as his scholarly publications in determining the nature and future course of Anglo-Saxon studies.

Although the controversy began in 1834, it had been apparent for some time that the differences between the "new Saxonists" and the old were too numerous and too important to be resolved without open discussion, though no one could have foreseen the bitter personal attacks which soon became one of its prominent features. The old Saxonists were antiquaries in the English tradition rather than philologists and were heavily represented in the publishing societies, especially in the Society of Antiquaries. The new Saxonists stood for the Continental philology of Rask and Grimm, with Thorpe and Kemble as their chief representatives. Before the controversy began to subside two years later, it had touched every aspect of philological scholarship and settled the issues in favor of the new philology.

The controversy opened with Kemble's review of Thorpe's *Analecta Anglo-Saxonica* in the *Gentleman's Magazine* for April 1834,[63] in whose columns it was fought; but Kemble had already the previous year introduced the most explosive issue in a review of Thorpe's *Caedmon* in the same magazine.[64] The text was, according to the policy of the Society of Antiquaries, printed in

[63] New Series, I, 391-393. For a list of items in the controversy and ascriptions, see "Bibliotheca Anglo-Saxonica" in *Anglo-Saxonica*, eds. P. de Larenaudière and Francisque Michel, Pt. II (Paris and London, 1837), 152-154, which forms part of Michel's bibliography in which Kemble seems to have had a hand. This information is repeated in Richard Wülker, *Grundriss zur Geschichte der Angelsächsischen Litteratur* (Leipzig, 1885), p. 54. See also Dickins.

[64] CIII (April, 1833), 329-331.

the old Saxon characters, a practice to which Kemble naturally objected vehemently, hoping "that in England the good example set by Continental editors would be followed." He supported his case with references to Rask, Grimm, and a number of German editions, including Karl Lachmann's *Nibelungen Lied* and Schmeller's *Heliand*.[65] In the very favorable review of the *Analecta*—which, though printed by Richard Taylor, was not issued by the Society of Antiquaries—Kemble found occasion to commend Thorpe for his rejection, "with a true knowledge of their no-value," of "the silly characters which people call Saxon, except in the case of *th*, and *dh*." But showing his fiery temperament, Kemble also made other statements that were almost certainly calculated to create controversy and discussion. He insulted the Society of Antiquaries by calling the use of the old type "bibliomaniacal foppery," and in the same context complained about the price of the book. Worse yet, he waved the red flag by contrasting the superiority of Continental scholarship to the "incompetent ignorance" witnessed in England before Thorpe's translation of Rask and the *Caedmon*. Talking about the Anglo-Saxon professors "at one of our universities," he said that "had it not been for the industry of Danes and Germans, and those who drew from the well-heads of their learning, we might still be where we were, with idle texts, idle grammars, idle dictionaries, and the consequences of all these—idle and ignorant scholars." Instead of following the careful procedure of classical scholars, the English Saxonists had "begun by editing books which they could not hope to understand" with the result, Kemble said, that "we could mention, were we so inclined, Doctors, yea, Professors of Anglo-Saxon, whose doings in the way of false concords,

[65] Between the 1st and 2nd editions of the *Grammatik*, Grimm had, under Rask's influence, become a strong advocate of Roman type, which he used for the 2nd edition.

false etymology, and ignorance of declension, conjugation, and syntax, would, if perpetrated by a boy in the second form of a public school, have richly merited and been duly repaid by a liberal application of ferula or direr birch." Thus, in addition to the key issue concerning the characters to be used in the printing of texts, Kemble introduced two others: the incompetence of English scholars and the harm done by the bibliomaniacs. All these issues were to figure prominently in the controversy, which later branched off into a general attack on the universities. Countercharges and new charges followed in quick succession with increasing asperity.

The first communication to take up the challenge was a letter dated "Oxford, July 20," which appeared in the *Gentleman's Magazine* for August of the same year, 1834.[66] It called the review "flippant," its statements incorrect, and the writer a mere "tyro," who himself could be proved more guilty of errors than the scholars against whom the attack was aimed. Next month there followed another letter against the review of the *Analecta*, dated August 2.[67] Without identifying the writer of the review, this letter opens with a confident avowal that the editor of the magazine and English scholars are "too alive to the real worth of Old England, to be carried away by the fine-spun theories of German Literati, who, in divinity, philosophy, and even in philology, have winged their flight so far into the higher, or rather into the lower regions, as not only to enter into palpable darkness themselves, but by their mysticism have decoyed a few inexperienced followers." With clear reference to Kemble, it charges that "some of our half-educated countrymen,

[66] New Series, II, 140.
[67] New Series, II, 259-260. The letter is signed "T. W.," but identification with Thomas Wright is out of the question. He was led to the study of Anglo-Saxon by Kemble's encouragement and next month wrote a letter in defense of German scholarship, signed "M. N."

after spending a few months on the Continent, return surcharged not only with gloomy ideas on divinity, but even upon philology." The letter defends Lye's *Dictionary* as an excellent work, and mentions Turner, Bosworth, Conybeare, and Ingram with respect against the charge of "most incompetent ignorance." The last part of the letter takes issue with the practice, instituted by Rask and Grimm, of adding diacritical marks to indicate vowel length, citing Kemble's *Beowulf* as one of the offenders. Here the antiquary and the philologist stood opposed, for the former did not know, and might not have understood, that Rask and Grimm could establish vowel length by comparing old and modern dialects and languages and by observation of scribal practices. To the much maligned scholars "misled by the German school," these marks were one of the most significant results of the new philological method, whereas the antiquaries merely found their addition a violation of the sacred nature of the manuscripts, and proof that Kemble was "chained '*in* [Grimm's] *sound iron-bound system*' "—as the writer says, derisively quoting a phrase which Kemble had used in the Preface to his *Beowulf* edition. It is evident that there was no hope of compromise or understanding between the two parties.

Next month, October 1834, the *Gentleman's Magazine* carried no less than three letters directed to the controversy, one for the new philology, one against, and one that was impartial.[68] The first letter exposed the ignorance of the two attacks on Kemble and the inaccuracy, evident enough, of their charges against both Thorpe's *Analecta* and the review. The writer finds Thorpe's an admirable book, praises Kemble's *Beowulf*, defends the "accents" they had added, and advises the correspond-

[68] New Series, II, 362-364. The first, dated Cambridge, September 1, is signed "M. N." The second, dated Oxford, September 6, is signed "T. W." The third is signed "B." for Bosworth, dated Cambridge, September 5.

ents to "examine candidly this 'German system,' as they call it," and prove if they can that it is unsound. The second letter, which came from Oxford, was merely another ill-informed and ill-mannered attack on Kemble and his editing of *Beowulf*. The third letter was the first to attempt arbitration in the dispute; it pointed out that some accents after all are found in Anglo-Saxon manuscripts and commended both Kemble and Thorpe for their work, without openly giving offense to their attackers.

So far the dispute had been almost entirely confined to rather ill-tempered wrangling about the relative merits of two opposed attitudes. The wrangling itself was of some value, for at least it forced the parties to reconsider their principles and define their positions, but with that result already achieved, only a return to serious discussion and the introduction of fresh matter could justify a continuation. Fortunately two letters published in November and December accomplished this end. They were both signed "K. N.," which has been identified as the signature of Frederic Madden, since 1828 assistant keeper of manuscripts in the British Museum and known for his edition of *Havelock the Dane*, published in 1828.[69] Madden addressed himself to the aspect of the controversy which he was better qualified to deal with than any of his contemporaries, the principles of correct editing, of which he himself gave an excellent example in his edition of Layamon's *Brut*, published for the Society of Antiquaries in 1847.

In the opening of the first letter, Madden regrets that the dispute has degenerated into a mere "war of words," but finds that an impartial observer must admit that Kemble and the "modern school" are essentially in the right, holding with Kemble that "nothing but *malevolence*

[69] New Series, II (November, 1834), 483-486, dated October 15, and *ibid.*, pp. 591-594, dated November 6.

would cavil at the trivial errors which the very best scholars are daily found to commit." The letter then turns to
a discussion of Thorpe's glossaries to the *Caedmon* and
the *Analecta*, both of which Kemble, at the expense of
Lye, had praised for completeness and philological accuracy. Madden finds them useful and better than previous glossaries, but still inadequate. The greatest defect,
he thinks, is that the entries contain neither references to
the pages on which the words may be found nor the
oblique cases of nouns and the past tenses and participles
of the verbs, though all are indispensable to a correct
understanding of the grammatical structure of the language and its transition from Anglo-Saxon to Middle
English. Furthermore, Madden suggests that a collation
of the orthographical variations in different manuscripts
must be undertaken, for "these may often be found to
affect very considerably the *assumed* grammatical rules
at present laid down." Here Madden is touching very
important matters, to which the new philologists had paid
too little attention in the first flush of their enthusiasm.
If the old saxonists had known their business, they could
have made the same point. The issue can best be understood by reference to a passage in the first *Beowulf* Preface.[70] Here Kemble had said, in words that were later
cited against him—though he had in fact qualified his
statement by emphasizing the need always to give the
original reading:

All persons who have had much experience of Anglo-
Saxon MSS. know how hopelessly incorrect they in
general are; when every allowance has been made for
date and dialect, and even for the etymological
ignorance of early times, we are yet met at every turn
with faults of grammar, with omissions or redundancies of letters and words, which can perhaps only be ac-

[70] *Beowulf* (London, 1833), pp. xxiii-xxiv.

counted for by the supposition that professional copyists brought to their task (in itself confusing enough), both lack of knowledge, and lack of care. A modern edition, made by a person really conversant with the language he illustrates, will in all probability be much more like the original than the MS. copy, which, even in the earliest times, was made by an ignorant or indolent transcriber.

Naturally no careful editor could agree with these opinions. A mere philologist, however, could see little danger in such a procedure, for with Kemble he would not question Grimm's "sound iron-bound system," or, as Kemble pointed out using an interesting mechanical metaphor, the fact that "the laws of a language, ascertained by wide and careful examination of all cognate tongues, of the hidden springs and ground-principles upon which they rest in common, are like the laws of the Medes and Persians and alter not."

Behind this statement lies the conviction so fundamental to the new philologists, both Continental and English, that the study of language was as scientific as natural history, and that language was a sort of substance, subject to invariable laws, which once established had the same general validity and certainty as those that governed the "hidden springs" of matter and motion. If true, then the philological text might indeed be "much more like the original than the MS. copy." Still, nineteenth-century English philologists were more restrained than their German colleagues. The classical philologists, with a longer and independent tradition behind them, could have offered some useful advice on conjectural emendation and the "restoring" of texts, but they abstained from interference for many reasons, not all of them good ones. Madden's share in the great debate is therefore one of the most significant results of the controversy; his own editions clearly illustrated the philological utility of his principles. That they should, furthermore, be especially connected with the editing of a Middle-English text is perhaps no accident, for it forced him to pay attention both to the dialect and to the changes that had occurred from Anglo-Saxon. Kemble and Thorpe were almost exclusively concerned with Anglo-Saxon texts, which presented a relatively static picture that was not designed to force upon them an awareness of historical development. It was fortunate that Middle-English studies were introduced during the short time that now separated philology from the conception of the scheme for the *New English Dictionary*; for it would have been very different without Madden's model editions and without a clear view of the historical development of the language.

The bitter tone of the controversy returned with a signed article by Kemble on "Oxford Professors of Anglo-Saxon," dated November 15, and published in the December issue of the *Gentleman's Magazine*.[71] Earlier Kemble had just had time to read the letter against him in the August issue, before he left for his first visit to Grimm.[72] When he returned early in October, the controversy had taken the turn which he had anticipated, but this article was his first contribution since the original review. The title alone indicates that Kemble did not intend to let Oxford and the Anglo-Saxon professors off the hook. He makes no concessions, spares no one, and even suggests that the whole proceeding was "no more than one bubble of the effervescence produced by the installation of their new Chancellor," a reference to the election of the Duke of Wellington, whom Oxford had received on June 9 with the wildest enthusiasm, but a man for whose Toryism Kemble had no sympathy. Kemble especially levels his charges against Oxford's much

[71] New Series, II, 601-605.   [72] Dickins, p. 61.

admired Conybeare and his *Illustrations*, whose elementary errors he exposes in a couple of devastating pages. "These things may do at Oxford," Kemble comments, "but they will not do at Göttingen, at Munich, or at Cambridge." He concludes with a reference to the Oxford defender who had signed with the letters "T. W.": "I know not whether he has filled, does fill, or means to fill the Saxon chair in that University; but from the specimen of his ability which he has supplied in these letters, I can assure him that he is worthy to take his place in the long list of illustrious obscures who have already enjoyed that cheap dignity. His ignorance would have obtained for him the pity of my learned German friends, and of myself; his malice so happily tempered with impotence, has given him a juster title to that which he has obtained, our contempt." In a postscript to the article, Kemble promised a future letter on the principles of "accentuation."

This promise was fulfilled in a letter which appeared in July 1835; it was the last communication in the controversy to appear in the *Gentleman's Magazine*,[73] thus making Kemble appear to be the victor in the dispute. The letter is written "for the purpose of giving information to those who desire and deserve it." It is a clear, factual exposition, with tables and many examples, of the textual and philological bases for the correct determination of vowel length. Admitting that Rask in some cases would seem to have been misled by too ready acceptance of Old-Norse analogies, Kemble gives the first full account of the subject in English, as it had been explained by Grimm. In one illustration, Kemble, who had often been charged with mysticism, takes delight in dismissing the alleged "theosophic and psychological views of the Saxons respecting God and man, and good and evil." It had been held that "the Saxons were so deeply impressed

[73] New Series, IV, 26-30.

with the goodness of God and the wickedness of man's nature" that they had only two words for the four concepts: *God* for *deus* and *bonus,* and *Man* for *homo* and *noxia.* But Kemble points out that the vowel qualities of the Anglo-Saxon words for *bonus* and *noxia* are long, so that the four forms are in fact altogether different, which he proves by listing cognate forms in the other Old-Germanic languages. The point itself may appear trivial, but it shows clearly both the new philological method and its disinclination to make the phenomena of language the bases of metaphysical speculations, a danger which Dugald Stewart had already identified many years earlier. Kemble's letter does not end on a conciliatory note, for he concludes: "Against all quackery, and all quacks, I hold the old motto—'War to the knife!' " The reverberations of the controversy were felt for some time, but there was no longer any threat to the new philology.

In March 1835, a pamphlet against Kemble had appeared under the title *The Anglo-Saxon Meteor; or Letters in Defence of Oxford, Treating of the Wonderful Gothic Attainments of John M. Kemble, of Trinity College, Cambridge.* It was presumed to have been printed in Holland under the supervision of Joseph Bosworth, who had been English chaplain at Amsterdam and later at Rotterdam since 1829.[74] This scurrilous pamphlet does not seem to have had much effect, indeed its very nature

[74] Dickins, pp. 60-61. From a reference at the end of the second *Beowulf* Preface (liii-lv), it appears that the pamphlet used very devious means to slander Kemble, claiming that Grimm, to the question why he had spoken favorably of Kemble, should have answered: "Why, he has praised me, and one hand washes the other, one good turn deserves another." In a letter from Göttingen (July 14, 1837), Grimm wrote to Kemble: "Dem pamphletisten, sei es nun sicher Bosworth oder wer immer, haben Sie durch erwähnung seiner abgefeimten lüge zuviel vorschub geleistet; ich denke er wird schweigen, und wenigstens in dem halben dunkel bleiben" (Gürtler & Leitzmann, *Briefe,* p. 84).

seems to have aided Kemble's cause rather than harmed it. The controversy had shown that the old saxonists could make no constructive contribution to philology; they now had no more to say.

A few years later, Kemble found occasion to repeat some of the points he had made in the course of the controversy in his "Letter to Francisque Michel," which is in effect an introduction to Anglo-Saxon studies, written to accompany Michel's own *Bibliothèque Anglo-Saxonne*.[75] Here, in a letter to a scholar he respected, Kemble makes the same points as before about the defects of Lye's *Dictionary*, about bibliomania, the virtues of Thorpe's *Analecta*, and the use of Roman characters, and the addition of quantity signs in text editions—in short, all the points for which the controversy had secured acceptance and general agreement.[76] Kemble and Thorpe continued to edit texts according to their own principles, and they were soon joined by other scholars; while the antiquarians, the dilettantes, the amateurs, the exquisite connoisseurs, and the old saxonists withdrew to the sheltered confines of the exclusive publication clubs.

Even Joseph Bosworth made concessions. His *Dictionary of the Anglo-Saxon Language* was first published in 1838 after many years' work, with an introduction of no less than 208 pages, containing among other things a section on "The Essentials of Anglo-Saxon Grammar, with an Outline of Professor Rask and Grimm's Sys-

[75] *Anglo-Saxonica*, Pt. II; Kemble's contribution covers pp. 1-63 and Michel's bibliography pp. 67-168.

[76] Edwin Guest's *History of English Rhythms* (2 vols.; London, 1838), devoted part of Bk. III, ii (II, 4-17), to the Anglo-Saxon controversy, chiefly the matter of vowel quantity. His opinion of Grimm's account of "changes of letters" is curious; he found that "the *laws*, which regulate these changes, are barely glanced at." He was still looking for the causes of language, not merely its description.

tems."[77] In the Preface to that section, written in 1836—thirteen years after the appearance of Bosworth's own *Elements*—he made the following admission, carefully phrased in a passive construction: "It will be seen that, as information has increased, there has been a gradual approximation, in grammatical forms and accents, to the views of Professor Rask and Grimm."[78] An even more important concession, however, was Bosworth's choice of Roman type rather than the old Saxon characters, which he had used in his *Elements*: "After much consideration, the Roman character has been adopted in printing the A.-S. words, with the exception of the two peculiar letters þ and ð." His reason was the "thorough conviction that the Roman character would be the most legible, and would best show the identity of the present English with the Anglo-Saxon, as well as the clear analogy existing in the words of all the other Germanic languages," i.e. the very reason which Rask had first stated in his *Angelsaksisk Sproglaere* twenty years earlier. The dictionary filled a great gap in Anglo-Saxon scholarship and has survived, greatly expanded, to this day. Robert Meadows White, who was Rawlinsonian Professor 1834-1839, had also decided to prepare a dictionary, but abandoned his plan when he heard that Bosworth had nearly completed his.[79] Kemble had also several times stated his intention to make an Anglo-Saxon dictionary and mentioned in a letter that he was actively engaged in the work.[80] Kemble's and Thorpe's glossaries, published with

[77] Bosworth, *Dictionary of the Anglo-Saxon Language* (London, 1838), pp. clxxix-ccii.
[78] *Ibid.*, p. clxxxi.
[79] *Ibid.*, pp. clxxi, clxxvi.
[80] See second *Beowulf* Preface, p. li; and Brookfield, p. 178: "I am labouring in my vocation, that is getting on with my *Anglo-Saxon Lexicon*, which, if I complete my plan, will certainly be a book of some importance: but *Ars longa, vita brevis*! I aim at something rather more philosophical than the host of word-books, and I know that I cannot execute about a tithe of what I should

their editions, were important aids in the preparation of the *Dictionary* and deserve to be remembered. Financially Bosworth was undoubtedly the most favored Anglo-Saxon scholar that ever lived; his works brought him a fortune of 18,000 pounds, of which he in 1867 gave 10,000 to Cambridge University for the establishment of an Anglo-Saxon chair.

While competent Anglo-Saxon and soon also Middle-English scholars were laying the foundations of modern English philology, works of a wider appeal began to appear, proving that comparative philology was beginning to attract attention by virtue of its value to ethnography or, in Whewell's phrase, palaetiology, i.e. "those speculations which . . . refer to actual past events, and attempt to explain them by laws of causation."[81] Of these sciences, geology was the chief representative, but they included the study of languages, customs, forms of society, and political institutions, in which "we see a number of formations superimposed upon one another, each of which is, for the most part, an assemblage of fragments and results of the preceding condition." We may for instance say that "the English language is a conglomerate of Latin words, bound together in a Saxon cement; the fragments of the Latin being partly portions introduced directly from the parent quarry, with all their sharp edges, and partly pebbles of the same material, obscured and shaped by long rolling in a Norman or some

---

like to do; . . . When the root verb is *not found yet*, it will be given hypothetically in *italics*. . . . In old languages like Anglo-Saxon, the metaphorical uses of language have not overlaid the original system and vital vigour, and the metaphysics are readily comprehended. Moreover, '*Language in its spontaneous period is sensuous*,' which golden law write up on any Etymological Dictionary you possess. When a tongue becomes dead like the English of our own one day, Society keeps the key to its coffin" (letter to W. B. Donne, which by internal evidence can be dated 1840).

[81] William Whewell, *History of the Inductive Sciences* (3rd edn., London, 1847), III, 527-528 (1st edn., 1837).

other channel."[82] Language study was beginning to form an alliance with geology. It is significant, however, that two of the most popular and respected writers on philological matters also wrote extensively on ethnography, which seems to have been the chief end of their studies: J. C. Prichard and R. G. Latham. Prichard's chief philological work was *The Eastern Origin of the Celtic Nations Proved by a Comparison of their Dialects with the Sanskrit, Greek, Latin, and Teutonic Languages* (Oxford, 1831). It was the first work on comparative philology to be written by an Englishman and was often used as an authority of the same stature as Grimm's *Grammatik*. Prichard also wrote a work on *Researches into the Physical History of Man* (1813; and often reissued and enlarged). Latham was known both for his very popular *English Language* (1841) and for his *Natural History of the Varieties of Man* (1850).

In those years, geology was often used to support religious doctrine, and it was in this role that comparative philology made its appearance in two works. During Lent of 1835, Nicholas—later Cardinal—Wiseman delivered a series of twelve lectures in the drawing room of Thomas Cardinal Weld in the Palazzo Odescalchi in Rome. They were published at London the following year as *Twelve Lectures on the Connexion between Science and Revealed Religion* and had reached no less than six English editions by 1859. The first two lectures were devoted to the "Comparative Study of Languages," for "it is indeed by the simple history of this science, that we shall see the Mosaic account of the dispersion of mankind most pleasingly confirmed."[83] In spite of their ulterior purpose, these lectures provided a very adequate exposition of comparative philology. Another work of a similar nature was the Reverend W. B. Winning's *Man-*

[82] *Ibid.*, p. 484.
[83] (New York, 1837), p. 13.

ual of Comparative Philology, in which the Affinity of the Indo-European Languages is Illustrated, and Applied to the Primeval History of Europe, Italy, and Rome.[84] This work also made philology do service in religious matters, but in the process it gave a considerable body of philological information, though, of course, both Wiseman and Winning were convinced that comparative philology gave proof of the divine origin of language and of the biblical account of the Babylonian Confusion.

By the early 1840's, it was clear that Kemble and Thorpe had won the case for the new philology; they had also determined the future course of language study in England. Both had prepared careful, and fairly complete, glossaries to accompany the texts they published, and both had shown lively interest in early English history in general. Language study and history intersect in the historical dictionary. In his article on "English Lexicography"—a review of Charles Richardson's (1835), Webster's (1828), and Johnson's (1818 in Todd's revision) dictionaries—published in the *Quarterly Review*

[84] (London, 1838). Winning, it seems, was the first to use the term "Grimm's law," which is the title of a section on pp. 36-39. The first instance in the *OED* is three years younger, from Latham's *English Language*, p. 190: "In Comparative, or Historical Etymology, one of the most fruitful discoveries . . . is currently called *Grimm's Law*." Grimm used *consonanzvergleichung* for the act of observation, *lautverschiebung* for the facts established, but he used the word *gesetz* in a very different sense in connection with his notions of the *wesen* of a word, associated with the vowels and ablaut, and the *gestalt* of a word which resides in the consonants. Having listed the consonant variations according to Grimm, Kemble had referred to them as "this law." See his review of Ernest Jäkel, *Der Germanische Ursprung der lateinischen Sprache* (Breslau, 1830) in *Foreign Quarterly Review*, X (October, 1832), p. 382. (This was Kemble's first philological publication.) During the 1830's *gesetz* was widely used by Rudolf von Raumer and Bopp; see, e.g. *Vergleichende Grammatik*, 3rd edn., Vol. I (Berlin, 1868), 78, 92, 113, 119, 128, 130, 161, 164. A review of Grimm in the *Quarterly Review*, L (October, 1833), had talked of this "remarkable law" (p. 170).

in September 1835,[85] Richard Garnett had devoted the opening pages to a defense of philology; although it was new, and seemed—but merely seemed—excessively esoteric, could anyone doubt its usefulness?

It would have been equally easy to ask fifty or sixty years ago—and would at that time have sounded quite as plausibly—what can be the use of collecting and comparing unsightly fragments of bone that have been mouldering in the earth for centuries? But now, after the brilliant discoveries of Cuvier and Buckland, no man could propose such a question without exposing himself to the laughter and contempt of every man of science. Sciolists are very apt to despise what they do not understand; but they who are properly qualified to appreciate the matter know that philology is neither a useless nor a trivial pursuit,—that, when treated in an enlightened and philosophical spirit, it is worthy of all the exertions of the subtlest as well as most comprehensive intellect.[86]

Then, pointing to the use of language study, Garnett returned to the age-old puzzle of words and things: "The knowledge of words is, in its full and true acceptation, the knowledge of things, and a scientific acquaintance with a language cannot fail to throw some light on the origin, history, and condition of those who speak or spoke it." English language study was soon—before 1860—to seek the fulfillment of the promise contained in Garnett's words.

[85] LIV (September, 1835), 295-330.
[86] *Ibid.*, p. 296. This and other essays by Garnett are reprinted in *Philological Essays by the late Rev. Richard Garnett* (London, 1859), pp. 1-40.

CHAPTER VI

English Philology to 1860

The Philological Society of London and the Project for a New English Dictionary

Edwin Guest took the initiative in the formation of the Philological Society of London. On May 9, 1842, he issued a printed announcement with his signature, informing the recipients "that a meeting will be held on Wednesday the 18th of May, at One o'clock P.M., at the Rooms of the Statistical Society, No. 4, St. Martin's Place, for the purpose of forming a Philological Society." On the 28th, the *Athenaeum* carried a notice that the meeting had been held. With the Bishop of St. David's, Connop Thirlwall, in the chair, it had been resolved that a society be formed "for the investigation of the Structure, the Affinities, and the History of Languages; and the Philological Illustration of the Classical Writers of Greece and Rome." A council was formed, and during the next six months enough members were attracted to open the first formal meeting on November 25, with a reading of the list of original members, 203 in number. Most of the names were preceded by "Rev." and many followed by academic title, degree, and affiliation at Cambridge, London, Oxford, Dublin, Glasgow, and Edinburgh. Then the rules were read, the first being the statement of the Society's purpose given above, whereupon "Professor Latham commenced the reading of a paper on the dialects of the Papuan or Negrito race, scattered through the Australian and other Asiatic islands." Others who had also been active in the formation were Thirlwall, Thomas Hewitt Key, Henry Malden, Hensleigh Wedgwood, Dr. Arnold, and Dean Stanley, who had enlisted the support of members of Oxford University.[1]

The formation of the Philological Society marked the beginning of a new stage in the history of language study in England, as important and distinct as the period of a dozen years that began with the publication of Grundtvig's *Prospectus* and the translation of Rask's *Grammar*. Since 1830, the chief interest, methods, and results of the new philology had gained a respected position in English scholarship. The Anglo-Saxon controversy had taken up some of the issues that were bound to arise, and they had now, fortunately, been settled beyond reasonable disagreement. Still more important, English philology had assumed a certain character: the publication of texts accompanied by increasingly comprehensive glossaries, foreshadowing the renewed efforts which on this basis, though with a more definite purpose, were begun by the Early English Text Society in 1864. The work of the 1830's, however, had not been guided by any formal, scholarly organization, nor had any been needed, for Kemble and Thorpe had supplied the guidance, with the authority of Grimm, Grundtvig, and Rask behind them. By 1842 the initial impulse had run its course. Kemble became more and more absorbed in Anglo-Saxon history and archeology, and texts came more slowly from Thorpe's hands and were no longer sustained by the novelty they had at first enjoyed. On the other side, the positive achievement was balanced by very scant attention to the wider implications of historical and comparative phi-

[1] *Proceedings of the Philological Society*, I (1842-1844), i-vi ("Rules") and 1-6 ("List of Original Members"). The *Proceedings* were published every two years in six volumes until 1854. In that year the title was changed to *Transactions of the Philological Society*, published each year (without volume number). They will be cited as *PPS* and *TPS*. For Guest's role, see especially his wife's biographical sketch in the Prefatory Notice to the first volume of Guest's posthumous *Origines Celticae* (London, 1883), pp. ix-x.

lology, which had merely received popular exposition in a few works that made little pretense to originality. The institution of the Philological Society must in part be seen as an effort to redress the balance by extending the field of investigation beyond English.[2]

The Society has always been surprisingly reticent about its early history, but it has left a few traces. On April 11, 1851, the first item of business was that "the MS. Minute-book of a former Philological Society, which had its meetings at University College, London, was presented to the Society by Mr. Key, in accordance with the wishes of the Members of that Society."[3] This was the group which in the early 1830's had gathered around Friedrich August Rosen, including George Long, Key, and Malden, who were all originally classicists from Trinity College, Cambridge. Their chief concern had been comparative philology in the manner of Bopp's *Vergleichende Grammatik*. But it was also the Society's aim to pursue "the Philological Illustration of the Classical Writers of Greece and Rome." It proposed, in other words, to do both classical and new philology, a combination that was unusual at the time, and which it would seem reasonable to attribute to the common training, interests, and backgrounds of the original members. Did most of them per-

---

[2] The announcement in the *Athenaeum* (p. 463) had envisioned reports "upon the recent progress and present condition of the study of the Structure, Affinities, and History of Languages in other countries," and one of the first contributions to the first volume of the *Proceedings* was a 25-page "Notice of European Grammars and Lexicons of the Sanskrit Language" by Professor H. H. Wilson from Oxford, who was then also very active in the Royal Asiatic Society. In the first twenty years such reports were actually given very rarely, which is perhaps a sign of the Society's vitality.

[3] *PPS*, V (1850-1852), 61. Recent issues of the Society's *Transactions* carry a note informing the reader that "the Philological Society was established in its present form in 1842, consisting partly of members of a Society of the same name established at the University of London in 1830."

haps have ties before they met in the Society? Philology aside, was there an initial community of outlook, apart also from their scholarly work and their academic positions in 1842? A detailed examination of the list of original members, their education and earlier history, will show a very close connection with Cambridge, and especially with Trinity College, of whose importance in this respect we have already encountered unmistakable evidence: the "Apostles' Club," Kemble, and the Anglo-Saxon controversy. Trinity was also the college of the later Dean of Westminster, Richard Chenevix Trench, who at Cambridge was a close friend of Kemble.

The evidence is striking. Looking at the original list, we may confine our attention to those members 1) who were listed as then holding positions at Cambridge, Oxford, or in London; 2) who were high dignitaries in the Church; and 3) whose names alone strike us though they do not fall in either of the first two categories, e.g. Henry Hallam and George Grote, who are merely listed with name and address. The search yields one hundred names, or nearly half the total. Twenty-one of these had London affiliation, most of them with the University and a few with the British Museum and the Record Office. Twenty-six held positions at Oxford or received their education there. But fully 53 can be traced to Cambridge; of these again no fewer than 27 graduated B.A. from Trinity between 1810 and 1830, and 24 of these were past or present fellows of their college. Furthermore, the connection between Cambridge and London stands out. Five of the original members counted under Cambridge above, where they had also held fellowships, were now, in 1842, in important positions at the University of London— Archdeacon Lonsdale as Principal of King's College and the other four as professors. Among these four were R. G. Latham, formerly fellow of King's College and since 1839 professor of English Language and Literature in University College; T. H. Key, one-time fellow of Trinity and now occupying the chair of Comparative Grammar in University College; and Henry Malden, also a former fellow of Trinity, and since 1831—until 1876—professor of Greek in the same college as Latham and Key. All three had distinguished careers in philology, were members of the council of the Society from the beginning, and for many years remained among the most frequent contributors to its publication.[4]

The preponderance of Cambridge men is also evident in the original council, a situation that only gradually shifted toward London in the course of the first twenty years. Connop Thirlwall was president and remained in that post until 1868, when he was succeeded by Key. The three vice-presidents were Charles James Blomfield, the Bishop of London; Edward Maltby, Bishop of Durham; and Thomas Musgrave, Bishop of Hereford. All four were classical scholars of distinction and, except for Musgrave, former fellows of Trinity. Until 1867 the treasurer was Hensleigh Wedgwood, a former fellow of Christ's College; and among the remaining Cambridge members, in addition to Key, Malden, Latham, and Guest, were Kemble, William Hodge Mill, Richard Craven Hawtrey who was now headmaster of Eton, T. F. Ellis, and the Master of Trinity, William Whewell.

[4] George Long did not become a member of the Society until 1860, but he was also a former fellow of Trinity; in 1828 he became the first professor of Greek at the London University, a post he gave up in 1831 to devote his time to editorial work. He was succeeded by Malden, and in turn, in 1842, followed Key in the Latin chair at University College, when the latter moved into comparative grammar. Key was one of the founders of the London Library, where the Society held its meetings until May 1856, when the Society accepted the offer of the Royal Astronomical Society to hold its meetings in Somerset House. (See *TPS*, 1856, pp. 360-361.) During the 1840's, the secretary of the London Library was Kemble's and Trench's friend and contemporary at Cambridge, William Bodham Donne, who was also one of the original members of the Society.

On September 30, 1851, when Whewell wrote to his friend Julius Charles Hare, he was perhaps influenced by the mention earlier that year of the "former Philological Society," which had met at University College, London. He said: "You will think I am very idle if I try to call back your thoughts to etymologies, but I do not want you to do much. . . . You will recollect with pleasure our old Etymological Society of (I think) 1832, though so many of the members have been called away from this world of words to the realities beyond the grave. I want to send a few memoranda respecting that society to the existing Philological Society of London. I have all the papers belonging to our old Society, and some of them may throw some light on similar labours which others are pursuing. You were always the great workman with us."[5] He apparently received the information he had asked for and wrote the letter he had in mind. On February 20, 1852, the Friday-night assembly of scholars in the London Library again broke the Society's silence about its early history. Edwin Guest, the secretary, prefaced his reading of Whewell's recent letter with a few remarks to the effect that it was desirable to have a record of previous societies which had also devoted their efforts to philology, for "without it, the history of English scholarship could hardly be considered as complete; and there was danger, lest in subsequent inquiries questions might be opened which had already been sufficiently investigated." But, Guest continued, "the members . . . of the Philological Society would be pleased to hear, that with respect to one Society, to which many of them once belonged, they had now the means of supplying the want complained of."[6] Guest then read Whewell's letter, which

[5] I. Todhunter, *William Whewell, D. D., Master of Trinity College, Cambridge*. An account of his writings with selections from his literary and scientific correspondence (2 vols.; London, 1876), II, 368.
[6] See *PPS*, V, 133-142.

gave an account of the history and work of the Etymological Society, which held informal meetings at Cambridge during the early 1830's.[7] The whole Society having first agreed on certain classes of words "marked by some peculiarity in their relation or history," each member would take one class "with the injunction to collect as many specimens as he could of the Class, and to produce them at the next or some succeeding meeting of the Society"—a procedure in which it is hardly mistaken to recognize the influence of the German seminar or perhaps the method of the geological field trip with its classification, observation, discussion, and attempt to arrive at a "philosophical" arrangement of the material, which had in this fashion been brought together by the united efforts of the individual members. Whewell explained that the classes had headings such as "English words from Italian, Spanish, etc.," "Words derived from names of persons," "Hawking terms," and "False etymologies." He also gave examples, with profound apology for the inadequacy of their etymologies measured by the "far more complete and philosophical manner" that had been developed during the intervening twenty years. The work of the Society was, furthermore, directed toward a definite end; Whewell concluded: "In particular we had a grand, but I fear hopeless, scheme of a new Etymological Dictionary of the English language; of which one main feature was to be that the three great divisions of our etymologies, Teutonic, Norman, and Latin, were to be ranged under separate alphabets"—corresponding, so to speak, to ge-

[7] Whewell does not give the dates, but says (p. 142) that "some of our speculations were inserted in the *Philological Museum,* which was published at Cambridge in 1832 and 1833." One of its editors and most frequent contributors was Julius Charles Hare, who was one of Whewell's closest friends and, of course, himself a member of the Etymological Society. It seems likely that the Society lapsed when Hare, in 1832, accepted the living at Hurstmonceux, thus abandoning etymology for the "higher duties."

ological layers. In this plan it is tempting to see one of the first suggestions of the great project and joint enterprise which the Society soon undertook. And indeed, the audience did not fail to see the implications. The reading of the letter was, according to the secretary's report, "followed by a long and interesting conversation as to the best mode of promoting the objects of English scholarship. It was suggested that an organization of labour, such as was adopted in the Etymological Society of Cambridge, promised advantages that could not be expected from the isolated efforts of individuals; and the impression seemed very general, that a more systematic investigation of our language might lead to a much more satisfactory knowledge of its peculiarities."

In his letter Whewell also gave a list of twenty scholars who were members of the Society, seven of whom had later become original members of the Philological Society, including Whewell himself; John Lodge, the University librarian; James Prince Lee, then fellow of Trinity, "one of the most distinguished classical scholars ever known in the university"[8] and now the first·bishop of Manchester; Malden, Musgrave, Thirlwall, and Julius Charles Hare. Two promising members had died in the meantime: John Wordsworth and Hugh James Rose, the friend and teacher of Trench, who held his first ecclesiastical office as Rose's curate at Hadleigh in Suffolk. These men were all at Cambridge at the same time, most of them at Trinity, either as undergraduates or fellows or both, and a close friendship existed between several of them, especially between Rose, Thirlwall, Hare, and Whewell, who was very dependent on Hare in all serious matters, as their correspondence testifies.[9]

[8] See *Alumni Cantabrigienses*, Pt. II, s.v. "James Prince Lee."
[9] See Mrs. Stair Douglas, *The Life and Selections from the Correspondence of William Whewell, D. D.* (London, 1881), pp. 51, 205-249 *passim*, 285-292. Late in 1841, Whewell wrote to

Most of the members of the Etymological Society wrote for the *Philological Museum*, and in our effort to get at the community of background, outlook, and philological interest shared by the influential Cambridge scholars, we may briefly consider that publication. Hare, who shared the editorship with Thirlwall, explained in the Preface to the first of the only two volumes that were published, that English scholars in the 1820's had contributed little more than a "mite" to the knowledge of classical antiquity, having instead imported their knowledge from abroad and allowed their intellects to "lie waste." To remedy this deplorable situation, it became the purpose of the *Museum* to foster the "spirit of philological criticism," chiefly relating to Greek and Latin, but "no inquiry that comes under the head of philology . . . will be altogether excluded . . . nor will the philology of the modern languages be regarded as forbidden ground." Actually the majority of the articles were on classical subjects, with Thirlwall the most prolific contributor. But the *Museum* also contained several articles on English and the new philology, of which Kemble's

---

Hare that he had used his influence as Professor of Moral Philosophy "to introduce an Anti-Lockian philosophy, and intend to use it for other good purposes" (p. 248). This desire was of course related to Whewell's interest in language and etymology, a frequent subject in the correspondence with Hare (see, e.g. the letter to a young lady concerning improved spelling of participles such as *lopt, confest, intrencht* (pp. 202-203), a practice which Hare always followed and to which he had devoted an article "On English Orthography" in the *Philological Museum*, I, 640-678). Whewell was impressed by the importance of a systematic scientific terminology; as Professor of Mineralogy, he had in 1828 published an *Essay on Mineralogical Classification and Nomenclature.* He gave Lyell the terms *eocene, miocene,* and *pliocene.* He supplied Faraday with *anode, cathode,* and *ion.* See S. Ross, "Faraday Consults the Scholars: The Origins of the Terms of Electrochemistry" in *Notes and Records of the Royal Society,* XVI (November, 1961), 187-220.

"On English Praeterites"[10] was the most important, being the first exposition in English of Grimm's analysis of the forms of the verb in Germanic. It was still, however, one of the main objects of the journal "to acquaint the English student of classical literature with the new views that have been taken, and the discoveries that have been made, of late years by the scholars upon the Continent, that is to say, by a very pardonable synecdoche, the scholars of Germany."[11] To this end, it contained a number of translations from the German of Savigny, Niebuhr, Buttmann, and both Dindorfs, together with several communications in Latin from August Boeckh. Insofar as its chief subject was classical studies, the *Philological Museum* was, as Hare made clear in the Preface, designed to meet the same need as the *Museum Criticum,* which had had a short run at Cambridge a few years earlier under the editorship of James Henry Monk and Charles J. Blomfield, both fellows of Trinity, and Blomfield of course later one of the founders of the Philological Society.[12]

Thus, in all these scholars, of whom some were Porson's students, we see at last the sources of the philological spirit which in the course of the years made Trinity College, Cambridge, so important in this respect. Good classicists themselves and eager to read and absorb the work of the German scholars they admired so much, they could not help gaining wider interests than Latin and Greek studies. They traveled in Germany, read its literature, and first and last mastered German, which was

[10] *Philological Museum*, II, 373-388.
[11] *Ibid.*, I, 150. In June of 1831, Grundtvig spent two weeks at Trinity as the guest of Whewell. He found that his *Prospectus* was already known there and remarked in his letters that there was more "Germanism" at Cambridge—by which he meant Trinity—than anywhere else in England. He met a number of people who were active in the Etymological Society.
[12] The first volume of the *Museum Criticum* appeared in 1814, the second and last in 1826.

then a very rare accomplishment among students in the English universities.[13] The spectacular rise and high quality of German classical scholarship in the late eighteenth century were, of course, the foundation of this interest; but its sudden impact in England was determined by the Continental Blockade between 1806 and 1812, for, as Blomfield's younger brother Edward Valentine Blomfield, who was also a classical scholar, wrote in October 1813, "the Milan and Berlin Decrees, which prohibited our coffee and our sugar, have been no less severe upon the literary goods of Leipzig."[14] The return of free communication meant that in a very short time the German influence reached a rather large number of contemporary English scholars, who by their numbers alone could not help passing it on with greater vigor and persistency than ordinary circumstances would have produced. The effect was much the same as the acceleration of Oriental philology after the Sanskrit collections in London and the English works on Sanskrit became accessible to Continental scholars, though Hamilton's residence in Paris during some of those years helped reduce the scholarly disadvantages of the blockade.

The Philological Society did not create a forum for the new philology in England. On the contrary, its reports on contemporary Continental scholarship being many fewer than had been anticipated in the original announcement in the *Athenaeum*, the most striking fact about the Society's work during the first twenty years is the virtual absence of non-English, Germanic philology. The Society was based on a native tradition which emphasized three

[13] When Hare, who had lived in Germany as a boy, entered Trinity in 1812, after some years at Charterhouse with Thirlwall and George Grote, he already knew German, which was then very unusual.

[14] See "Account of the Present State of Classical Literature in Germany" in the *Museum Criticum*, I, 273-278. For the ascription, s.v. "E. V. Bloomfield" in the *DNB*.

kinds of work: classical philology; the investigation of the forms, dialects, and etymologies of English; and the ethnologically oriented philology that turned to distant non-Indo-European languages, such as the "dialects of the Papuan and Negrito race." During the first fifteen years there was a careful balance between these three categories. Key, Malden, and several others read on Greek and Latin subjects; Latham and a few others took care of non-Indo-European; and Hensleigh Wedgwood led the contributors on English with his many papers on English etymology.[15]

The articles published during these years have little claim to our attention today, and least of all, perhaps, those which were considered most important by the members who then listened to them. Where scholarship mattered, Wedgwood's etymologies were not even *au courant*, though he and his fellow etymologists were strong in tracing the English history of words, their English origins, and their shifting meanings. One paper, however, deserves attention because it implies a motive which has not previously been mentioned and which occurs with increasing frequency in these years. On February 22, 1850, the year before the Great Exhibition, Thomas Watts read a paper "On the Probable Future Position of the English Language."[16] Watts pointed to the vastly increased distribution of English in the last hundred years and to the fact that "English is essentially a medium language" uniting, "as no other language unites, the Romanic and the Teutonic stocks." On this basis he concluded that English may become the most widely spoken language on earth, a state of affairs which would be an equal blessing to religion and to literature. Five years later, Trench referred to Watts's article, with the addition

[15] In Indo-European there were also a few papers on Spanish, Russian, and Welsh, which was the special interest of Garnett
[16] See *PPS*, IV (1848-1850), 207-214.

of further support from Jacob Grimm, hopefully concluding that with the aid of language "the English Church ... may yet in the providence of God have an important part to play for the reconciling of a divided Christendom,"[17] the very consequence which two centuries earlier had also been Bishop Wilkins' hope for his philosophical language.

The Philological Society and its work exhibit one very important feature, which emerges as soon as we fix our attention on what the Society did not do rather than on what it did. This feature is the Society's fortunate detachment and common sense about language study, even when that study was given a central position in one of the great arguments of the day. This was the controversy over science and natural theology, which took so much time and space and occupied so many minds in the last 25 years before the *Origin of Species* was published in 1859. Cardinal Wiseman and the Rev. W. B. Winning had already in the 1830's used language to support the truth of Scriptures and revealed religion, but it was Chambers' *Vestiges of the Natural History of Creation* which, in 1844, pushed language into the center of the discussion. Its argument was chiefly erected on astronomical and geological evidence, but a chapter on the "Early History of Mankind" used ethnographical philology to supply additional proof of Chambers' thesis. Here, in conformity with the development hypothesis which was the core of his argument, Chambers had introduced the shocking doctrines that the original state of mankind was barbarous rather than civilized, that animals possessed a kind of gesture and sign language on which speech was

[17] Richard Chenevix Trench, *English Past and Present*, pp. 28-29. I use the edition in Everyman's Library (No. 788), which includes both *On the Study of Words* (1851) and *English Past and Present* (1855) with separate paginations. Hereafter referred to as Trench, *Words* and Trench, *English*.

merely a refinement peculiar to man, and that language consequently was not of miraculous origin, but had a material source in man's constitution, mental as well as physical, for "such an arrangement of mutually adapted things was as likely to produce sounds as an Eolian harp placed in a draught is to produce tones."[18] The entire thesis of the *Vestiges* was an outrage, though the writer, who remained anonymous until some years after his death, had not meant it to be so. Adam Sedgwick spoke for many when he charged that the book had *"annulled all distinction between physical and moral."*[19] Though most eighteenth-century writers had in fact taken Chambers' argument for granted, it seemed especially heinous that such a use should be made of language, and it was at this point that the upholders of more orthodox natural theology followed Sedgwick's suggestion and sought refuge in language and philology as most likely to supply a replacement of the arguments which science no longer lent religion.

To counter the *Vestiges*, Whewell in 1845 hastily put together some sections from the *History* and the *Philosophy of the Inductive Sciences* "in which, as he considered, the opinions of the author of the *Vestiges* had been anticipated and condemned."[20] The result was a small volume called *Indications of the Creator*. Here in a section on the "Origin of Languages," significantly placed in a chapter entitled "Doctrine of Catastrophes and Uniformity," Whewell briefly argued that the history of languages, being a science "beyond the domain of matter," will lead us "to regard the present order of the world as pointing towards an origin altogether of a differ-

[18] Robert Chambers, *Vestiges*, 4th edn. from the 3rd London edition (New York, 1846), p. 217.
[19] Adam Segwick, "Natural History of Creation" in the *Edinburgh Review*, LXXXII (July, 1845), 3.
[20] Todhunter, *William Whewell*, I, 155.

ent kind from anything which our material science can grasp," since "we cannot place the origin of language in any point of view in which it comes under the jurisdiction of material causation at all."[21] Thus the burden of the theological argument was shifted from the physical to the moral, from body to mind and its manifestations in language and religion. To meet the demand, philology would have to produce proof, or at least the likelihood, that mankind had a single origin, and that the origin of language was not material, i.e. neither onomatopoeic in any form nor to be conceived on the principle of the Eolian harp placed in the wind. At its meeting in Oxford in June 1847, the British Association rose to the occasion and listened to no less than five papers on ethnographical philology, which together filled more than half the pages of the ensuing report. The *pièce de résistance* was Christian Bunsen's ponderous report. It proved all that any one could have desired, largely due to Bunsen's truly astounding obtuseness, which enabled him to drive toward his preconceived conclusions amid a welter of mutually contradictory facts and authorities. It is therefore impossible, and happily unnecessary, to give a reasoned account of his argument, which furthermore is much better known from the equally strange lucubrations of Bunsen's protégé Max Müller. A later pronouncement by Müller will indicate the drift, though not the precise nature and the details, of the argument: "There is no thought without words, as little as there are words without thought." And Darwin's comment on those words will settle the matter: "What a strange definition must here be given to the word thought!"[22]

[21] (London, 1845), pp. 119-121.
[22] *Descent of Man*, 2nd edn. revised and augmented (New York, 1913), p. 90; Darwin discusses language, pp. 85-93. On page 87 Darwin called Horne Tooke "one of the founders of the noble science of philology."

But the storm that broke over the *Vestiges* is still a puzzling phenomenon. The explanation, however, is simple: Chambers had presented the conventional account of the natural history of language. The promptings of nature and the needs of man were sufficient to explain the slow but steady and uniform progress of man from the primitive state of the savage to civilization. Aided by nature alone, man had invented language, as Condillac had shown a hundred years earlier. Its development was as natural and uniform as geological formations, its understanding independent of indications of design in the Creator. Being aware that his doctrine was very unpopular in some circles, Chambers had deliberately rejected the opinion that "has of late years been a favorite notion with several writers, that the human race was at first in a highly civilized state, and that barbarism was a second condition."[23] He had produced a sharp confrontation of the doctrine of invention with the antimaterialist romantic and religious belief in divine inspiration or at least aid. Rousseau had long ago discovered a serious weakness in the invention argument, for it presupposed prior agreement or compact, which in turn would seem unthinkable unless language was already available as the medium of effecting agreement—hence he could not decide whether language or society came first. Reid had altogether rejected the invention of language for the same reason: "There must be compacts or agreements before the use of artificial signs; but there can be no compact or agreement without signs, nor without language."[24] It was this

[23] *Vestiges*, p. 207.

[24] RH, pp. 117-118 in *An Inquiry into the Human Mind* (1764), IV, ii. Reid therefore argued that the artificial, invented language must have been preceded by a common natural language. Condillac had not denied that, but later writers either ignored that part of his argument or, more cogently, still saw the transition from natural signs to arbitrary signs as an insuperable barrier. Herder's postulate that man must create language by his very

weakness that was used to overturn the old doctrine. Friedrich Schlegel had, with the effect of plain statement, implied that the Indo-European languages at least had a higher origin, but in England these new arguments were borrowed from two French writers rather than directly from the Germans. Both de Bonald and especially de Maistre strongly influenced Julius Charles Hare and his circle. Both were ultramontane opponents of the Revolution, the Ideologists, atheism, and materialism. Their arguments were ready-made for attacks on the Utilitarians and all forms of freethinking. With common aims but, it seems, independently of each other, both had argued that language could not have been invented by man, but had been revealed to him, that the primitive state of man is one of wisdom and altogether different from that of the savage, and that the history of mankind is not a record of steady improvement and progress but of corruption and degeneracy—unless checked by faith and divine favor. The impossibility of inventing language proved the existence of God. "Il est nécessaire que l'homme pense sa parole avant de parler sa pensée," de Bonald had said; here was the secret that explained "le mystère de l'être intelligent"—"qu'on cesse donc de s'étonner si nous avons mis une si haute importance à la question de la révélation de la parole. Toute la dispute entre les deux partis qui divisent l'Europe savante, les

---

nature had avoided the problem. Monboddo's ingenious compromise was either disregarded or more often misunderstood as the most debasing naturalism. Fichte had faced the problem in "Von der Sprachfähigkeit und dem Ursprunge der Sprache" (1795), in which he argued that intellectually superior members of primitive groups had imposed their own invented terms on the rest, though only after natural signs had come into use; he had also presupposed man's possession of reason, a point on which Condillac was at best vague—though perhaps because he, by taking it for granted, failed to make enough of it. A. W. Schlegel used the same argument as Reid, in *Vorlesungen über Schöne Litteratur und Kunst* (1801-801), ed. J. Minor (3 vols.; Stuttgart, 1884), I, 273.

théistes et les athées, les chrétiens et les sophistes, se réduit à ce fait, à ce seul fait: là est la preuve de l'existence de Dieu, le motif des devoirs de l'homme, la nécessité des lois et de la société."[25] De Maistre wished to have good dictionaries of savage languages, convinced that in them he would find "restes évidents d'une langue antérieure parlée par un peuple éclairé. Et quand même nous ne les trouverions pas, il en résulterait seulement que la dégradation est arrivée au point d'effacer ces derniers restes."[26] Language, therefore, was a "véritable baromètre dont les variations annoncent infailliblement le bon et le mauvais temps."[27] No wonder that he found Condillac "le plus coupable de tous les conjurés modernes."[28] From de Maistre, Julius Charles Hare and his brother Augustus William borrowed many observations and arguments for their popular *Guesses at Truth* to sustain the conviction that "Philology, in its highest sense, ought to be only another name for Philosophy. Its aim should be to seek after wisdom in the whole series of its historical manifestations."[29] Chambers was right, when

[25] *Législation primitive* (3 vols.; Paris, 1817), I, 56, 337, 81 (1st edn. 1802).

[26] *Oeuvres complètes de Joseph de Maistre* (Paris, 1884), IV, 106 in "Deuxième Entretien" of *Les soirées de Saint-Petersbourg* (1st edn. 1821); this *Entretien* is devoted to language, but de Maistre frequently returns to it in other places. This passage is followed by an example drawn from the language of the savages of New Holland, which Trench used in *Words*, p. 20.

[27] *Oeuvres*, I, 301 in *Essai sur le principe générateur des constitutions politiques* (1st edn. 1814).

[28] *Oeuvres*, XIV (1886), 138, in letter of July 10, 1818, to de Bonald on receiving his *Recherches philosophiques*—"Vous parlez comme un ange, Monsieur le Vicomte, sur les langues, qui sont à peu près toute la métaphysique. Il faut être possédé de quatre ou cinq diables pour croire à l'invention des langues."

[29] *Guesses at Truth by Two Brothers* (2 vols.; London, 1847-1848), II, 326 (1st edn., 1827 and often reissued with additions). Hare's copy of the *Soirées* in the 1st edition is in the Library of Trinity College, Cambridge, heavily marked throughout. *Guesses*, I, 337, cites the *Soirées*, prefaced by this remark: "Here let me

he stated that several writers believed the "human race was at first in a highly civilized state," which explains why his book caused such consternation among Hare's friends and students. Their sacred cause was at stake. One of his best students was Trench, who without becoming involved in arguments about the origin of language still found a remedy that served the cause.

The Société Linguistique, formed in 1866, has been praised for the second clause of its statutes, which expressly banned any communication about the origin of language; but the Philological Society had acted as admirably by not allowing itself to be drawn into the contemporary controversy in spite of the temptation and in spite of the services which the Society by the nature of its subject matter might have been expected to render. The etymologies of Hensleigh Wedgwood, who was Darwin's brother-in-law, did in fact show some leanings toward the "bow-wow" and the "pooh-pooh," the imitative and the ejaculatory, theories of the origin of language, as Wedgwood himself in 1872 made plain in his long essay "On the Origin of Language," written for the second edition of his *Etymological Dictionary*. But his position was not made a matter of policy with the Society, and if he erred, he did at least, unlike Müller, stay this side of absurdity and nonsense. Having advocated the "ding-dong" theory in one of his many carelessly un-

---

cite a passage from one of the wisest and most delightful works of recent times, which, though its author is sometimes over-fanciful, and not seldom led astray by his Romish prejudices, is full of high and holy thoughts on the loftiest subjects of speculation." On February 17, 1832, Whewell wrote to Hare of a visiting Frenchman who was "a philosopher of the school of Bonald, an intimate friend of De Maistre and of Schelling, and a most earnest Catholic, enthusiastic about painting, music, and languages—now should you not like to know *him*? as girls sometimes say to one another." Todhunter, *William Whewell*, II, 159 (he gives the year 1833, but an examination of the letters shows that it should be 1832).

reasonable moments, Max Müller was never quite able to disavow it, for whether he believed it or not, it was the sort of extravagance in which his sentiments, such as they were, were bound to spend themselves.[30] Only in 1873, when the controversy between Müller and the Darwinians was at its height, did the president, Alexander J. Ellis, in his annual address comment on the origin of language. He stated what had for long been the Society's practice:

> I conceive such questions to be out of the field of philology proper. We have to investigate what *is*, we have to discover, if possible, the invariable unconditional relations under which language, *as we observe it,* forms, develops, changes, or at least to construct an empirical statement of definite linguistic relations, and ascertain how far that statement obtains in individual cases. Real language, the go-between of man and man, is a totally different organism from philosophical language, the misty ill-understood exponent of sharp metaphysical distinctions. Our work is with the former. We shall do more by tracing the historical growth of one single work-a-day tongue, than by filling wastepaper baskets with reams of paper covered with speculations on the origin of all tongues.[31]

Ellis may have been thinking of the Society's *New English Dictionary*, the great project, which was then going forward and which owed its inception largely to Richard Chenevix Trench, who along with Sir William Jones deserves to be remembered in the history of language study for the truly Faradayan saintliness he carried to the enterprise.

Trench became a member of the Philological Society

---

[30] See Max Müller, *The Science of Thought* (2 vols.; New York, 1887), I, 205-209. He once asked: "What would Hobbes and Locke have given for Bopp's Comparative Grammar?"

[31] *TPS*, 1873-1874, pp. 251-252.

in March 1857 and was elected ordinary member of the council at the anniversary meeting in May of the same year. He had been Rector of Itchenstoke near Winchester from 1845 to 1856, and since 1846, professor of divinity, and later of exegesis of the New Testament, in King's College, London. In October 1856 he succeeded William Buckland as Dean of Westminster, a post he retained until he was appointed Archbishop of Dublin in November of 1863, following another man who, like Buckland, had served the cause of natural theology, Richard Whately. It was during the first four of his seven years at Westminster that Trench performed his important work with the Philological Society. No new member could have come with better credentials than Trench, who had already, in several widely respected and popular works, contributed to the understanding of the Scriptures and to language study. Trench was, first of all, a teacher with a remarkable gift for clear and interesting exposition; to him, theology and exegesis were bound up with philology since both served the cause of Christian instruction in the tradition of the English Church and gave promise of an ultimate reunion of divided Christianity. Like Sir William Jones and Grundtvig, with whom he had so much in common, Trench did not believe in language study for its own sake, but saw its justification in the light it might shed on other matters. His motives and his educational use of the English language and its history will explain his interest in a new dictionary as well as the nature of the proposal which brought the project for the dictionary into being.

We have seen that Trench in his youth at Trinity College met many of the men he now rejoined in the Society. His outlook had early guided him toward language, and in the "Introductory Essay" to his *Notes on the Parables of our Lord* (1840), he made some comments that define the position which he later retained with remarkable consistency. In essence, its foundation was in Augustine's distinction between words and things, as was appropriate in a work devoted to the parables. Here he insisted that for preachers, "it is well that they should be conscious, and the more conscious the better, of the wonderful thing which language is,—of the power and mystery, of the truth and falsehood, of words; and as a part of this acquaintance, that the truth, and that which is the vehicle of the truth, should for them be separable; . . . it should be even for them as soul and body."[32] For besides the revelation in words, "God has another and an elder, and one, indeed, without which it is inconceivable how that other could be made, for from this it appropriates all its signs of communication. This entire moral and visible world from first to last . . . is from beginning to end a mighty parable, a great teaching of supersensuous truth, a help at once to our faith and to our understanding." Or in other words "the whole of Scripture, with its ever-recurring use of figurative language, is a reawakening of man to the mystery of nature, a giving back to him of the key of knowledge, of the true *signatura rerum*."[33] Here was safer ground than geology and the contemplations on—and in—antediluvian caves, which in England's smoky coal fields had occupied Buckland, Sedgwick, and Whewell.[34] But in language lies also a danger,

for somewhere or other every man is a liar . . . so that

[32] Revised edition (New York, 1874), p. 24.

[33] *Ibid.*, pp. 16-17. The *Signatura Rerum* is the title of a work by Jacob Boehme, whose doctrine of the Adamic language has certain points in common with that of Trench.

[34] Though unusually tolerant, Trench never showed much interest in natural theology. On October 24, 1838, he wrote to his friend W. B. Donne: "Our faith is here such a timid thing, leaning on such strange supports, exulting if a sea-shell be found on the top of a hill, and frightened out of its wits if some bones are found in a wrong stratum." [Maria Trench, ed.], *Richard Chenevix Trench, Archbishop; Letters and Memorials* (London, 1888), I, 229. Hereafter referred to as *Letters and Memorials*.

of the truths of God in the language of men (this language of course including man's acts as well as his words), of these sons of heaven married to the daughters of the earth, it may truly be said, "we have this treasure in earthen vessels." And we must expect that somewhere or other the earthen vessel will appear, that the imperfection which cleaves to our forms of utterance, to men's words and to their works, will make itself felt either in the misapprehensions of those to whom the language is addressed (as at John III, 11), or by the language itself, though the best that human speech could supply, by the men themselves, though the noblest, it may be, of their age and nation,—yet failing to set forth the divine truth in all its fulness and completeness.[35]

Language must constantly be recalled to truth. We cannot disengage ourselves wholly from sensuous images, and to reach "the hearts and understandings of his hearers," the teacher must make the fullest possible use of the "parabolical element." "To do this effectively will demand a fresh effort of his own; for while all language is, and must be figurative, yet long familiar use is continually wearing out the freshness and sharpness of the stamp . . . so that language is ever needing to be recalled, minted and issued anew, cast into novel forms, as was done by Him of whom it is said, that without a parable spake He nothing," a passage in which Trench brilliantly appropriates and reverses the famous image which Hobbes had derived from Bacon. Trench returned to this image again and again with further illustrative elaborations to exorcise the spectre of nominalism and the doctrines of the false prophets of more recent days, the Utilitarians.[36]

[35] *Parables*, pp. 21-22. Trench considered De Quincey the greatest living master of English prose. See Trench, *English*, p. 25.
[36] *Ibid.*, p. 25. The metaphor is classical (Quintilian) and has had a long career in Bacon, Hobbes, Locke, Leibniz, and Robert

Trench soon carried into action the program for teaching through language which he had outlined in the "Introductory Essay." Toward the end of February 1845, he wrote to Archdeacon Wilberforce that he would deliver a lecture to the students in the Diocesan Training School in Winchester "On Language as an Instrument of Knowledge," which he found "a large title for such a lecture as I think to deliver."[37] He gave not one but five lectures, which in somewhat altered form were published in 1851 as *On the Study of Words*. He published the lectures in order to reach a wider audience, for, as he explained in the Preface, "it seems to me that the subject is one to which it is beyond measure desirable that their attention, who are teaching, or shall have hereafter to teach, others should be directed; so that they shall learn to regard language as one of the chiefest organs of their own education and that of others." A few years later, in the spring of 1854, he delivered a similar course of four lectures to the pupils of King's College School, London. They were repeated the same autumn to the Training School in Winchester, and appeared the following year as *English Past and Present*.[38] Both books did far more than any previous

---

South, whose sermons were much admired by both Hare and Trench. South, like Trench, used it both of words and of man's knowledge of God and creation: "The whole business of our redemption is, in short, only to rub over the defaced copy of the creation, to reprint God's image upon the soul, and (as it were) to set forth nature in a second and a fairer edition. The recovery of which lost image, as it is God's pleasure to command, and our duty to endeavour, so it is in his power only to effect." *Sermons* (London, 1823), I, 52. De Bonald used it in the same manner in *Législation primitive*, I, 99: "La parole est donc, dans le commerce des pensées, ce que l'argent est dans le commerce des marchandises, expression réelle de valeurs, parce qu'elle est valeur elle-même. Et nos sophistes veulent en faire un signe de convention, à peu près comme le papier-monnoie, signe sans valeur."

[37] *Letters and Memorials*, I, 275.
[38] See Trench, *English*, p. 3. On September 29, 1854, Trench

publication to make language study popular, and without that popularity it seems unlikely that the *New English Dictionary* would have been able both to get the readers it needed and to arouse the general interest which sustained it. The *Words* reached its nineteenth edition in 1886, the year of Trench's death; *English Past and Present* had its fourteenth three years later, and both have since been reprinted several times. The work that went into them also prepared Trench for the writing of his report *On some Deficiencies in our English Dictionaries*.

The form and the contents of *On the Study of Words* are admirably adapted to the original audience in the Training School in Winchester. Its style is simple, it contains few learned references, the important points are repeated with sufficient frequency to be retained in the minds of the listeners, and its many examples are drawn from familiar sources. For our purposes, however, the chief interest lies not in the details, but in the view of language, its nature, and its study, which the book sets forth. What are the characteristic features that give the

---

wrote to his son Richard at Cambridge: "I am just preparing some lectures for publication. They contain a brief sketch of some changes which the English language has undergone. 'English, Past and Present' is to be the name. If they succeed as the 'Words,' they may do something toward paying your college expenses" (*Letters and Memorials*, I, 304). In the meantime he had also published, in 1854, his *Synonyms of the New Testament*, "being the substance of a course of lectures addressed to the theological students, King's College, London," which treated the Greek words in much the same manner as the other works had dealt with English words, though of course on a higher level. The nature and significance of Trench's work was plain to his contemporaries. Shortly· after Trench had been installed in office at Westminster in January 1857, Dr. Liddon, later the famous Canon of St. Paul's, wrote: "His great work for the English Church was his drawing attention to the philosophy (so to call it, for the want of a better term) of religious language. I well recollect my great delight at the appearance of his 'Synonyms of the New Testament.'" (*Letters and Memorials*, I, 316.)

book and its author such a significant position in the history of language study in England? These features are best understood if we compare the views which Trench argued against and rejected with the ones which he advocated.

Trench made it clear at the outset that he was not interested in philosophical speculation on the origin of language, for "here, as in everything else that concerns the primitive constitution, the great original institutes of humanity, our best and truest lights are to be gotten from the study of the three first chapters of Genesis." Having first been endowed with reason, man also received language from God "(for what is man's word but his reason coming forth, so that it may behold itself?) . . . because he could not be man, that is, a social being, without it," though of course he did not begin with a ready-made dictionary and grammar, not *with names*, but *with the power of naming*." Man began with the capacity which was evoked when God brought the animals before Adam to be named; here was "the clearest intimation of the origin, at once divine and human, of speech."[39]

This view had two consequences. Like de Maistre and Hare, Trench felt bound to reject the notion that the primitive state of man was illustrated in the savage, who far from being the seed of civilized man was like a "dead withered leaf, torn violently away from the great trunk of humanity," not the child of man but rather "the man prematurely aged, and decrepit, and outworn."[40] The second

[39] Trench, *Words*, p. 17.

[40] *Ibid.* Julius Hare had expressed the same view in *Guesses at Truth*: "The ultimate tendency of civilization is toward barbarism" (II, 234). Hare's *Guesses at Truth* contains many passages on language and related matters, which anticipate Trench, both where the latter quotes and mentions Hare and where he does not. For a contemporary account of Hare's role, see A. P. Stanley's "Archdeacon Hare" in the *Quarterly Review*, XCVII (June, 1855), 1-28, written shortly after Hare's death. The Dean notes that Trench, "more than any other of Hare's pupils, imbibed

consequence of Trench's account of the origin of language was quite as important, for he was compelled to admit that "man makes his own language, but he makes it as the bee makes its cells, as the bird its nests." Language is a mystery, "even as every act of creation is of necessity such."[41] Thus Trench very adroitly made a convincing transition from orthodoxy to the already familiar notion of the organic nature of language; yet, thanks to his orthodoxy about ultimate beginnings, he was not forced to accept, or even consider, the implications of all the fanciful theories which that view had encouraged. Trench's solution was practical and hence fruitful; the fact of inexplicability was absorbed in reverence for the admitted mystery of all being. Furthermore, if things at least might have been more perfect in the beginning than they later became, then the belief in progressive development, or growth, would have to be abandoned for a concept of change, a view which is not likely to be accompanied by irrelevant and distorting prejudices. The study of language becomes observation of the ways in which words have behaved in shifting contexts through the ages.

This was the position at which Trench fortunately arrived, owing in part to his good common sense, and in part to the religious and national outlook which determined his interest in the study of words rather than in the structure of language. He did, in fact, present a good argument to show that structure did not fall within his province: "The great logical, or grammatical, framework of language (for grammar is the logic of speech, even as logic is the grammar of reason) [man] would possess, he

---

from him the accurate discrimination which has produced the series of delightful little volumes on 'Words,' 'Proverbs,' and 'the English language' " (p. 6). In the "Deuxième Entretien" of the *Soirées*, de Maistre used the same metaphor of the savage having been torn from the trunk of humanity. See *Oeuvres*, IV, 63, 81-82.

[41] Trench, *Words*, p. 18.

knew not how; and certainly not as the final result of gradual acquisitions, but as that rather which alone had made those acquisitions possible."[42] All men, barbarous as well as civilized, equally shared the universal gift of reason, which belonged to their being. Structure itself, therefore, could yield no lessons to show how well the nations had used their God-given talents. The evidence must be sought by observing how men have "unconsciously worked, filling in this framework by degrees with these later acquisitions of thought, feeling, and experience, as one by one they arrayed themselves in the garment and vesture of words."[43] Thus, by making the substance of language—the words—the object of inquiry, Trench placed himself firmly in the English tradition, which had its beginning in Locke. There was one important difference, however. Trench shared with the Lockeian school, Tooke and the Utilitarians, the belief that words contained information about thought, feeling, and experience, but unlike them he did not use this information to seek knowledge of the original, philosophical constitution of mind, but only as evidence of what had been present to the conscious awareness of the users of words within recent centuries; his interest was not in etymological metaphysics, not in conjectural history, but in history; not in material philosophy, but in the spiritual and moral life of the speakers of English.[44] Here also lies the reason why Trench showed little interest in remote etymologies. In fact, he had only a limited knowledge of

[42] Trench, *Words*, p. 21.
[43] Trench, *Words*, pp. 21-22.
[44] Trench had, in fact, learned a great deal from Tooke and was not ashamed to admit it; in the Preface to the *Words*, he wrote: "Whatever may be Horne Tooke's shortcomings, whether in occasional details of etymology, or in the philosophy of grammar, or in matters more serious still, yet, with all this, what an epoch in many a student's intellectual life has been his first acquaintance with *The Diversions of Purley*."

the new philology and hence, with greater modesty than most, confined his observations and conclusions to the English language since 1500, which he undoubtedly knew better than any of his contemporaries, as is amply demonstrated by the astounding scope and number of references in all his works on English. Since "in the historic period of a language it is not permitted to any man to bring new roots into it," Trench's study rested on foundations that were known; his purpose was to see what man had done "to evolve what is latent therein, to combine what is apart, to recall what has fallen out of sight."[45]

Trench's eminently practical historical study of words may, of course, be apprehended apart from its background. Here in fact is the key to its success; its fulfillment was not likely to be crossed by controversy. But its particular character cannot be understood apart from the general considerations which transformed his parochial motives into a universal program for language study, a program which was sufficiently powerful and English to command the best philological efforts of the country for many years to come. In the midst of the tensions of the mid-century, came an answer to the fears which Julius Charles Hare some years earlier had expressed in a sermon on "The Healer of the Deaf and Dumb," when he talked of "the thoughts and feelings of the world" which stifled the "feeling in the heart, wherewith it can love God" and the "discernment in the mind, wherewith it can behold the things of God." For, Hare continued,

> We live as it were in a smith's forge, with the flames of the world roaring, and the sledgehammer of the world knocking with ceaseless din in our ears, sometimes too ourselves blowing the flames, and sometimes ourselves wielding the sledgehammer; so that every word from without, which might drop on us, like the song of a

[45] Trench, *Words*, p. 75.

lark, from heaven, and might stir us to look toward the spot it came from, is drowned in the clash of noises. Amid this hubbub of noises we live: amid it we have grown up from our childhood: and therefore, as those who live and have been bred up within sound of a great waterfall, lose all ear for sweet and soft music, so do such as live within the roar of the great fall, down which the world is ever rushing with riotous speed into hell, lose their inward ear for the sweet and soft music of heaven.[46]

In these words Hare was not merely creating the familiar image of the satanic clamor of industrialism. He also had a more literal meaning in mind; for, as he made plain elsewhere, the din of the world had made itself heard even in language, in the Utilitarians and especially in the "new gibberish" of Bentham, who, "as he ever rejoiced to see society resolving into its elements, seemed desirous to throw back language also into a chaotic state," and who, "unable to understand organic unity and growth, ... lookt upon a hyphen as the only bond of union."[47]

Trench, naturally, had no fondness for the "false prophets," but according to his method, they could receive their due without distorting or perverting the principles of language study. Here is perhaps his most striking compromise between personal motives and correct scholarly standards. Language being a "faithful . . . record of the good and of the evil which in time past have been working in the minds and hearts of men," it may be considered "a moral barometer, which indicates and permanently marks the rise or fall of a nation's life. To

[46] *Sermons Preacht in Herstmonceux Church* (London, 1841), p. 252. This sermon is perhaps the clearest statement of Hare's view of language.

[47] *Guesses at Truth*, I, 209. Factually, the observation is strikingly perceptive. On Hobbes, Bentham, and the "selfish philosophers," see also I, 205-206, 300.

study a people's language will be to study *them*, and to study them at best advantage; there where they present themselves to us under fewest disguises, most nearly as they are." Then he adds a comment directed against the Utilitarians: "Too many have had a hand in it, and in causing it to arrive at its present shape, it is too entirely the collective work of the whole nation, the result of the united contributions of all, it obeys too immutable laws, to allow any successful tampering with it, any making of it to witness other than the actual facts of the case."[48] Hence, according to the axiom *vox populi, vox Dei,* rightly understood, usage is all, and we need not be misled by the abuses of the "modern 'false prophets,'" who would gladly explain away all such phenomena of the world around us as declare man to be a sinful being and enduring the consequences of sin," by telling us "that

[48] Trench, *Words*, p. 40. It has been noted above that de Maistre used the same metaphor. Cf. *Guesses at Truth*, I, 216: "Languages are the barometers of national thought and character," which is immediately followed by an anecdote about Tooke, which makes the same point about tampering with language as Trench does in the quoted passage. Tooke, Hare says, had tried to "fix the quicksilver for his own metaphysical ends" much like the schoolboy "who screwed his master's weatherglass up to fair, to make sure of a fine day for a holiday." It is worth noting that Trench does not mention Tooke in this context. In the *Words* he several times draws on the *Diversions* without adverse comment, see, e.g. pp. 33-34: "A 'kind' person is a 'kinned' person, one of kin; one who acknowledges and acts upon his kinship with other men, confesses that he owes to them, as of one blood with himself, the debt of love. And so man*kind* is man*kinned*. . . . We do in fact every time that we use the word 'mankind,' declare our faith in the one common descent of the whole race of man." Cf. also p. 120: "Thus 'heaven' is only the perfect of 'to heave,'" and pp. 75-76: "By 'things' I mean subjects as well as objects of thought, whatever one can *think* about." These etymologies are all in the *Diversions*. When Trench, a few years later, wrote *English Past and Present*, he did not, though it would otherwise have served his purpose, repeat Tooke's etymology of "kind," but gave examples leading to the conclusion that "The '*kindly* fruits' are the '*natural* fruits'" (*English*, p. 116).

pain is only a subordinate kind of pleasure, or, at worst, that it is a sort of needful hedge and guardian of pleasure."[49]

In his critique of Tooke, Dugald Stewart had made the same point about usage, and he had also proceeded to the same corollaries. Firstly, Stewart had ridiculed the practice of referring to the "Woods of Germany" for authority in matters of style; so likewise Trench insisted that "it is not of necessity that a word should always be considered to root itself in its etymology, and to draw its life-blood from thence. It may so detach itself from this as to have a right to be regarded independently of it." It is, for instance, no absurdity to call a weekly news-paper a "journal," and not self-contradictory to talk of a "white blackbird"; and it was "a piece of ethical prudery, and an ignorance of the laws which languages obey, when the early Quakers refused to employ the names com-monly given to the days of the week, and substituted for these, 'first day,' 'second day,' and so on."[50] Secondly, just as Stewart had argued against etymological meta-physics, Trench asserts that names are not "co-extensive with things, . . . that a multitude of things exist which, though capable of being resumed in a word, are yet with-out one, unnamed and unregistered; so that, vast as is the world of names, the world of realities is even vaster

[49] Trench, *Words*, p. 31.

[50] *Ibid.*, pp. 63-64. Cf. StH, V, 182. Trench does not refer to Stewart in the *Words*, and I have not elsewhere in Trench found any mention of him. But it is striking that Trench, in talking of old errors that have left traces in languages, should say "The mythology, for example, which our ancestors brought with them from the forests of Germany is as much extinct for us as are the Lares, Larvae, and Lemures of heathen Rome; . . . 'lubber,' 'dwarf,' 'oaf,' 'droll,' 'wight,' 'hag,' 'nightmare,' 'wicked,' suggest themselves here, as bequeathed to us by that old Teutonic demonology" (p. 63). He used the phrase again in *English*: "There are those who may seek to trace our language to the forests of Germany and Scandinavia, to investigate its relation to all the kindred tongues that were there spoken" (p. 10).

still."[51] Or, in different terms, "as shadows attend substances, so words follow upon things." For this reason, the insistence on usage does not, of course, preclude that particular great men could add important words to the language, fashioned out of the old material, as Augustine did when he—with his "strong good sense"—made "no scruple about employing 'Salvator'; observing well, and with a true insight into the law of the growth of words, that 'Salvator' may not have been, and indeed was not, good Latin before the Saviour came; but when He came, He made it to be such."[52] Indeed, it has been one of the results of Trench's study of words that the great men of all ages in the history of the nation can be known by their words. In his own way, Trench had proved the sense of Stewart's belief that the study of language must be an historical discipline.

It was the virtue of Trench's exposition, however, that his listeners and readers could grasp the sense and absorb the conclusions of his argument without necessarily being intellectually aware of the complexities that lay behind it, much as sympathetic minds can learn to see the beauty of a landscape in its forms and in the patterns of the fields, the farms, the trees and roads and hedges and all the other signs of many living and working generations, without knowing the geology of the region. They would see that "many a single word . . . is itself a concentrated poem, having stores of poetical thought and imagery laid up in it," a phenomenon that was in turn the effect of "some deep analogy of things natural and things spiritual."[53] Thus language was, in the words of "a popular American author" (who of course is Emerson), "fossil poetry" and, Trench added, "fossil ethics" and "fossil history" as well. He devoted a chapter of *On the Study*

[51] Trench, *Words*, pp. 75-76.
[52] Trench, *Words*, p. 73.
[53] Trench, *Words*, pp. 11-12.

of Words to each of these, crammed with examples designed to reawaken the reader to the meaning which the history of the word would bring out, thus recreating the image which long currency had worn down until the form retained only the value of a mere counter. Who could fail to see the inspiring lesson contained in the history of "tribulatio,"[54] or the sad evidence of moral decline contained in "pastime," which shows that the "amusements and pleasures" of the world "do not really satisfy the mind and fill it with the sense of an abiding and satisfying joy; they are only 'pastime'; they serve only, as this word confesses, to *pass* away the *time*, to prevent it from hanging, an intolerable burden, on men's hands"?[55] The distinction between "instruction" and "education" also contains a lesson. The etymology of "education" tells us that it is not a process of "the filling of the child's mind, as a cistern is filled with waters brought in buckets from some other source." It is, on the contrary, "the opening up of its own fountains," for "education must educe, being from 'educare,' which is but another form of 'educere'; and that is 'to draw out,' and not 'to put in.' "[56]

[54] Trench, *Words*, pp. 12-13.

[55] Trench, *Words*, p. 14; the example is, as a footnote indicates, from Bishop Butler's Sermon XIV, "Upon the Love of God."

[56] Trench, *Words*, p. 111. The example is from *Guesses at Truth*, I, 319: "No small part of the blunders made by modern theorizers on education may be traced to their ignorance or forgetfulness that *education* is something more than *instruction*." Cf. II, 144: "The true principle of Education . . . is to *educe*, or bring out, that which is within, not merely, or mainly, to *instruct*, or impose a form from without." See also Douglas, *Life of Whewell*, p. 264. This thought comes remarkably close to the Platonic element in the German spiritualists of the late sixteenth century; cf. Valentin Weigel in *Studium Universale* (Newenstadt, 1618): "Studieren und Lernen eine Erweckung ist dess, das in uns ist, *nemlich* das ich erkenne, und gewahr werde, dess das in mir, und in allen Menschen verborgen liegt. Denn das Himmlische und das Irdische lieget in mir verborgen. *Dannenher* auch die *Platonici* gesagt *Discere esse reminisci.*" Quoted in A. Koyré, *Mystiques, spirituels, alchimistes du XVIᵉ siècle Allemand* (Paris, 1955), p. 84.

These arguments may make us somewhat uneasy, especially when we learn that the practice of saying "love-child" instead of "bastard" throws "a flimsy veil of sentiment over sin" and is a direct "source of mischief in all our country parishes," because it may for many young women "have helped to make the downward way more sloping still."[57] But the occasion for discomfort, if any, is removed in the later chapters "On the Rise of New Words," and "On the Distinction of Words," which are full of illuminating word histories.

These chapters also point forward to Trench's next book on the language, called *English Past and Present*. Here the emphasis is more firmly on the plain history of English words, without far-reaching exploration of the moral and theological lessons, in which he had previously engaged. Its tenor is consequently also more national, for

> the love of our own language, what is it in fact but the love of our country expressing itself in one particular direction? If the great acts of that nation to which we belong are precious to us, if we feel ourselves made greater by their greatness, summoned to a nobler life by the nobleness of Englishmen who have already lived and died, . . . what can more clearly point out their native land and ours as having fulfilled a glorious past, as being destined for a glorious future, than that they should have acquired for themselves and for those

[57] Trench, *Words*, p. 38. "Love-child" is, for at least two obvious reasons, not Bentham's. It is a translation of *enfant d'amour*, and it is the very sort of word Bentham wished to avoid. In a strictly legal context he will use the word "illegitimate," but otherwise he will simply say "the child" or "the son." In the *Principles of Penal Laws*, he points out, with his usual insight, that people sometimes try to create a sort of control over events by means of words, as for instance "by that barbarous maxim, that a *bastard is the son of no one*—a maxim which has a tendency, as much as it is in the power of words to give it, to deprive a man of all parental connexions" (*Works*, ed. Bowring, I, 473).

who came after them a clear, a strong, an harmonious, a noble language?

Hence, quoting F. Schlegel, Trench could affirm: "The care of the national language I consider as at all times a sacred trust and a most important privilege of the higher orders of society."[58] He was not a jingoist, however, and the exclusion of foreign words from the language, where possible, was not one of his concerns. On the contrary, he seemed to take special delight in collecting as many words from foreign sources as he could, perhaps with a feeling that there was something catholic about the English language which might point toward a great destiny.[59] But the most significant aspect of Trench's new book is its very large number of quotations from English authors; the citations show both the wide scope of his reading and his careful notetaking as well as the direction in which his studies were now moving. Most of the material could not have been derived from already existing word collections and dictionaries, and he now made it a practice to add in a parenthesis the name of the author in whom he had found the word, not because he wished to suggest that the word was in any way peculiar to that author, "but only to give one authority for its use."[60] Thus, in the space of a single page, Trench gives no less than 85 examples of the feminine termination in -ess, 19 from Wiclif's Bible, 8 from Chaucer, and 58 in 30 different authors from Udall to Addison.[61] Elsewhere he gives 140 sets of words with double forms, such as "divers" and "diverse"; "cónjure" and "conjúre"; "ghostly" and

[58] Trench, *English*, pp. 8-9.

[59] See, e.g. Trench, *English*, pp. 13-16, which contain lists of words from different languages: Hebrew (16), Arabic (65), Persian (13), Turkish (7), Hindustani (10), the New World (20), Italian (67), and Spanish (60); altogether 258 words.

[60] Trench, *English*, p. 34n.

[61] Trench, *English*, pp. 96-97.

"ghastly"; and "lurk" and "lurch."[62] Trench had openly
admitted that he had neither the knowledge nor the time
to make philology "the subject of especial research,"
but he did count himself among those who "have yet an
intelligent interest in their mother tongue, and desire to
learn as much of its growth and history and construction
as may be reasonably deemed within their reach."[63] It
was to such an audience that he addressed himself, but
his insight and his faithful work carried him far beyond
the studies of an enlightened amateur. *English Past and
Present* clearly established him as the best student of the
history of English; at the same time, he had also, of necessity, acquired the most extensive knowledge of the existing dictionaries and their deficiencies. He was, by the
same token, uniquely qualified to say what a better dictionary should be like.

Johnson's *Dictionary* was now a hundred years old,
and still the revered ancestor of the many lexicographical
efforts which had appeared in print in the meantime—as
well as many that never reached the printer's office.[64] In
relation to its varied offspring, it had come to occupy
much the same position as Henri Estienne's famous
Thesaurus Graecae Linguae of 1572, which for over 250
years had a multitude of successors that took the *Thesaurus* for their only source instead of seeking out the
original material on which it was based. Both saw a
stream of abridgments, expansions, books of synonyms,
and adaptations for every conceivable purpose. But to all
who still used and admired Johnson's great work, it was
becoming increasingly evident that it was no longer fully
adequate, partly because so many new words had since
been added to the language, partly because it bore the

[62] Trench, *English*, pp. 61-62.
[63] Trench, *English*, p. 10.
[64] See Allen Walker Read, "Projected English Dictionaries,
1755-1828," *JEGP*, XXXVI (1937), 188-205.

magnificent stamp of an age which had steadily been losing a sympathetic audience. We must not forget that Johnson's *Dictionary*, in addition to being a wonderful intellectual autobiography written in terms of the atoms of meaning, i.e. the words Johnson himself acknowledged and used, was also a profound and typical expression of its age. This is nowhere so evident as in its concept of "true meaning," which, in spite of all the personal features, was close to that of Nathaniel Bailey's *Universal Etymological English Dictionary*. Bailey sought meaning in etymology, much as Johnson wished to exhibit first the "natural and primitive signification" of each word, as e.g. in "to *arrive*, to reach the shore in a voyage."[65] To Bailey and the eighteenth century, etymology was altogether different from what it later became in the new philology. It was understood in Lockeian terms: etymology showed "the Original of Words, in order to distinguish their true Meaning and Signification," and an etymologist was "one skilled in searching out the true Interpretation of Words." It was a matter of discovery through skill, rather than knowledge through study.[66] Professor W. K. Wimsatt, in his truly excellent study, remarks on this aspect of the *Dictionary*: "There was . . . a strain in the empirical writers whose books Johnson read, a character of the very tradition, which promoted

[65] Johnson, *Works*, II (London, 1824), 20-21 ("The Plan of an English Dictionary").

[66] *Op.cit.* (4th edn., London, 1728), s.v. "Etymology," "Etymologist." Johnson's view of language was, of course, by no means so simple as Bailey's. In the "Plan" he would in the same context say that language may be "laid down, distinct in its minutest subdivisions, and resolved in its elemental principles," then express the wish, still in the material metaphor, "that these fundamental atoms of our speech might obtain the firmness and immutability of the primogenial and constituent particles of matter," only to shift quickly to the consideration "that language is the work of man, of a being from whom permanence and stability cannot be derived" (*Works*, II, 17-18).

the metaphor between matter and spirit and hence the metaphoric use of scientific terms."[67] This metaphor, which to the eighteenth century contained the essence of etymology, was not congenial to the nineteenth century, and here lies perhaps the chief reason why Johnson's many unusual words—even to well-informed readers— became a source of embarrassed amusement rather than enlightened understanding.[68] The first half of the nineteenth century did, however, see two developments in lexicography which had a profound influence on the men who planned the new dictionary: Charles Richardson's *New Dictionary of the English Language* and Liddell and Scott's *Greek-English Lexicon*.

Charles Richardson (1775-1865) early committed himself wholeheartedly to Tooke's philology, and through his *Dictionary* he carried its principles and their results to a vast audience which may never have understood what Tooke was up to or even heard his name. Richardson remembered Tooke's severe criticism of Johnson,[69] and as early as 1815 he had in his *Illustrations of English Philology* provided an exposition of the "Grammatical Principles of the Diversions of Purley" followed by "A Critical Examination of Dr. Johnson's Dictionary," which devoted nearly two hundred pages to a word-for-word exposé of Johnson's violation of "every just principle of philology."[70] Richardson's point of departure, which he also made the fundamental principle of his own lexicography, was a passage from Tooke, which stated the argu-

[67] *Philosophic Words* (New Haven, 1948), pp. 42-43. Cf. also pp. 46, 66, 109ff.

[68] See Hare's critique of Johnson and the *Rambler* in *Guesses at Truth*, II, 258-260.

[69] See, e.g. *DP*, I, 223, 345ff., 428-429, 458-459, 472; II, 5, 49, 179.

[70] (London, 1815), p. 248. Pages 251-292, the concluding portion of the work, is a Tookeian refutation of Stewart's "On the Tendency of some late Philological Speculations."

ment for etymology against usage as determining the one and only fundamental meaning of each word: "Interpreters, who seek the *meaning of a word singly* from the passages in which it is found, usually connect with it the meaning of some other word or words in the sentence. A regard to the individual etymology of the word would save them from this error, and conduct them to the *instrinsick meaning of the word, and the cause of its application.*"[71]

Richardson was soon given an opportunity to enshrine Tooke's philology in a dictionary. In 1817 Coleridge had been engaged to superintend the publication of the *Encyclopedia Metropolitana*, to which he would, among other things, contribute "for the first time, a Philosophical and Etymological Lexicon of the English language; the citations selected and arranged chronologically, yet including all the purposes of a common Dictionary,"[72] but Coleridge did not "produce." Instead, Richardson took charge of the dictionary, which was published serially as part of the *Encyclopedia*, before it came out in two very large volumes (1836-1837), with Richardson's long introduction on language and the principles of lexicography.[73]

---

[71] *Illustrations*, p. 257.

[72] Alice D. Snyder (ed.), *S. T. Coleridge's Treatise on Method as Published in the Encyclopedia Metropolitana* (London, 1934), pp. vii, 76; the quotation is from the "Prospectus."

[73] Richardson's principles were more radical than Tooke's, for he had, by "a train of general reasoning" been led to the belief "that all written words are formed of the written signs of spoken sounds; each sound having its own distinct meaning; and each written letter being the sign of that meaning; of whatever numerical series of such written signs any word may be connected or composed," though he cautiously admitted it was unlikely "that evidence to particular cases, should be carried very far among the complexity of words, consisting of many letters. Corruption will commence with the very elements, . . . and the means of decomposing into the simple parts will soon elude the eye of the most vigilant sagacity" (*New Dictionary* [London,

The chief and most admired feature of the *New Dictionary* was the copious quotations that accompanied each entry, extending as far back as 1250; this has generally been identified as the source of the historical method on which the *New English Dictionary* was founded, and it is of course true that it can in effect be so interpreted. Holding with Tooke, that "each one word has one radical meaning, and one only," Richardson confined his explanation of meaning to a brief statement at the head of each entry, always beginning with the radical meaning and discovering whenever possible "the thing, the sensible object, . . . the sensation caused by that thing or object (for language cannot sever them), of which that word is the name." The quotations were designed to guide the reader to these intrinsic meanings of words and to trace "their lineal and co-lineal descent from a radical meaning to their present form and use"; it was to etymology in this sense that "the researches of the Dictionary have been generally limited."[74] Here is the rationale of Richardson's "explanatory formulary" for each entry: "The etymology, and the literal meaning; literally, metaphorically, and consequentially, employed,—with the words of similar application."[75] It was on these grounds that Richardson made so much of

---

1839], I, 7 [Preliminary Essay]). In a somewhat different form, this notion of literal roots is the same as Walter Whiter's.

[74] *New Dictionary*, I, 41-43.

[75] *Ibid.*, p. 44. When Trench said that Richardson's was the only dictionary "in which etymology assumes the dignity of a science," he understood Richardson and his sense of etymology correctly, as the context makes perfectly clear (*Words*, p. 135). Trench's words were by no means "an extravagance which should have caused the Dean acute embarrassment," as James H. Sledd and Gwin J. Kolb suggest in their *Dr. Johnson's Dictionary* (Chicago, 1955), p. 187. They were quoting Trench out of context from the prefatory material to Worcester's *Dictionary of the English Language* (Boston, 1860).

the quotations, and especially of those that were drawn
from early English sources, a practice in which he merely
followed Tooke's extensive citations from Chaucer,
Gower, and the Scottish Chaucerians. Thus Richardson's
Dictionary became in effect a great improvement over all
previous dictionaries, and it amply illustrated the advantage of the historical method. But Richardson's own intentions were of an altogether different order and did not
by any means constitute an encouragement to basing a
dictionary on historical principles, a fact that was perfectly obvious to the men who a hundred years ago began
to plan a more complete and better dictionary. It was the
design of Richardson's *Dictionary* to demonstrate the
history of thought and mind, not to tell the history of
English. The principles they needed they found fully developed in another source, of whose importance they
were all fully aware.

Liddell and Scott's *Greek-English Lexicon based on
the German Work of Francis Passow* first appeared in
1843 and was immediately recognized as greatly superior
to all previous efforts in lexicography in England. Its
completeness and the neat arrangement of the individual
entries—which the *New English Dictionary* in turn borrowed—were important virtues, but its most remarkable
feature lay in its fundamental principle, which the com-
pilers, who were both original members of the Philological Society, stated in the admirably brief six-page Preface: "Our Plan has been that marked out and begun
by Passow, viz. *to make each Article a History of the
usage of the word referred to.* That is, we have always
sought to give the earliest authority for its use first," so
that, "in most cases the word will tell its own story: the
passages quoted will themselves say whether it continued
in use, and whether it was used or no both in Poetry and
Prose; for there are few words that do not change their
significations more or less in the downward course of

Time, and few therefore that do not need many references."[76] Today this practice of making each article the biography—or rather the autobiography—of the word seems so self-evident that we can hardly imagine any other, just as we would take a strict alphabetical arrangement for granted, though even that was the exception rather than the rule until about 1800. Previously most lexicons had followed the *Thesaurus Graecae Linguae* in arranging only the roots alphabetically, with the derivatives ranged under them, an arrangement which Richardson had also used according to his Tookeian principles, defending it by the consideration that "the very fact, that this arrangement presents a stumbling block (and such may be the case), to hasty and impatient reference, confirms the propriety of adopting it."[77]

Franz Passow (1786-1833) was a German classical scholar and lexicographer. In 1812 he brought out a brief commentary on the deficiencies of Johann Gottlob Schneider's recently published *Griechisch-Deutsches Wörterbuch* (1797-1798). Its title was *Über Zweck, Anlage und Ergänzung Griechischer Wörterbücher*, and it set forth the principles which Passow himself followed less than ten years later in his *Handwörterbuch der Griechischen Sprache* (1819-1823), which was based on Schneider's work.[78] In his little treatise Passow clearly explained his method. It had its source in the romantic and scholarly outlook, which he stated with great conviction:

> Der sinnige Forscher der Natur wird im unscheinbarsten Halm, im farblosesten Stein heilige Andeutungen wahrnehmen, und so auch das Kleinste gross achten. Selbst der Alterthumsforscher ist längst gewohnt, die kunstloseste Münze, verwitterte Scherben

[76] (New York, 1852), p. xx.
[77] *New Dictionary*, I, 53.
[78] In the 4th edn., published in two volumes in 1831, the reworking had been so extensive that Schneider's name disappeared from the title page.

und verstümmelte Marmorbröckel, wenn ihnen irgend ein Stempel alterthümlicher Bedeutung aufgeprägt ist, eben so sorgsamer Prüfung und Betrachtung zu würdigen, wie die vollendetsten Denkmaale antiker Kunst. Und gleiche Ansprüche haben unstreitig alle Überreste jeder Sprache, der man ein tieferes Studium zuzuwenden sich geneigt fühlt: wieviel mehr jeder Laut eines Idioms, dessen unerreichte Trefflichkeit hier als anerkannt vorausgesetzt werden darf! Jeder Stamm nicht nur, auch jede Ableitung, jede Zusammensetzung, jede durch Zeitalter oder Volkseigenthümlichkeit oder Dichtergebrauch umgestaltete Form ist organisches Glied Eines Körpers, und darf nicht als zu gering übersehn werden, wo es einen vollen Überblick des Ganzen gilt.[79]

The principles which he derived from this fundamental notion of the nature of language seem so obvious today that we are in danger of overlooking their great historical importance. He held that all geographical, mythological, and historical words had no place in a dictionary, whose only function was to indicate the place of each single word in the body of the language.[80] He was strongly convinced of the necessity never to include a single word without at the same time citing the authority. This requirement led to the third principle, the one on which he placed the greatest emphasis: the citation of authorities for the use of the word implied chronological order; hence the opening citation should not be the first and best that came to mind, or the one that most neatly illustrated the common meaning of the word, but the earliest on record; to place any other citation first, no matter how good it might otherwise be, ran counter to the very purpose of quotation.[81]

[79] Passow, *Über Zweck*, pp. 3-4.
[80] Passow, *Über Zweck*, p. 21.
[81] Passow, *Über Zweck*, p. 32. Still committed to Stephanus' al-

Following these principles in practice, Passow could confidently make this statement in the Introduction to his own dictionary:

Das Wörterbuch soll . . . die Lebensgeschichte jedes einzelnen Wortes in bequem geordneter Ueberschaulichkeit entwerfen: es soll Auskunft geben, wo und wann ein jedes (natürlich immer *soviel wir wissen*) zuerst gefunden werde, in welchen Richtungen es sich fortbildete, welche Veränderungen es in Hinsicht auf seine Formen oder in der Entwicklung seiner Bedeutung erfahren habe, endlich um welche Zeit es etwa aus dem Gebrauche verschwinde und durch ein andres ersetzt oder verdrängt werde. Weit entfernt also, jemals gesetzgeberisch einschreiten, vorschreiben oder hemmen zu wollen, begnügt es sich, treu zu berichten, was es vorgefunden, und das Vorgefundene, wo es nöthig seyn könnte, hinlänglich zu belegen.[82]

When, in 1860, Herbert Coleridge wanted to explain the scheme of the Society's projected dictionary to the public, he stated without qualification "that the theory of lexicography we profess is that which Passow was the first to enunciate clearly and put in practice successfully—viz., 'that every word should be made to tell its own story' —the story of its birth and life, and in many cases of its death, and even occasionally of its resuscitation."[83]

---

phabetical arrangement of entries according to roots alone—in the service of etymology—Passow was against ranging all the single words alphabetically, for the empty mechanism of the alphabet killed the life and spirit of the language, "welches sich erst dann erzeugt, wenn das Verwandte mit dem Verwandten zu Familien, Geschlechtern, und Stämmen wiedervereinigt wird" (p. 25). The convenience of the alphabet was only for the indolent; but a few years later, in the first edition of his own dictionary, he was already willing to compromise in order to secure the desired distribution for his work.

[82] *Handwörterbuch*, 4th edn. (Leipzig, 1831), I, xxvii.
[83] Trench, *On some Deficiencies in our English Dictionaries*,

In England, Passow's dictionary had been noted with interest before 1843. The most extensive review, appearing in the *Quarterly* in March 1834, gave a very thorough exposition of its method, showing that the work "by its chronological history of the significations of words . . . established a principle which must be the basis of all future lexicography,"[84] and concluded with "an outline of such a Greek-and-English lexicon as we would wish to see undertaken."[85] Eleven years later, the same writer contributed another article to the *Quarterly*, this time on "Greek-and-English Lexicography" and chiefly devoted to a very favorable review of Liddell and Scott, with renewed illustration of the virtues of the new lexicography, which thus was not allowed to escape the notice of any serious student. And who would not regret that no dictionary of a similar cast was available to help the reader's understanding of English words and meanings? In his wonderful book on *Learned Societies* (1847), Abraham Hume had asked: "Where are the improvements in our lexicography? How happens it that a learned Englishman often knows less of his own language and literature than of those of two or three other countries?"[86] Both of Trench's books contained a wealth of word histories, which, had the words been Greek instead of English,

---

2nd edn. (London, 1860), p. 72, in Herbert Coleridge's letter to Trench, dated May 30, 1860. The first edition of the *Deficiencies* had appeared very early in 1858. Hereafter cited as Trench, *Def.*

[84] *Quarterly Review*, LI (March, 1834), 151.

[85] *Ibid.*, p. 170. The review was by J. R. Fishlake (1790-1868), a former fellow of Wadham College, who in 1836 brought out a translation of Philip Buttmann's *Lexilogus* (for the ascription see Liddell's and Scott's Preface). As early as March 1820, the *Quarterly* had published a long review of the first parts of Valpy's annotated reissue of Stephens' *Thesaurus*. This review, by Ch. J. Blomfield, gives a very good survey of Greek lexicography (XXII, 302-348).

[86] (London, 1853), p. 50. Hume (1814-1884) was elected a member of the Philological Society on January 16, 1846 (see *PPS*, II, 177).

could have been found in Liddell and Scott. Trench soon brought out another book, which showed the inadequacies of the existing dictionaries even more clearly than his two previous books. In the spring of 1857, Trench had nearly completed the little work that came out two years later, his *Select Glossary of English Words Used Formerly in Senses Different from Their Present.* Though the glossary did not aim at completeness—"there would have been no difficulty whatever in doubling or trebling the number of articles admitted into it"—it still contained almost one thousand passages "adduced in proof of the changes of meaning which [the words] have undergone," but only twenty-five of those passages, at most, were drawn from existing dictionaries.[87] The proportion which Trench himself had used in his earlier books on the language was equally small, since he conscientiously made it a practice not to use the same material twice.

When Trench became a member in March 1857, it was already a reasonable guess that the Society would soon do something about the lack of a systematic, historical record of English. The first volume of Grimm's *Deutsches Wörterbuch* had appeared in 1854; yet there is no evidence that this event had had any direct influence on the decisions of the Society, though most of the members must have known of it, just as they must have remembered that both of the Grimms were honorary members of the Philological Society. Nor is there any reason to believe that the Society took up lexicography merely in consequence of a curious piece of business which required the attention of the regular meeting on February 4, 1857. The annual report said: "A copy of Richardson's English Dictionary, interleaved, was presented by Messrs. Bell and Daldy, on the condition that

[87] Trench, *Select Glossary* (London, 1859), Preface (dated May 25, 1859).

they might be allowed to use any notes made in it"[88]—
the two gentlemen being the publishers of the Society's
Transactions. But a few months later occurred one of the
major events in the history of language study. On June
18, the Society held the last meeting before it adjourned
for the summer. The report of that meeting says: "The
appointment of Messrs. Herbert Coleridge and Furnivall
and Dean Trench by the Council, as a Committee to
collect unregistered words in English, was announced,
and that they would report to the next Meeting of the
Society in November."[89] A year later it had already been
resolved to publish a new English dictionary.

' But when the Society met again on November 5, it
was not to listen to the report of the Unregistered Words
Committee. Its place was taken by the first part of
Trench's paper "On some Deficiencies in our English Dictionaries," which was concluded at the next meeting two
weeks later. The paper made such an impression that it
was immediately resolved "that The Dean of Westminster
be requested to publish his interesting and valuable
Paper," a request to which he acceded.[90] Thus the report
of the Committee became the business of the third rather
than the first meeting of the new term, a reversal which
again shows that Trench, as James A. H. Murray later
pointed out, gave the chief impulse to the making of the
new dictionary.[91] The report of the Committee was fol-

[88] *TPS,* 1857, p. 139. Bell and Daldy were the publishers of
Richardson's *Dictionary.*
[89] *TPS,* 1857, p. 141.
[90] *Ibid.*
[91] *Evolution of English Lexicography* (Oxford, 1900), pp. 45-
46. On July 27, 1857, Whewell wrote to Trench that he had received "a printed paper with your name appended to it, containing a proposal for the collection of materials for completing
our English dictionaries, especially as regards etymology"; here,
as elsewhere in Trench, "etymology" meant the English history
of the word. Whewell concluded: "I have no doubt that under
your guidance we shall find out good ways of doing the good
thing to which you invite us" (*Letters and Memorials,* I, 317).

lowed by a resolution "that for the present this Report be received and laid on the table," this resolution being passed "in consequence of a statement that a larger scheme, for a completely new English Dictionary, might shortly be submitted to the Society."[92] This scheme was introduced and accepted in the first meeting of the new year, on January 7, 1858,[93] and now followed in quick succession the familiar events which gave form and substance to the plan. Trench's paper "On some Deficiencies" was published early in 1858. The plan to publish a new dictionary was publicly announced in August 1858,[94] and was within a year followed by two editions of a *Proposal,* which set forth the scope and nature of the dictionary, asking for "such further help in the reading and noting of books as will enable the plan to be carried out satisfactorily," and secondly, providing the readers with a detailed set of rules and directions, both to "direct them to the principal points to be attended to in perusing and analysing the books they may undertake, and also ensure general uniformity in the results arrived at."[95] In the summer of 1859 also appeared Herbert Coleridge's *Glossarial Index to the Printed English Literature of the Thirteenth Century,* which was made the essential guide to the early texts. Late that year Coleridge was appointed general editor, and in that capacity he prepared the "Canones Lexicographici"[96] which, after extensive revision both by a committee set up for that purpose[97] and by the whole Society in three successive meetings, finally appeared in the summer of 1860, under the same title.

The original *Proposal* and Coleridge's own version of the "Canones" had closely followed Trench's essay "On

[92] *TPS,* 1857, p. 142.
[93] *TPS,* 1858, p. 198.
[94] Trench, *Def.,* p. 72 (Coleridge's letter to Trench).
[95] *Proposal,* p. 2.
[96] The "Canones" were read as a paper on November 24, 1859 (see *TPS,* 1859, p. 295).
[97] *TPS,* 1859, pp. 295-296.

some Deficiencies," proposing a single work according to the recommendations of that essay. The revisions of the plan called for three parts: (1) the "main" dictionary as suggested in Trench's essay; (2) a vocabulary of technical and scientific terms as well as a vocabulary of proper names, both of persons and of places; (3) a separate etymological appendix.[98] The revisions were regretted by Coleridge, who was relieved, however, that the main part would still stand as at first suggested.[99] Everyone knows that these changes in the plan were discarded, and that the first volume, when it appeared more than twenty years later, followed the first plan very closely, a fact which clearly shows Trench's influence, his clear insight, and his good sense for the efficient and the practical. But the actual work was done by other hands. Coleridge died in his thirty-first year in April of 1861, and Trench soon became entirely absorbed in his work at Westminster.

[98] See "Canones," p. 3.

[99] Trench, *Def.*, p. 77 (Coleridge's letter to Trench): "I do not feel that it would be proper for me in this place to enter into a criticism of these changes with respect to which very various opinions may be, and certainly will be, formed: I am glad, however, to be able still to say that all the essential features of your scheme have been preserved, and that while much has been added, nothing has been introduced which contravenes the positions of the Essay" (Cf. "Canones," pp. 10-11). Coleridge's letter was occasioned by the criticism of Derwent Coleridge, who felt that the function of a dictionary was "eminently regulative . . . either silently, in the way of exclusion, like the Dictionary of the French Academy, or by careful obelism." If followed, this suggestion would have altogether removed what to Trench was the chief virtue of the dictionary. Derwent Coleridge also argued for much wider inclusion of dialect words, a recommendation that was followed in the final version of the "Canones," but later abandoned. See "Observations on the Plan of the Society's proposed New English Dictionary" in *TPS*, 1860-1861, pp. 152-168 (read May 10, 1860, but previously communicated to H. Coleridge). Very similar points were made by the *Edinburgh Review* in an article on "Dr. Trench on English Dictionaries," CIX (April, 1859), 365-386.

On some Deficiencies in our English Dictionaries is the modest title which Trench assigned to the essay in which he achieved two objectives; he clearly demonstrated that the existing dictionaries were very deficient, and at the same time created a plan for a new dictionary which would remove the deficiencies. In this respect the essay closely resembled the critique of Schneider's *Wörterbuch* which Passow published as *Über Zweck, Anlage und Ergänzung* in 1812. The essay owed its success to three factors. First of all, it was timely. Secondly, it exhibited Trench's usual clear and systematic exposition, his convincing examples, and his good common sense. Thirdly, there was really nothing new in it; the audience had been prepared for the acceptance of the essay's argument by Trench's own books *On the Study of Words* and *English Past and Present* and by the Liddell and Scott *Lexicon*. These books had created an interest in language which made all intelligent readers feel the want of an historical dictionary, and the *Lexicon* had illustrated the principles and the method which made such a dictionary a simple thing to plan. A survey of the contents of the essay will therefore constitute a review of material that has already occupied us.

Trench was not afraid to say what the "true idea" of a dictionary is. A dictionary is "an inventory of the language," and becomes a standard of the language only insofar as it is complete. It is the lexicographer's job to make that inventory, a job he can perform only if he is the historian and not the critic of the language—"it is no task of the maker of it to select the *good* words of a language." A dictionary created according to this idea thus becomes "an historical monument, the history of a nation contemplated from one point of view. And the wrong ways into which a language has wandered, or been disposed to wander, may be nearly as instructive as the right ones in which it has traveled: as much may be learned, or nearly as much, from its failures as from its successes, from its follies as from its wisdom."[100] It was in this sense that language was a moral barometer. It is evident that this view of a dictionary and its function constitutes a mixture of Passow's principles and Trench's own concept of language and its study. The same mixture appears in his list of the seven chief deficiencies of the dictionaries: 1) Obsolete words were incompletely registered and those that were included were chosen arbitrarily, but the listing should be complete; 2) even the regularly formed derivatives should all be included to make families of related words fully represented, as they had not previously been; 3) the earliest occurrence of each word had rarely been listed, just as the latest use of a now obsolete word was often not recorded; 4) the listings of the meanings of words and their changing uses were often incomplete; 5) synonymous words were not distinguished as well as they should be; the remedy should be careful selection of illustrative passages to bring out the distinctions; 6) especially useful early passages in which the writer himself had noted that he introduced a new word, or explicated the meaning or the etymology of the word, had often been missed; 7) many dictionaries contained material that did not belong in them, such as technical terms that were not in the common language or matter that belonged in an encyclopedia rather than a dictionary, whose primary purpose was "to illustrate the *word*, and not to tell us about the *thing*."[101]

In the concluding pages, Trench added some practical remarks and suggestions which were later followed by the many people who made the dictionary. If the members of the Society counted it "worth while to have all the words, we can only have them by reading all books; this

[100] Trench, *Def.*, pp. 4-6.
[101] *Ibid.*, pp. 60-61; the seven points are listed on p. 3 and discussed separately in the following.

is the price which we must be content to pay."[102] This raised the need for readers and the arrangements which alone made the dictionary possible. The demands of the new dictionary also raised the question of texts. Here Trench urged very strongly that editors should take care to provide their editions with good glossaries with precise references to the occurrences of the words in the text, a practice which had been advocated many years before but was still by no means always followed. Trench did not here mention the harmful bibliomania which made many texts unavailable even when printed by the exclusive clubs, but this was a complaint that was at least twenty-five years old. The answer was the Early English Text Society, which Furnivall founded in 1864 to serve the dictionary's need for texts.

Thus the cooperative work that centered on the dictionary soon came to embrace all of English philology, and it is hardly an exaggeration to say that during the next half-century, English philologists directed their best efforts toward that center. And soon the philologists themselves and everyone else began to receive the benefits which radiated from it. Extending in time from the 1860's until the 1920's, the *New English Dictionary* became in effect a unique sort of learned periodical, in which the items were alphabetically arranged and the contributions almost anonymous. Most of the early workers were dead when the *Dictionary* was finished, but in the end it recorded, as Trench had wished, the history of a people in terms of its language.

[102] *Ibid.*, p. 69.

Index

abbreviation of discourse, 27, 60, 69; in Horne Tooke's theory of language, 46ff, 51ff; in Port-Royal Grammar, 48f; in Condillac, 49; in de Brosses, 49; in du Marsais, 49; in Locke, 50; in Pascal, 50; in Galileo, 50n

Abhandlung über den Ursprung der Sprache, see Herder

abstract ideas, denied by Horne Tooke, 62f

abstract nouns, Horne Tooke's etymology of, 62f

abstraction, 43, 51; Monboddo on, 38; Locke, 50f; and abbreviation, 60; a contrivance of language, 61f; and subaudition, 64f

Adam and Eve, 21

Adamic language, 232n, 234n

Adelung, J. C., 111

adjective, not necessary, 65f

adverb, 25

Advocates' Library, 178

Aelfric's Grammar, 189

Aelfric Society, 190

affinity of languages, Alexander Murray on, 85-86

alchemy and metaphysics, 89

Alfred, King, 168

Althorp, *see* Spencer

American War of Independence, 117

analogy, Thomas Reid on, 99

analysis in chemistry and philosophy of mind, 91, 94; and Horne Tooke, 92

andrometer, 118n

Anglo-Saxon, 56-57, 61, 76, 119; studies in England, 167ff, 196f; in English universities, 169; in Germany, 181; versification, 183; use of Anglo-Saxon letters in print, 183-85, 196, 206; text publi-

cation, 185ff; use of Roman type, 190-91, 196, 206; controversy, 191-205, 212, 214; vowel quantity, 198, 203-204

"Anniversary Discourses" and F. Schlegel, 156. *See also* Jones

Arnamagnean Institution, 162

Arnold, Thomas, 212

Antiquarian Society, Kemble on, 169

Apollonius of Tyre, 189

Arnauld, Antoine, 10; and *Grammaire générale*, 14. *See also* Port-Royal Grammar

Art de Parler, see Port-Royal Grammar

article, 25; Horne Tooke on, 60-61

Asiatic Researches, 122f

Asiatic Society, 121ff, 137

association of ideas, 88, 94-95

atheism, 227

attention, 19-20

Augustine, 232, 243

Bacon, Francis, 6, 74, 92n, 100, 122, 160, 233; Dugald Stewart on, 100n

Bailey, Nathaniel, on etymology, 248

Bain, Alexander, 91n, 93n

Barclay, John, 112n

Beadon, Richard, 44, 45, 55, 58, 60, 64

Beattie, James, 41, 88

Beauzée, Nicolas, 15n; on Sanskrit as a philosophical language, 153

Bede, 167n

Bell and Daldy, Publishers, 257

Belsham, Thomas, 73

Benecke, G. F., offered position in Edinburgh, 178

Benfey, Theodor, 7, 156f

Bentham, Jeremy, 6, 73, 88,

materialism, 35-36, 227
material metaphor, 248-49
Maurice, F. D., 192
meaning, Reid on, 100-101;
Stewart on, 103-105; and etymology, 105-106
Meiner, Johann Werner, *Ver-
nunftlehre oder Philosophische und Allgemeine Sprachlehre*, 143
memory, dependent on *liaison
des idées*, 20
Mercury, wings of, 46-47
"mere philology," 122, 124n
metaphor and false philosophy,
108-109
metaphysics, experimental, 34;
and language, 43, 58, 65-66,
94-95, 230; and alchemy, 89;
physiological, 100; and universal grammar, 127. *See also*
etymological metaphysics.
Michaelis, J. D., 112, 143-47,
180; and Stewart, 102n; on
aim and method of language
study, 112; *On the Influence
of Opinions on Language*,
102n, 143-47; eds. and trs. of,
144n; and d'Alembert, 143n;
and Lowth's lectures, 144n;
and philosophical language,
145; on etymology, 146; on
language and folk-spirit, 146-
47; on botanical nomenclature, 146n
Michel, Francisque, 205
Middle English, 200, 202, 207
Mill, James, 6, 73, 92-96, 186n,
192; his review of Thomson's
System of Chemistry, 91n,
93n; on abstraction, 93; his
review of the *Diversions*, 93;
*Analysis of the Phenomena
of the Human Mind*, 94-95,
142; and Hartley, 94-95; and
Horne Tooke, 94-95; on naming, 94; *History of British India*, 140-42; opinion: of the

Hindus, 140; on Sanskrit,
141-42; of Jones, 142; of
Sakontala, 142
Mill, J. S., 88, 94n, 95n
Mill, William Hodge, 215
Milnes, Richard Monckton, 192-
93
mind, passive, 13, 29, 35-36, 97-
98; active, 13, 36-38, 40, 98f,
101, 105; natural history of,
14; progress of, 30, 38; material basis of, 31-32, 74;
names of its operations, 32-
33; and language, 36-40, 47;
and study of language in
Germany, 42; has sensations
only, 52; study of and natural
science, 88ff; Reid and Stewart on, 97f; mind-body analogy, 99, 107-108
Minsheu, John, 70
mixed modes, 29
Monboddo, 6, 11, 58, 88, 101,
183, 227n; and Condillac,
37n, 41n; definition of language, 38; and Locke, 38n;
reputation in Germany, 41-
42; *Of the Origin and Progress of Language*, 36-41;
German tr. of, 41-42
Monk, James Henry, 220
Montesquieu, 167
mood, 15, 95; Horne Tooke on,
68
morphology, 10
Müller, Max, 156f, 225, 229-30
Munich, 193, 203
Murray, Alexander, 81-88, 258;
*History of the European Lan-
guages*, 81ff, 164; his method,
82-83, 85-86; on origin of
language, 82-83; and Horne
Tooke, 82, 87; on development of English, 84; on Teutonic, 85; on affinity of languages, 85-86; and association of ideas, 86; on linguistic